The Poems of Edwa[rd...]
Seventeenth Earl of
Robert Devereux, Second Earl of
Essex (Studies in Philology, Volume 77)
By Steven May (1980)

↑

Edward de Vere (1550 - 1604)
                                    buried at
Master of Arts degree   Hackney
          Dec 6, 1566

Anthology Bio in (~~????~~ Paradise of Dainty Devices, ~~????~~)
              (E.O.)   (Revised))   (1810)
              poems on p. 24/69, 70/75, 76/77, 78
                        ↑

~~in B10~~
     " Fancy and ~~Desire~~"

(p.24) - "His good name being blemished, he
                                          bewayleth"
first line~~-~~ Fraud is the fortune past all recoverie, "

~~????~~ " the Judgement of Desire"
(p.69-70) first line - The lively larke did stretche her wyng. "
~~????~~
p 75-76 - " A Lover Rejected Complaineth"
           The tricklyng teares That fales along my cheeks. ~~
~~
p. 77-78
        " Not attainying to his desire, he complaineth"

      "His ~~????~~ mynde not quietly settled, he
              writeth thus. "

The Poems of Edward de Vere, 17th Earl of Oxford . . . and the Shakespeare Question

Volume I: He that Takes the Pain to Pen the Book

Roger Stritmatter, General Editor

Volume I of the Brief Chronicles Books Series

On our cover: Robert Greene writing
from within a death shroud.

P.O. Box 66083
Auburndale, MA 02466

shakespeareoxfordfellowship.org

They have been at a great feast
of languages, and stolen the scraps.
                    –Moth, *Love's Labour's Lost*

Even as the wind is hush'd before it raineth,
Or as the wolf doth grin before he barketh,
Or as the berry breaks before it staineth,
Or like the deadly bullet of a gun,
His meaning struck her ere his words begun.
                    – *Venus and Adonis*

One of these men is Genius to the other;
And so of these, which is the natural man,
And which the spirit? who deciphers them?
                    – Solinus, *Comedy of Errors*

There's something in the heart of a prophet
That wants you to remember his name
                    – 27, Motopony

To the Honorable Justice John Paul Stevens —
Who knows how to evaluate evidence.

Contributors

Editor: Roger Stritmatter, PhD, Professor of Humanities, Coppin State University. Stritmatter serves as the General Editor and Designer of the Brief Chronicles book series.

Gary Goldstein is the current editor of *The Oxfordian*, an annual peer reviewed journal of the Early Modern Period and Shakespeare's works in particular. He formerly served as Managing Editor of *Brief Chronicles* (2009-2011), an annual journal of authorship studies, and as founder and editor of *The Elizabethan Review*, a peer reviewed history journal of the English Renaissance (1993-2001), and here writes on "Assessing the Linguistic Evidence for Oxford."

Robert R. Prechter, CMT, is president of Elliott Wave International, a financial forecasting firm. He and colleague Dr. Wayne Parker presented a new theory of finance in "The Financial/Economic Dichotomy: The Socionomic Perspective," published in the Summer 2007 issue of *The Journal of Behavioral Finance*. Prechter also funds the Socionomics Foundation, which supports academic research in the field. He here follows his passion for authorship studies in "Verse Parallels between Oxford and Shakespeare."

Bryan Wildenthal, JD, Special Editor for the Canonical Poems project (this volume), is Professor of Law Emeritus, Thomas Jefferson School of Law (San Diego, California). While obtaining his JD from Stanford University, he served as an editor of the *Stanford Law Review*. He has served since 2016 on the Shakespeare Oxford Fellowship Board of Trustees.

Thank You's

Many contributed their expertise and resources to this project, starting with the Shakespeare Oxford Fellowship, which kindly made available a production grant. Julie Sandys Bianchi, Gary Goldstein, John Hamill, Ron Hess, Maria Hurst, Wally Hurst, Heidi Jeanne Jannsch, Lynne Kositsky, John McCormick, Robert Prechter, Theresa Lauricella, Shelly Maycock, Tom Regnier, Markley Roberts, Richard Waugaman, James Warren, and Sue Weigand, provided ideas, editorial services, and/or constructive criticism that have greatly improved this book in its gradual development over the last several years from idea to accomplished product. Special thanks are also due to Mark Anderson and the ShakesVere Discussion Group for facilitating useful discussion about the book as it has developed over time and the Cosmos Club for its hosting of many important discussions about the authorship question.

Research for this project has been enabled by The Huntington Library, The British Library, University of Louisiana Library, The University of Maryland Library system, Coppin State University, Virginia Tech Libraries, *Early English Books Online (EEBO)*, *The English Short Title Catalog* online *(ESTC)*, and OpenSource Shakespeare.

Special thanks are due, first to the Shakespeare Oxford Fellowship for its subvention, and also to Elisabeth Waugaman for her perceptive critique of the MS in draft, Alex McNeil for his laborious help with editing and proofreading, and Kurt Kreiler for his detailed knowledge of all aspects of the inquiry into Oxford's early poetry, from which I have learned much.

Remaining errors are solely the responsibility of the General Editor.

Contents

Key to Abbreviations

Shakespeare Plays

A&C = *Anthony and Cleopatra*
All's Well = *All's Well That Ends Well*
As You = *As You Like It*
Caes. = *Julius Caesar*
Cor. = *Coriolanus*
Cym. = *Cymbeline, King of Britain*
Dream = *A Midsummer Night's Dream*
Edw. III = *Edward III*
Errors = *The Comedy of Errors*
Ham. = *Hamlet, Prince of Denmark*
1 Hen. IV = *King Henry IV, Part 1*
2 Hen. IV = *King Henry IV, Part 2*
Hen. V = *King Henry V*
1 Hen. VI = *King Henry VI, Part 1*
2 Hen. VI = *King Henry VI, Part 2*
3 Hen. VI = *King Henry VI, Part 3*
Hen. VIII = *King Henry VIII*
John = *King John*
Kins. = *The Two Noble Kinsmen*
Lear = *King Lear*
LLL = *Love's Labour's Lost*
Lover's Comp. = *A Lover's Complaint*

Lucrece = *The Rape of Lucrece*
Mac. = *Macbeth*
Meas. = *Measure for Measure*
Merch. = *The Merchant of Venice*
Much = *Much Ado About Nothing*
Oth. = *Othello, the Moor of Venice*
Per. = *Pericles, Prince of Tyre*
P&T = *The Phoenix and the Turtle*
Rich. II = *King Richard II*
Rich. III = *King Richard III*
R&J = *Romeo and Juliet*
Shrew = *The Taming of the Shrew*
Sonnets = *Shake-speare's Sonnets*
Tem. = *The Tempest*
Timon = *Timon of Athens*
Titus = *Titus Andronicus*
Troil. = *Troilus and Cressida*
Twelfth = *Twelfth Night, or What You Will*
Two Gent. = *The Two Gentlemen of Verona*
Venus = *Venus and Adonis*
Win. = *The Winter's Tale*
Wives = *The Merry Wives of Windsor*

Other Literary Sources

EEBO = *Early English Books Online*
End. = *Endymion*
ESTC = *English Short Title Catalog*
Eng. Hel. = *England's Helicon (1600)*
F1 = *Shakespeare First Folio (1623)*
Hy. = *BL Harleian MS 7392 (2)*
Iron. = *Edmund Ironside*
Meta. = *Ovid's Metamorphoses*
OED = *Oxford English Dictionary*
Paradise = *Paradise of Dainty Devices (1576)*
Pass. Pilg. = *The Passionate Pilgrim (1599)*
Phoenix = *Phoenix Nest (1593)*
Ra. = *Bodleian Rawlinson poet. MS 85*
Tamb. =*Tamburlaine*

Other Abbreviations

Cf. = *compare*
EME = *Early Modern English*
e.g. = *for example*
f.p. = *first published*
i.e. = *that is*
J.T.L. = *John Thomas Looney*
MS= *manuscript*
s.d.= *stage direction*

Oxford's Poems and the Authorship Question

Roger Stritmatter and Bryan Wildenthal

In 1872 the distinguished Victorian scholar-editor, Alexander Grosart, briefly remembered the subject of these two volumes, in his *Worthies of the Fuller Memorial Library:* Edward de Vere, 17th Earl of Oxford (1550-1604), was a poet possessed of touches of the "singer"; his prose preface to *Cardanus Comforte* is "in various ways extremely interesting and characteristic, graceful and gracious." "An unlifted shadow," concluded Grosart, "lies over his memory" (IV: 359).

In 2019 the shadow remains, but progress has been made.

Grosart was not alone in his suggestion that there was more to the literary legacy of "E.O.," as the Earl typically abbreviated his signature to his published work, than meets the eye. Alexander Courthope, writing in his 1895 *History of English Poetry*, placed emphasis on the Earl's legendary wit. Tom Nashe in 1592 had already called him "a little fellow but one of the best wits in England" (McKerrow I:300; Ward 1928 191-92). Courthope likewise saw Oxford as one who, like Falstaff, was "not only witty in himself, but the cause that wit is in other men" (2 *Hen. IV* 2.1.9-10). On top of this, he was a "great patron of literature" who, while being "careful to conform, in his verse at least, to the external requirements of chivalry" had nevertheless "headed the literary party at Court which promoted the Euphuistic movement" (312-13), a literary style often associated with Oxford's secretary John Lyly. In epigrams such as E.O. 16, concluded Courthope, "his studied concinnity of style is remarkable" (313).

In truth these Victorian scholars were only echoing previous testimony by Oxford's contemporaries. In dedicating his translation of the *Histories of Trogus Pompeius* to his fourteen-year-old scholar and nephew, Arthur Golding noted "how earnest a desire your honor hath naturally graffed in you to read, peruse, and communicate with others, as well the Histories of auncient tyme, and things done long ago, as also for the present estate of things in our days, and that not without a certain pregnancy of wit and ripeness of understanding " (Chiljan 1994 5-7). The Anglo-Saxon scholar Laurence Nowell, the young Oxford's tutor and possessor of the MS of *Beowulf*, wrote to Oxford's guardian William Cecil, in 1563 when the Earl was thirteen: "I clearly see that my work for the Earl of Oxford cannot be much longer required" (cited in Ogburn 440). And the translator playwright George Chapman in 1613 still saw in him a "spirit passing great/Valiant and learn'd, and liberal as the sun" (cited in Ogburn 401).

As an adult Oxford would become known as the patron of literary men like Robert Greene, Thomas Nashe, Thomas Watson, and Angel Day. If his "doings could be found out and made public with the rest" (Arber 75), added *The Arte of English Poesie* in 1589, he would be known as a foremost comic dramatist. And to Gervase Markham, writing in 1624, within months of the publication of the 1623 Shakespeare First Folio, "the bounty which Religion and Learning daily took from him, are trumpets so loud, that all ears know them" (17). Markham was citing Matthew 6.1-4: "When thou givest thine almes, thou shalt not make a trumpet to be blowen before thee, as the hypocrites do in the Synagoges and in the stretes, to be praised of men. Verely I say unto you, they have their reward. But when thou does thine almes, let not thy left hand knowe what thy right hand doeth,/ That thine almes may be in secret, & thy Father that seeth in secret, he wil rewarde thee openly." Markham's allusion to these verses becomes more interesting when we realize that these verse numbers are underlined by hand in red-orange ink in de Vere's Folger Library copy of the Geneva Bible (AA4$^{r\text{-}v}$).

This seemingly random fact turns out to have an enhanced significance when we realize the potent implications of these verses for any 16th century reader who remembered the story of William Tyndale's anonymous and banned 1525 English translation of the New Testament. Asked why he had, against the edicts of Henry VIII, published a Bible translation without putting his name to it, Tyndale's published confession cited Matt. 6.1-4 in his defense. Markham's accolade for Oxford comes about as close as one could imagine to a contemporary witness crediting Oxford with some great but unacknowledged "alms" for the world, alms that would feed rich as well as poor.

Naturally, given such a reputation and history, since 1920, when he was first proposed as the mystery man behind the Shakespearean oeuvre, Oxford has been damned, in the revealing pejorative of one recent work, as a "monstrous adversary," a Timon-like waster of his own estates, and a contemptuously bad poet and rotten speller. So who was Edward de Vere — really? What sort of man, poet, dramatist, dramatic producer, and scholar was he? Without attempting a definitive or final solution to this question, these two volumes of his poetry hope to supply the reader with some of the formative ingredients that must go into such an account.

Consider. The man with the comic wit that could readily be compared to Falstaff's also patronized and underwrote the production of the 1572 translation of "Hamlet's Book" (as Hardin Craig among others has termed it), *Cardanus Comforte*, from Latin into English. He did this a year after patronizing the translation of Castiglione's *Courtier* from Italian *into Latin* even though Thomas Hoby's English translation had been available in England since 1560. Castiglione's anti-Machiavellian sensibility pervades *Hamlet* as much as *Cardanus Comfort* does. These are chief among the books we know Shakespeare had to have read to write *Hamlet*. To rephrase and focus these facts, de Vere was the patron of two of the most important Renaissance books that shaped the author's conceptions of both play and protagonist.

It was once fashionable for books on the authorship question to apologize in advance for imposing again on so "disreputable" a topic. Here the apology will be spared. The authorship question is the largest and most consequential debate of longstanding public awareness in the humanities curriculum of the Anglo-American world and perhaps the rest of the world as well, wherever Shakespeare is taught or studied. Many informed persons insist that the topic deserves more, not less, attention from academicians and scholars.

Since 1920-21 the most plausible case for an alternative author has been Oxford, as confirmed by the density of the materials assembled in James Warren's 2017 (3rd Ed.) *Index to Oxfordian Publications*, which lists over 9,000 books, reviews, and articles. This book brings to the already persuasive case for Oxford's authorship a detailed comparison between his poetry — both the poems of his youth (Vol. I) and middle years (Vol. II) — and the lyrical, linguistic, and conceptual patterns visible in the Shakespearean works.

Thus, in these two volumes are gathered a carefully curated collection of the poems and song lyrics of the man whom a growing number of modern literary scholars and historians already regard as the mind behind the mask of the greatest works of English literature, the plays and poems attributed to "William Shakespeare."[1] Even from this brief résumé, we hope the reader can tell that there is substance to the hypothesis that de Vere, Earl of Oxford, is "after all comparisons of truth, truth's authentic author to be cited" (*Troil.* 3.2.181), the true spirit and life behind the works we now study under another man's name.

Historical Context and Contents of the Two Volumes

In Volume I are twenty-one "canonical" poems published or extant in MS copies attributed to the 17th Earl. The attribution of sixteen of these poems has generally been accepted for many decades, starting from the time of J. Hannah's *Courtly Poets* (1870), which reprinted five of de Vere's lyrics and attributed twenty-one more to him in notes. Grosart's *Worthies of the Fuller Memorial Library* (1872-76) established the first reasonably complete collected edition of these "canonical" poems, then numbering in his estimation twenty-two. Figure 1 illustrates the comparative contents of the five major collections of Oxford's poetry from 1870 to 2019:

---

[1] See, for example, Looney (1920), Ogburn (1984), or Anderson (2005).

Edition	Number of Poems Attributed to Oxford
Hannah (1870)	26
Grosart (1872)	22
Looney (1920)	24 including "Elizabeth" verses and Sidney's reply to E.O. XX.
May (1981)	Retains 16/22 as by Oxford, reclassifying two as "possibly" by Oxford (E.O. 17, 19) and adding four (E.O. 12, 13, 18-18b and 20), two of them (18-18b and 20) to "possible" list, while reattributing 6 (DP 4 and 6-10, Appendix C) to other writers.
Stritmatter and Wildenthal (2019)	21+ 11

Figure 1. Comparative contents of five major collections of Oxford's poetry (1870-2019).

Twenty of the poems included in Volume I are listed by Steven May of Georgetown College, the leading Stratfordian authority on Oxford's poetry, as by Oxford; sixteen (E.O. 1-16) he classifies as definitely by Oxford, and four (17, 18 & 18b, 20, and 21) as "possibly" by him. One more poem (E.O. 19) is rejected by May but is accepted by all other authorities. The four poems classified by May (38-42, 79-84) as "possibly" by Oxford are more confidently attributed to him here with close comparison revealing many underlying similarities of form and content with the sixteen May agrees are definitely by Oxford. Another eleven poems, published with attributions to "E.O.," "E. of Ox.," "E. of O." and "Content" (as in "I am content") have been assigned (mistakenly, we believe) to other authors, but in the interest of thoroughness are reproduced in facsimile in Appendix A.

In 1975, Professor May added the much-loved "My Mind to Me a Kingdom Is" (18 & 18b), formerly attributed to Fulke Greville, to the growing list of "canonical" de Vere poems. Five years later May reproduced twenty poems with analytic commentary and traced the MS variants to their sources, rejecting some works that Grosart, Hannah and/or Looney had ascribed to Oxford, but also adding (in addition to E. O. 18 and 18b) E.O. 12 and 13, poems which, ironically, have furnished many of the most intimate and telling connections between de Vere and "Shakespeare." Following the methodology first developed by Fowler in his 1986 *Shakespeare Revealed in Oxford's Letters*, Joseph Sobran (1997) subsequently examined these poems for their Shakespearean resonances. That study is pursued here in a systematic and thorough study of the poems.

Another of Steven May's contributions to the present volume is his discovery and publication of E.O. 12 and 13, poems that are especially rich in close affinities to many Shakespeare texts as well as to other Oxford poems. May might be surprised to learn that, among the approximately 25,000 *EEBO* records before 1623, only Shakespeare and the Earl of Oxford use the phrase "winged with desire," but his own showing of the poem's attribution to Oxford is the precondition of that knowledge, a fact for which all students of Oxford's poetry should be grateful.

Volume II reproduces 85 English and two Latin poems (with translation) written by de Vere, that where either published anonymously or under one of several pseudonyms or were mistakenly identified as the work of his contemporaries. These are now all formally attributed in Volume II (in many cases following the lead of previous researchers such as J. Thomas Looney or Richard Waugaman) to Oxford. These include song lyrics from the plays of Oxford's secretary John Lyly (written during a period of close association between the two theatrical men during the 1580s); poems first published with attribution to "William Shakespeare" in *Passionate Pilgrim* (1599), or in *England's Helicon* (1600) under the pseudonyms of "Ignoto" and "Shepherd Tony," as well as various other pseudonymous or anonymous poems published between 1590 and 1614. Many of these attributions are unoriginal, having been first set forth in J. Thomas Looney's *Poems of Edward de Vere* (1921), but they deserve the more systematic analysis set forth here.

Like the poems of Volume I, those of Volume II disclose many striking poetic modes tied together by a set of common ideas and phrases without being otherwise attributed to any other credible author (except in a few cases that will be discussed in detail, such as Anthony Munday's alleged authorship of the "Shepherd Tony" lyrics).

There is both plurality and and underlying unity in this collection. The most striking contrasts of literary modes and "voices" are present, from the comical operatic lyrics written to accompany John Lyly's plays to the testy pre-*Richard III* tone of Ignoto's bawdy "I Love Thee Not for Sacred Chastity," or the dry ironic wit of Oxford's "To Play With Fools, O What a Fool was I." Assessed as a group, the poems of both volumes exhibit a range of common strategies and motifs: their rhythmic and lyrical fluency, even when the ideas seem trite, recalls epithet "honey-tongued" that so many of the Shakespeare's contemporaries applied to him; testing the limits of lyric and narrative forms, they incorporate elements of dialogue, soliloquy, and scene setting; their psychological richness owes much to their strong Ovidian and Senecan influences and early appropriation of Montaigne's subjectivity (see, e.g., E.O. 2); they employ a dazzling variety of linguistic and literary devices later recycled in more sophisticated usage by "Shakespeare," but above all, the experimentation tends toward the musical dramatic and constitutes an extended meditation on Shakespeare's "great theme," as Herb Coursen has called it, of the discrepancy between truth and appearance and the prevalence of dissimulation in human affairs. As the speaker of E.O. 5 declares, "I am not as I seem to be, for when I smile I am not glad." Such discrepancy between the inward state of emotion and the external sign is an essential ingredient of Shakespeare's dramaturgical imagination: "I am not merry, but I do beguile the thing I am *by seeming otherwise*," echoes Desdemona (*Oth.* 2.1.125).

The Reception of Past Studies of Oxford's Poems and Prose

Aesthetic judgments of the merits of these poems vary; they were once held in high esteem by both the Elizabethans and the Victorians, and at least one (E.O. 18 and 18b) has been continuously reprinted since 1588, being ranked among "the most popular verses in the English language," one exhibiting an "extraordinary and enduring popularity," in the words of Professor May. Yet, following J. Thomas Looney's 1920 book identifying their creator as the concealed author of the "Shakespearean" works, they have been subjected to a sadly predictable fall from official grace, reduced to the status of graduate school samizdat. No matter. The evidence of these two volumes illustrates that de Vere's poetry, however one chooses to rate it on aesthetic grounds, is, or at least comprises a significant part of, Shakespeare's lost juvenilia.

Yet while Fowler's and Sobran's books have been systematically ignored by orthodox Shakespeareans, Looney's original claim that the de Vere poems contribute to the case for his authorship of the Shakespearean canon has been vigorously disputed. Departing from the broad truism that "Elizabethan poets drew upon a broad, common range of motifs, rhetorical devices, allusions, and adages," Steven May in 1980 implausibly contended that Oxford's poems "fail *in any way* to connect [him] with Shakespeare" (12), later insisting (2004) that "*nothing* in Oxford's canonical verse *in any way* hints at an affinity" to the Shakespearean writings (242, emphases added), and even, in a startlingly unwarranted final leap, that there is "a gulf between the two" bodies of writing that actually "rules out" de Vere's candidacy as the true Shakespeare (221).

The misleading absolutism of these statements, we submit, is contradicted by the detailed and cumulatively expressive testimony of these two volumes. Instead these poems disclose an intellectual and artistic continuum, emerging out of the early phases of poetic experimentation, leading towards and ultimately merging into Shakespeare's most mature literary vocabulary and syntax. In many instances we find distinct impressions of the developmental trajectory of an idea or linguistic unit, sensing the outlines of a sequence starting from the earliest of Oxford's poems in Volume I, through the various collections of later work in Volume II: the Lyly song lyrics, the poems of Ignoto and Shepherd Tony.

In other words, the materials documented in these two volumes are a part of the developmental stream passing through *Venus and Adonis* (1593), *Rape of Lucrece* (1594), *Two Gentlemen of Verona*, *3 Henry VI*, and other early plays, and on into the author's mature mellowing and the greater suppleness of the writing in the last works, such as *Lear, Hamlet,* and *Anthony and Cleopatra*. Throughout, the language and ideas echoed in *Shake-speares Sonnets* (1609), where "every word" reverberates to "almost sell" the poet's name (Sonnet 76).[1]

---

[1] Q prints "sell," not the popular emendation "tell." Both readings are starkly incompatible with orthodox beliefs.

While postmodernism has expediently called into question the value of any consideration of authorship as a literary category, this book demonstrates that it does matter who speaks. Comparing related but strategically varied expressions from more than one play, it is clear that in Shakespeare the speaker and the dramatic situation unavoidably give rise to the particularities of any linguistic expression. Thus, while often revolving around a core idea or phrase, their variations are solely attributable to their imagined situational use, including both the character and circumstances of the speaker. To the literary historian, saying that the author does not matter is like claiming to a director that the characters do not matter. Of course they matter.

As any student of 16th century rhetoric understands, it not only matters *who* is speaking, but also in what sociological, cultural, historical, or fictive contexts he or she is speaking. To consider one telling example, the author of the Shakespearean plays uses the adjective *lasting* in at least fifteen plays, but only once in each play, each time coupled to a different noun unambiguously expressing the themes or motifs of the particular play in which it is used. Only in *Lucrece* is it used twice, in *lasting shame* and *lasting date*. Likewise, numerous passages from different plays are built on the same underlying aural, conceptual, or idiomatic patterns, each time adapted to the particularities of their respective dramatic situations.

In our view, with almost four decades of combined experience following the main outlines of contemporary Shakespeare scholarship, the discipline in 2019 is perhaps only now beginning to recover from several decades in which honest and consequential debate about authorship has been vigorously suppressed. The doctrine of the "death of the author" may have had some redeeming value in 1968, the year in which the United States decided to save a village in Vietnam by destroying it. Today, to learn anything worth knowing about the historical Shakespeare or to rediscover the electric current between life experience and literary expression in early modern literature, we must shift our frame of reference and consider a new paradigm.[2] Today's students are curious about the aesthetic wholeness that results from finally comprehending the Shakespearean works with a knowledge of their real author.

This brief summary of the reception of the canonical de Vere poems printed in this volume would not be complete without mention of the most complete collection of Oxford's verse published to date, namely Kurt Kreiler's bilingual *Der Zarte Faden, Den Die Schönheit Spint/ The Thriftless Thread which Pampered Beauty Spins* (2013), which prints 100 of Oxford's poems, including many from the fustian 1573 poetry "anthology" *A Hundredth Sundry Flowers*.

---

[2] See, in addition to resources cited in the previous footnote, Waugh and Stritmatter (forthcoming 2020).

The Use of Linguistic Evidence in Authorship Studies

In assessing this poetry, it is prudent to remember that many other forms of evidence already exist for the hypothesis of de Vere's authorship of the Shakespeare canon. Be that as it may, on the other hand, any study relying primarily on the application of linguistic evidence to draw conclusions about the historical "Shakespeare" must consider the historical misuses of such linguistic evidence in authorship studies. Travis D. Williams surveys the sad history:

> Many studies in the 19th and early twentieth centuries looked for and found verbal correspondences in every corner of Shakespeare's and Montaigne's respective oeuvres. The results often presented proverbs and commonplaces which might be found in hundreds of contemporaneous locations, as evidence of unique and nuanced influence.

In other words, researchers should take care to consider the range of possible causes of any given parallelism, which could result from coincidence or from influence as well as common authorship. Any of these may produce a parallelism, and it may sometimes be difficult to distinguish one cause from the other, especially on the basis of limited data. A useful case in the point is Calvin Hoffman's impressive study documenting idiomatic parallelisms between Shakespeare and Marlowe (MacMichael & Glenn 117-22). As Figure 2 illustrates, these parallelisms frequently amount to several words expressing the same complete thought or together exhibiting some clear pattern, at least, of evidently purposive association.

Marlowe	Shakespeare
The glory of this happy day is yours (*II Tamb.* 3664)	To part the glories of this happy day (*Caes.* 5.5.51)
For he that gives him other food than this,/ Shall sit by him and starve to death himself (*I Tamb.* 1533-34)	There let him starve, and rave, and cry for food; If any one relieves him or pities him, for the offense he dies (*Titus* 5.3.180-81)
My mind presageth fortunate success (*I Tamb.* 1628)	My dreams presage some joyful news at hand (*R&J* 5.1.2)

Figure 2. Linguistic Parallels in Marlowe and Shakespeare.

It is clear, from the evidence Hoffman assembled, that Marlowe and Shakespeare, if they were not the same person, at least belonged to the same "speech community" of London theatre professionals, who frequently borrowed or parodied one another; the data show clear indications of "overhearing" and participation in a shared idiolect. That this is a more robust hypothesis than the idea that Marlowe was Shakespeare, is suggested by the fact that many similar parallelisms can also be detected, plausibly for similar reasons, between the plays of John Lyly and those of Shakespeare, as Warwick Bond had proven by 1902 (Bond 1:169-75); later, Jonson, Chapman and Marston (among others) plundered the Shakespearean texts for the purposes of parody, and consequently imitate many popular Shakespearean topoi, such as Richard III's "a horse, a horse, my kingdom for a horse" (a line that inspired both abundant imitation and extravagant parody).

To find the same parallelisms between the Shakespeare plays and private correspondence or poems circulated only in MS would be more surprising and would provide stronger evidence of shared authorship, as distinct from influence, which is one reason for the impressive clarity of William Plumer Fowler's 1986 results on the de Vere letters. In the case of such published or widely staged documents as the texts of *Tamburlaine, Julius Caesar, Titus Andronicus,* or *Romeo and Juliet,* on the other hand, it is plausible to explain these parallels as a result of two separate authors participating in a shared speech community.

To assess the significance of the evidence we must not only consider the types of documents being compared, but also seek to rule out the hypothesis of common authorship with further testing. That similar parallelisms are long known to be available between Shakespeare and Lyly, as we have seen, already complicates the case for Marlowe's authorship if based solely on the demonstration of a shared density of linguistic association in the data sets. Do other types of evidence support, or call into question, this skepticism?

Unfortunately, the remaining Marlovian evidence is weak or implausibly interpreted (requiring, among other things, faked government documents of Marlowe's death by murder in 1592 and an elaborate conspiracy to ferry MS written in Italy back to England over a long period of time). For this reason we are permitted to conclude that however impressive Hoffman's linguistic findings were, they are more likely to be the result of influence than a sign of identity.

Use of *EEBO* to Evaluate Rarity of Expression

Following in the footsteps of William Plumer Fowler's magisterial 1986 *Shakespeare Revealed in Oxford's Letters,* this book subjects these poems to a comprehensive analysis devoted to reconstructing their relevance as evidence in the authorship question. Just as Fowler found "Shakespeare's" letters in Oxford's, we shall find that these poems, when properly assessed, help us to envision the artistic and cognitive scope of Shakespeare's development, both as lyricist and dramatist.

They connect the plays to the sources of their inspiration and development in Shakespeare's juvenilia and in his life, furnishing an autobiographical component to the study that is often missing or ignored, perhaps even tabooed, in early modern studies under the watchful gaze of Stratfordian authority. Often written long before the name "Shakespeare" became the publicly acceptable authorial fiction for the poems with *Venus and Adonis* in 1593 or Francis Meres's 1598 announcement of "Shakespeare" as the author of a dozen plays, these poems pioneer techniques and themes later put to more sophisticated uses in the plays to come.

Another type of mistake is assuming that the frequency of a particular rare word or phrase can be determined without proper investigation. One relevant category of evidence is vocabulary. Wherever possible, authentically rare combinations of words are recorded in the notes. Beyond the dense accumulation of phrases or word combinations of more general currency, a significant number of the parallelisms cited in this book are quite idiosyncratic in their occurrence in early modern texts, as has been established through control data harvested from *EEBO* (Early English Books Online), a data base containing 132,363 documents published in England between 1473 and 1900. It is easy to be deceived on such a question unless you check. Some things that might seem likely to be common turn out to be rare. Only Shakespeare and E.O. use the phrase "did print," for example (*EEBO* 1473-1623), but some phrases that sound odd to the modern ear will generate dozens or hundreds of hits in *EEBO*. A useful case in point is the legal language of York's speech condemning Richard II for appropriating Bolingbroke's estate:

> If you do wrongfully seize Hereford's rights,
> Call in the letters patents that he hath
> By his attorneys-general to sue
> His livery, and deny his offered homage,
> You pluck a thousand dangers on your head. (*Rich. II* 2.1.201-06)

Rebecca Lemon assures us that "while phrases such as 'letters patents' and 'sue his livery' may be unfamiliar to modern ears, an early modern audience would be accustomed to these legal terms" (182). Perhaps so, but if *EEBO* is any guide, the reality is more complex than the scholarly conclusion: while "letters patent" was commonplace (563 hits in 211 records before 1623), "sue his livery" was in fact quite rare (only 4 hits in 2 records before 1623). Nor is it difficult to see the reason for the disparity, when we place these terms in a comparative context: "Letters patent" were ubiquitous legal instruments used in many transactions daily in an urban center like London, and indeed throughout Britain and elsewhere. To "sue one's livery," by contrast, pertained only to a small number of upper nobility who, like Edward de Vere or the 3rd Earl of Southampton, Henry Wriothesley, were, like Bertram in *All's Well*, raised as wards of the court. The phrase refers to the legal process by which a ward could demonstrate a legal claim to ancestral properties that had been partially alienated through third-party management.

In considering the accumulated evidence of these two volumes, excessive weight should not be *individually* attached to the vast majority of these parallels, many of which are commonplace phrases. It is, rather, the *accumulation* of the linguistic *and* conceptual parallels, converging as densely as they do, which contributes a meaningful context even to some of the less individually striking elements of evidence documented here. We are seeing a mind that functions through the use of certain core linguistic elements found throughout the totality of the sample in closely related combinations but in a bewildering variety of speech context that help to motivate their formulation.

By the same token, the rarity of an expression should not be judged by the length of the expression or any other extrinsic factor. Even a one or two-word parallelism, if it is rare, has evidentiary value. While the definition of "rare" may be open to legitimate discussion, we can illustrate the principle in a single example.

In Oxford's January 1602 letter to Robert Cecil (Fowler 652-53), he uses the Latin proverb: *finis coronat opus* ("the end crowns the work"). This proverb occurs three times in the Shakespeare plays, but only in English or Anglo-French versions, never in Latin. The Latin suited the reserved rhetorical context of a rather formal family correspondence between brothers-in-law. When the proverb occurs in varied permutations in *All's Well* and *Troilus and Cressida* (Figure 3), each iteration is adapted to its own narrative, textual, philosophical, and auditory context.

Oxford	Shakespeare
Finis coronat opus The end crowns the work	La fine couronne les oeuvres (*2 Hen. VI* 5.2.28) Still, the fine's the crown./ Whate'er the course, the end is the renown (*All's Well* 4.4.35-36) The end crowns all,/ And that old common arbitrator, Time,/ Will one day end it (*Troil.* 4.5.224-26)

Figure 3. Three Shakespearean versions of the proverb *finis coronat opus* ("the end crowns the work").

Was every hypothetical author, from Francis Bacon to William Stanley, likewise deploying what is, after all, a proverb?

As it turns out, no; Oxford in his 1602 letter and Shakespeare in three different plays are among only a handful of English writers before 1623 who used the proverb in either English or Latin (Figure 4).

EEBO 11/4/18 search results: You searched on: Keyword(s): *finis coronat opus*; Date: **1473** to **1623** - Your search included variant spellings: Your search produced 3 hits in 3 records, dated 1607-1622.

You searched on: Keyword(s): **the end crowns the work**; Date: **1473** to **1623**- Your search included variant spellings: Your search produced 2 hits in 2 records, dated 1613-1621.

Figure 4. The "End Crowns the Work" Proverb in both Oxford and Shakespeare.

If *EEBO* does not contain the sum total of all early modern English documents, it is still the largest such archive in the world, including 123,000 books published between 1473 and 1900, including all but a handful of known books before 1623, the date used as a cutoff for most of the searches reported in this book. If an English word or phrase is rare in *EEBO*, that means that, by the best available data, it is rare in written sources in England during the period searched. Interestingly, over the ensuing years of the 17th century the Latin version of the proverb becomes more common (20 hits in 19 records, 1623-1900) while the English remains more obscure (5 hits in 5 records, 1623-1900).

By any measure this proverb is rare before 1623. In the Latin version, Henri Estienne (1607), Edmund Bolton (1610), and Gerard Malynes (1622), use "finis coronat opus" before the publication of *All's Well* in 1623; in English, only Sébastien Michaelis (1613) and George Hakewell (1621) are known to do so. Evaluating this evidence honestly requires assessment of prior probabilities. None of these worthy gentlemen has ever been accused of writing the Shakespeare works, while the hypothesis of Oxford's authorship has been explored or endorsed, by latest count, in over 9,000 publications (Warren 2017). For this reason, we may regard even one semantically rich parallelism like this one as, perhaps, having significant evidentiary weight. Yet there are at least twenty-eight such overlapping phrases, occurring less than twenty times in the *EEBO* data, in common between the twenty-one canonical poems and Shakespeare (Appendix A).

Given the difficulty of distinguishing identity from influence in the history of debates about authorship, some will find an obvious but largely irrelevant point of debate to insist that the parallelisms documented in this study simply *must be* the result of multiple writers all operating within a shared speech community. While ignoring the totality of the case here presented, including the references to such foundational works as Fowler's study of the de Vere letters, such critics merely display their own unpreparedness for paradigm shift. Once we *go there*, placing the earl of Oxford as a central figure in a pattern of literary exchanges that also includes Shakespeare, Ignoto, and Shepherd Tony as well as Oxford's quondam literary secretary, John Lyly, we are on a slippery slope. Why should the Earl of Oxford be the literary intimate of those other four?

It is easy to find a reason to disregard a conclusion we dislike on instinct; the question is, what should go in its place? Professor May's careful and important study of "My Mind to Me a Kingdom Is" (E.O. 18-18b) greatly enhances Oxford's poetic reputation and supplies readers with opportunity for profound insight into the mind that would eventually create a character who could be a "king of infinite space" but who finds his mind "bounded by a nutshell."

The Poems and their Sources in a Developmental Model

Of the twenty-one "canonical" poems, eight originally appeared under the initials

"E.O." in the first and most popular of the Elizabethan poetry anthologies, *Paradise of Dainty Devices* (1576 and subsequent editions); the others, attributed to Oxford in MS or published sources, have generally been accepted by at least two of Oxford's previous editors. Although juvenilia, these twenty-one poems not only establish a stylistic baseline against which to compare the others (in both volumes), but also serve to focus attention on a longstanding problem of orthodox Shakespeare studies, namely the absence of a credible developmental model of Shakespeare's literary art. Although the eight poems first published in *Paradise of Dainty Devices* must have been written before 1576, their composition dates are indefinite except for a clear *date before which*. To some, that date is 1566, when Richard Edwardes, the volume's purported editor, died. To others it is 1576, when the collection first appeared in print. Other poems afford more definite biographical clues to their compositional stratum. Since some surviving MSS attribute E.O. 17 to de Vere's onetime mistress, the great court wit and beauty Anne Vavasour (c. 1560-c. 1650), the poem most likely dates to c. 1579-83. But whether it was written in 1579 or 1583, it represents the first definite expression in this body of work of the deep imprint that Ovid had already left on the youthful Earl.

The source of this Ovidian influence is well known: the 1565-1567 translation of the *Metamorphoses,* published as the work of de Vere's uncle and Latin tutor Arthur Golding, left a durable impact on the young scholar. Charlton Ogburn (1984, 442-48), Robert Prechter (2007) and Richard Waugaman (2018) (among others) have credibly identified the student as the most likely prime mover in the Ovid translation subsequently attributed to the tutor. Scholars agree on the profound imprint it left on the young Shakespeare. "The phraseology of Golding's translation so frequently reappears in Shakespeare's page, especially by way of subsidiary illustration," writes Sir Sidney Lee (1909), "as almost to compel the conviction that Shakespeare knew much of Golding's book by heart" (119); Gordon Braden (1978) attests that in the Golding translation of *Metamorphoses,* "we can trace *the beginnings of a particular poetic world* that Shakespeare twenty years later would bring to its fullest development" (36; my emphasis), and that is "in various ways close to the sensibilities of the early Shakespeare comedies" (48).

Another, a more sobering influence, was the Latin tragic playwright and stoic philosopher Seneca, whose reflections on the capacity for human evil, royal absolutism, or the healing powers of sleep or the experience of the natural world outside the "court" all show up in *Macbeth, Titus, Richard III,* and even *3 Henry VI* and *Midsummer Night's Dream.* Oxford's "Kingdom, Cottage, or Grave" lyric (E.O. 16) shows the direct influence of Seneca's stoicism on Oxford, who was evidently fascinated by the idea of *Thyestes' immane regnum est posse sine regno pati* ("it is a vast kingdom to be able to cope without a kingdom") (455-70).

Oxford's first acknowledged poem, a prefatory offering to a translation of "Hamlet's book," *Cardanus Comforte,* which he "commanded" to be published over the alleged objections of the translator, is situated at the philosophical intersection of Seneca and Jerome Cardan, the great philosopher and mathematician. The poem concerns the alienation of the literary work and announces what may be the first "reader response" manifesto in the English Language: "He that takes the pain to pen the book/Reaps not the gifts of goodly golden muse/But those gain that who on the work shall look/And from the sour the sweet by skill doth choose." The reader, implies de Vere, must become the laborer.

Essential later in Shakespeare's own theory of communication, the theme of nature echoing back the beloved's name as manifest in Oxford E.O. 17 is indebted to Ovid's account of the death of the beautiful young boy Hyacinthus, who is killed by Phoebus Apollo (god of music and poetry) in a discus competition in Book Ten of the *Metamorphoses*. In atonement for his lethal error, Apollo imposes the judgment of metamorphosis:

> You should have lived forever in my sight . . .
> But this [death] runs far beyond the laws of Fate,
>> Yet certain accents of your name shall echo,
>> "Ai, Ai," with the music of my lyre
>> And shall be printed letters on frail flowers.
>>> (Gregory 276; 10.162-219)

Ovid here gives an etiology of writing, a history of the transference of the acoustic sign to the visual one, the way writing fixes and preserves the voice on paper. As always, Ovid's treatment is comprehensive, for in this account the printed letters, originating in the voice, are given renewed acoustic life through the "echo," an achievement print cannot accomplish without the reader's consent and human voice.

The idea of the echo of the name, morphed into an image, is fundamental to the Shakespearean ethos and aesthetic. In *Twelfth Night,* Viola's desire for Olivia prompts her to "Halloo *your name* to the *reverberate* hills/And make the babbling gossip of the air/ Cry out, 'Olivia!,' *O,* You should not rest/ Between the elements of air and earth,/ But you should pity me!" (1.5.272-76). In E.O. 17, where the author's name, first articulated inadvertently in his leading lady's soliloquy, reverberates back in nature, *Vere, Vere, Vere,* it becomes apparent that the writer had already embodied in himself the myth of Hyacinthus, and somehow thinks of himself as Apollo's victim, whose name will resound on the page, through the agency of his readers, "like printed letters on frail flowers."

Another lyric that embodies great psychological insight and even wisdom, as many readers have long understood, is E.O. 18, the Senecan consolation poem, "My Mind to Me a Kingdom Is." For over a century and a half wrongly ascribed to Edward Dyer, and only identified as Oxford's by Steven May in 1975, it is evident that E.O. 18 originally represented a psychological breakthrough for the poem's speaker. Today it still embodies a damning contradiction to orthodox belief that the Earl of Oxford was a mediocre poet.

"My Mind to Me a Kingdom Is" has echoed across the generations of the English lyric tradition since it first achieved anonymous publication in William Byrd's 1588 *Songs and Sonnets*, and May terms it "among the most popular verses in the English language," one that "has been almost continuously in print since 1588" (25). Readers of all kinds have found in it a masterpiece of lyric consolation embodying a zen-like message of stoic self-reliance. Those troubled by the apparent arrogance of the final line of the E.O. 18 version should continue reading the additional twenty-four lines of E.O. 18b from Byrd (1588).

Nor did this internationalist poet ignore the work of his own English antecedents; the 16th Earl of Oxford had owned a Chaucer MS, and was the patron of John Bayle, the fiery inventor of the protestant drama of English history plays, and the young de Vere's Anglo-Saxon tutor Lawrence Nowell was in possession of the Beowulf MS during the adolescent's schooling at Cecil house. As poet and literary historian Warren Hope has stated, the de Vere poems form a palpable literary link between Shakespeare and his own antecedents, not only Ovid, Petrarch, Seneca and Montaigne but also Chaucer and Surrey, the latter being Earl Edward's maternal uncle before losing his head to the Tudor crown in 1547; Surrey's poems of love and loss were published in *Tottel's Miscellany* in 1557, when de Vere was seven, and must have also been among his earliest deep influences.

Such admissions are half-truths verging on a fuller reality. As Richard Waugaman observes, "among the most implausible features of the traditional authorship theory is the assumption that Shakespeare began writing at the height of his creative powers, with no developmental trajectory" (2018, 7). The answer to this riddle is embodied in these two volumes of verse.[3] The mature works of "Shakespeare" are preceded by two decades of exploratory and foundational work of the type made visible in this volume. Examining the paper trail of de Vere's juvenilia, translations and lyrical songs, Waugaman further suggests, can help us to find "a more realistic picture of the maturation of his genius from precocious child to author of Shakespeare's mature works" (7).

Thus the Oxfordian solution explains a double problem: 1) where are the mature works of the Earl of Oxford, including the comedies that his contemporaries attributed to him? and 2) Where are the apprentice works of "Shakespeare"?

Each enigma, as Looney had already recognized in 1920, answers the other.

What is the Rationale for these Attributions?

The poems of the two volumes are distributed into several groups according to their respective origins. The twenty-one poems featured in the first volume have nearly

---

[3] To this should of course be added the underappreciated research of E. Everitt, Seymour Pitcher, Eric Sams, Michael Egan, Ramon Jiménez and others on Shakespeare's dramatic juvenilia, which is entirely in accordance with the arguments presented here.

always been attributed to Oxford; many were published under his initials and those that were not survive in one or more MSS attributing them to him. To these this volume adds, in Appendix C, eleven others attributed to Oxford in print which have sometimes been (incorrectly, we believe) parceled out to other writers despite seemingly credible printed attributions to Oxford. As the authorship of these poems is in dispute, they must be separately considered. Likewise, the poems of Volume II arrive to us under cover of various pseudonymous or artificial attributions that have led them either to remain without coherent attribution or to be wrongly attributed to Oxford's collaborators John Lyly, Anthony Munday, or Robert Greene.

In both volumes a congruity of thought, diction, vocabulary, and figurative devices connects these works to one another as well as to those published under the name "Shakespeare." Attributing these works primarily to one highly idiosyncratic and prolific writer reveals to the student of the creative process a much more coherent developmental arc, starting from the poems first published in *Paradise of Dainty Devices* (1576) and ending in such mature works as *Hamlet*, *Lear*, or *Anthony and Cleopatra*.

The full data on some 150 rare (1-12 occurrences) or somewhat rare (13-30 occurrences) phrases or words common both to Oxford and Shakespeare is attached in volume I as Appendix A and in volume II in tables appended to the conclusion of each section (A-E). The Earl of Oxford and Shakespeare are the *only* known writers before 1623 to use several phrases, including *I am not glad*. Both employ the same description of fortune's *restless rolling stone*, and they are the only two to use the phrases *stricken deer*, or *winged with desire*. Surely this commonality of usage not only invalidates Professor May's dicta, but also supplies probative value as a starting point for further inquiry.

Numerous further phrases, although occurring somewhat more frequently in the published writings of the period, demonstrate the existence of what must be regarded as evidence for very strong influence if not identity, a trend already observable by Fowler as long ago as 1986. In the data of these poems, unusual common phrases include *I muse why*, *her soft hand*, *each passion*, *did print*, *pipes of corn*, *when I am alone*, *who taught thee?*, *thy mortal foe*, and *I am abused*. All appear in fewer than sixteen total *EEBO* records, including both Shakespeare and Oxford's poetry. The full significance of these parallelisms of vocabulary may be better appreciated by considering the larger question of "Shakespearean style."

The Shakespearean Style Defined

Virginia Tufte opens her *Artful Sentences: Syntax and Style*, with this keen observation:

> Anthony Burgess is right: it is the words that shine and sparkle and glitter, sometimes radiant with an author's inspired choice. But it is syntax that gives words the power to relate to each other in a sentence, to create rhythms

and emphasis; to carry meaning — of whatever kind — as well as glow
individually in just the right place.   (9)

Beyond vocabulary, consultation of established studies of Shakespearean syntax may
furnish more telling constructive comparison. In his 1953 study, the *Composition of
Shakespeare's Plays,* Albert Feuillerat established a list of eight foundational elements
which "will enable us to define what properly characterizes Shakespeare's poetic
style" (59). These Feuillerat describes as characteristic of the "young Shakespeare,"
being devices used in complexly modified formulations and recombinations in the
later plays and poems. He also cautions that "because they are to be found in the
poets of the age, these mannerisms cannot be considered a distinctive mark of
Shakespeare's style. Were it not that *they are found in excessive numbers* they would
hardly deserve to be mentioned" (65):

1. A strong tendency to form isocolonic structures, "dividing a thought into
symmetrical and balanced parts of more or less equal length" (60);

2. Frequent use of anaphora—the repetition of a word or the same grammatical
construction at the start of two parallel clauses (primarily in poetry) (61);

3. "The association of two words—nouns, adjectives or verbs—expressing two
aspects of the same idea and connected by a conjunction such as 'and, or, nor'"
(hendiadys per se and analogous forms) (61);

4. Antithesis "for itself," using "two opposing parts not necessarily balanced or of
equal length (i.e., antithesis as a sensible figure 'of thought,' not merely an auricular
figure 'of ornament'") (62);

5. The Italian *concetto* ("jingle"), which consists of "repeating a word or a phrase
either in its proper form or under a grammatically derived form, for the simple
pleasure the ear takes in the repetition of the same sound" (62);

6. The "more refined" *concetti* involving "the laborious development of farfetched
comparisons, ingenious sometimes to the point of extravagance, original by their
very strangeness" (63);

7. A habit of writers of the French Renaissance (Du Bartas et alia) in imitation of
the Greeks and Latins, praised by Philip Sidney in his *Defense of Poesie* (f.p. 1595),
of coining new words by combining two previously unrelated words or phrases,
especially formed from compounds or the additions of prefixes such as *un-* (64);

8. partiality towards words preserving an atmosphere of Norman consonance (65).

These elements constitute the closest thing we have to a DNA map of Shakespeare's
"style." No less than three (1, 3 and 4) are expressions of an underlying dualism, a
tendency often observed and emphasized by students of Shakespeare's cognitive
style. According to Edward A. Armstrong, "The foundation of Shakespeare's
imaginative thought. . . is the realization and expression of life's dualism. . . . To a
remarkable degree Shakespeare's imagery can be ranged into contrasts according to
such antitheses" (1946, 93).

A. Barton agrees: "Throughout his working life, Shakespeare displayed a marked predilection for analyzing situations by way of contraries or antitheses. . . . Certain words seem to summon up their opposites almost automatically, as much the result of an ingrained habit of mind as from the requirements of a particular situation or rhetorical pattern. . . . This is the case especially with the true-false antitheses, as even a quick glance at the two words in the Shakespeare concordance will reveal" (1980, 144-45).

This "deep structure" of dualism is also highly evident both in the letters reproduced by William Plumer Fowler in his 1986 comprehensive survey of Oxford's letters and in the poems printed here. A few samples of isocolonic structure, in which the two halves of the line echo and somehow seem to contradict or complement one another, will help illustrate the concept:

> And gladly shunned who gladly fled from me (*R&J* 1.1.123)
> To play with fools, oh what a fool was I (E.O. 19.18)

Along with dualism, *amplificatio* — a series of strategies for copiously developing a theme in writing — is fundamental to the Shakespearean style. Hendiadys says two things in place of one; in an isocolonic expression, every line must somehow be doubled. This is in contrast, for example, to Ben Jonson, whose terser style (as parodied in the laconic character of Nym in the Falstaff plays) valued brevity and compression as the ultimate poetic ideals. But to Shakespeare, if it was worth saying it was worth saying again in a different way. *Anaphora* — the repetition of the first elements of the line — in a passage from *Lucrece* and one from Oxford (E.O. 9) illustrates the closely parallel strategies of *amplificatio* in both samples:

E.O. 9 (pub. 1576)	*Lucrece* **(pub. 1594)**
And let her feel the power of your might	Let him have time to tear his curled hair
And let her have most desire with speed	Let him have time against himself to rave
And let her pine away both day and night	Let him have time of Time's help to despair
And let her moan and none lament her need	Let him have time to live a loathed slave
And let all those that shall her see	Let him have time a beggar's orts to crave
Despise her state and pity me.	And time to see one that by alms doth live
	Disdain to him, disdained scraps to give.

Figure 5: Anaphora in E.O. 9 and *Lucrece* compared.

"If these are not both from the same pen," concluded Looney, "never were there two poets living at the same time whose mentality and workmanship bore so striking a resemblance" (145).

Another parallelism of rhetorical figure is visible in the use of anadiplosis — the repetition of the second part of a previous line in the first part of a subsequent one, is visible in on the "E.O." lyrics in the edition of Sidney's *Astrophel and Stella* edited by Thomas Nashe and printed for Thomas Newman (1591) and later reproduced (in part) in *England's Parnassus* (1600) (Volume I, Appendix C). Despite these published attributions, orthodox scholars have cast doubt on the attributions, and have instead attributed several poems published as by "E.O." to Fulke Greville or Thomas Campion.

Comparison of one of the *England's Parnassus* poems with a corresponding passage from *Comedy of Errors* (Figure 6) does, on the other hand, supply a plausible reason why traditionalists have labored so assiduously to discover alternative attributions for the former poems:

> What plague is greater then the griefe of minde?
> The griefe of mind that eates in euery vaine :
> In euery vaine that leaues such clods behinde,
> Such clods behind as breed such bitter paine.
> So bitter paine that none shall euer finde
> What plague is greater then the griefe of minde.
>   E. of Ox.

> She is so hot because the meate is colde,
> The meate is colde, because you come not home :
> You come not home, because you haue no stomacke :
> You haue no stomacke, hauing broke your fast :
> But we that know what 'tis to fast and pray,
> Are penitent for your default to day.

Figure 6: Patterns of anadiplosis in E.O. in *Eng. Par.* (see Appendix C, DP 10) and *Comedy of Errors* (f.p. 1623) 2.1.47-52.

These two passages are so dynamically similar as to defy credible explanation outside of a hypothesis of shared authorship or some other very close textual affinity involving one author copying the pattern of the other. Both employ the literary figure known as anadiplosis, in which the first part of a subsequent line must repeat the terminal part of the previous one. Here the game is to produce long units of repetition and still maintain the logical forward momentum necessary to the lyric, which both these examples accomplish with considerable facility.

If Oxford's poetry typically expresses a tragic vision, we should not forget that he was primarily known during his own lifetime as a writer of stage comedy. Setting aside the artificial rhymes of the early Oxford lyric, the *Errors* passage more closely approximates natural speech, rhyming only in the concluding couplet, all of which suits the jaunty tone of the entire play with its distinctive Plautine slapstick routines.

Hendiadys (Feuillerat's #3) is another "Shakespearean" feature common in de Vere's poetry (and found in his letters). At least a dozen examples are found in the canonical poems of volume I: *shame and infamy* (4.2); *voice and tongue* (4.7); *cruel hap and hard estate* (5.25); *care or skill* (6.1); *rude and rascal race* (6.23); *pomp and prime of May* (11.2); *meat and daily food* (11.7); *wit and sense* (13.7); *firm and sure* (15.9); *clear and calm* (17.5); *health and perfect ease* (18.43); *hand and head* (20.28).

Probably no other single aspect connects these poems more obviously to Shakespeare than the frequent occurrence in them of antithesis as a figure of thought. The examples are myriad and can be found in nearly every poem, sometimes several per poem. In E.O. 1, *labor* is opposed to *reward*; in E.O. 2 the speaker "waste[s] in others' love" who "hath myself in hate"; in E.O. 3, the "more [he] follows on," like Apollo himself, "the more" Daphne "fled away." And so on.

Feuillerat defined the Italian *concetto* as the "repeating a word or a phrase either in its proper form or under a grammatically derived form, for the simple pleasure the ear takes in the repetition of the same sound." Again, the pleasure the ear takes in the repetition of similar sounds is a conspicuous feature of these twenty-one poems. They include such nonce-words or phrases as "Lalantida" (E.O. 3) or "Laridon tan tan" (E.O. 8), such alliterative displays as "wailful wights of woe," and such flights of concetti as "saw thereby she wanted what she saw,/ And so I see, and seeing want withal" (Ig. C. 16). In E.O. 17, the writer even composes an ingenious word play based on de Vere's heraldic motto, *Vero Nihil Verius* ("Nothing truer than the truth"):

> And I, that knew this lady well,
> Said Lord, how great a miracle,
> To her how echo told *the truth*,
> *As true as* Phoebus' oracle.

To the Italian *concetto* Feuillerat adds "laborious development of farfetched comparisons, ingenious sometimes to the point of extravagance." The category is exemplified by the entirety of E.O. 13, "Love Compared to a Tennis-Play," which in a fourteen-line Shakespearean sonnet finds "a pleasure mixed with pain" in both tennis and love.

Feuillerat also lists words prefixed by *un-* and compounds more generally, a feature praised by Sir Phillip Sidney as "one of the greatest bewties in a language" (Feuillerat 64). Compounds and words negated with *-un* account for a very large number of Shakespeare's coinages and are used more frequently by him than most other writers. The large number of compound words seen in these poems are compiled in volume II, Appendix E. The data suggest that as he aged, Shakespeare made greater and greater use of affixing *un-* to negate other known words: in the poems of this book, only a few *un-* compounds appear: *unfeigned* (11.10) or *untruth* (17.18) are examples. Such formations are much more common in the poems of Volume II, where at least twenty-three (Volume II, Appendix E) appear. Likewise, while compound words generally are not common in the poems of Volume I (see *dwelling-place* [11.19]), they abound in the later, more inventive poems. The later examples include such unusual combinations as *boy-like, fore-spent, rich-adorned, holy-heated, foul-maskt, holy-heated, and deep-wounded.*

Feuillerat's final category of the early Shakespearean style is words of Norman consonance. De Vere's fluency in French by the age of thirteen is attested in his earliest surviving letter, written August 23, 1563, to William Cecil (Fowler 1-18). It begins: "Monsieur, j'ay receu voz lettres, plaine du'humanitè et courtousie, et fort resemblantes à vostre grand'amour et singuliere affection envers moy" (Fowler 1). Later in his life de Vere would apparently fulfill an important *sub rosa* role in English diplomatic initiatives in France. The Norman linguistic influence, no doubt reinforced by his close familiarity with Chaucer, is detectable in the poems in such words as *manchet* (E.O. 1), *posterity* (E.O. 7), *advance* (E.O. 6, 21), *haggard* (E.O. 20), *purchase* (E.O. 20), *moisture* (Ig. C.16), *debonaire* (Ig. D.1), and in the letters in *commandment, opportunity, obscurement, dissembling, concealment, decipher, deface*, and *forfeiture*, or in such surviving spellings as *commaund* (E.O. 21), *daunce* (Ig. D.1), *inchaunting* and *coulers* (Ig. D.1) or *musique* (Ig. C.13).

 Most remarkably, the data distribution strongly confirms the developmental model; the majority of the concurrences detailed in this book link the Oxford poems to Shakespeare's two narrative poems, *Venus and Adonis* (pub. 1593) and *Lucrece* (pub. 1594) and to the earliest strata of the plays, especially the *Henry VI* trilogy (see Volume II, Appendix B). By examining the multiple occurrences of particular phrases or literary figures over time we see how the context of their usage evolves and radiates throughout the entirety of the sample.

Readers may best appreciate the weight of the evidence simply by plunging into the poems and their parallels. Many will have difficulty accepting the contention that all these resonant echoes can be explained away as mere poetic "commonplaces" recycled by "hundreds" of Elizabethan writers. Do "hundreds" of other writers (or several, or even one?) exhibit the remarkable thematic and verbal convergences leaping out from E.O. 4 (as just one example)?

Was it "common" for multiple Elizabethan poets to craft entire phrases and scenes (not just a single word or image here and there) eerily similar to those found in Shakespeare? For just three more examples worth a preliminary look, see E.O. 2 (lines 16-18), E.O. 9 (lines 34-36), or E.O. 17 (lines 1-4 & 9). We suspect close readers will emerge in the end feeling strongly, as we do, that the same mind produced these two bodies of work.

Editorial Conventions Used in This Book

The editorial conventions used in the two volumes in this series have been varied with a diverse readership in mind. In Volume I (Canonical Poems), the poems are given in modern spelling and without footnotes, with explanatory apparatus and linguistic parallelisms to Shakespeare texts given in the brief commentary following each poem. The poems are presented for their wry insights and clever flashes of brilliance as well as deeply soulful and often comic or ironic turns, worthy of appreciation for their own sake.

Each poem (in plain text, with line numbering) is followed by annotations identifying words and phrases drawn from these de Vere poems for comparison to parallel passages in the Shakespeare poems and plays, highlighting especially notable textual overlaps between these de Vere poems and the Shakespearean passages.

The parallels set forth in the annotations are divided into two broad categories: the "strongest" parallels to that poem followed by "additional" parallels. Within each category, the parallels are listed not in order of perceived strength, but simply following the line numbering. The "strongest" parallels are those which, even viewed in isolation, seem to us especially suggestive of common authorship. The "additional" parallels are those which seem to us not as strong but still significant, especially in a cumulative sense. As Looney noted (1920, 161), these poems contain many "minor points of similarity, which though insignificant in themselves, help to make up that general impression of common authorship which comes only with a close familiarity with [them] as a whole." (We hasten to add that we have *not* tried to identify every "minor point of similarity." Even with regard to the "additional" parallels, we have presented only those which we feel are in some way significant or noteworthy).

There is doubtless ample room for reasonable debate (which we welcome) about whether any given parallel properly belongs in one category or the other—or perhaps, in some cases, lacks the significance we perceived. At the same time, we have doubtless missed some parallels altogether, or some telling expansions or elaborations of ones that are presented here. We welcome constructive critical feedback on all aspects of this edition. A great deal of subjective discretion has likewise gone into defining the scope of each of the parallels. We make no claim of numerical precision.

We have identified in the twenty-one poems of Volume I a total of 450 passages, each containing one or more (often many) parallels in the works of Shakespeare. Many of these passages constitute elaborate sets or clusters of parallels, echoing multiple Shakespearean passages. We generally use the terms "parallel" and "echo" a bit loosely, to refer either to each *de Vere parallel passage* (identified by a line number or numbers) or to each separate *Shakespearean passage* echoing or paralleling that line or passage. The numbers summarized here refer strictly and conservatively to the *de Vere parallel passages*. Thus, it is important to note that the total number of parallels could be said to be much larger. But we do not seek to hype or artificially inflate the numbers.

Under this conservative definition, using *EEBO* comparative word counts as one factor in our weighting system, we have identified 105 passages as the "strongest" parallels, and the remaining 345 as "additional." The number of "strongest" parallels identified in each poem varies widely, from one (E.O. 13) to nine (E.O. 12 and 18), or even twelve if E.O. 18-18b are considered as one poem, with an average of 4.8 per poem, about one every five lines; the additional parallels occur at a rate of about 16.4 per poem, or .63 per line. The strongest parallels also deserve more weight, perhaps three times that of the others. We have thus calculated a "parallel score" for each poem by multiplying the number of strongest parallels by three, then adding the number of additional parallels.

Under this system, E.O. 16 has by far the highest "score per line" at 3.5, but it is only six lines. E.O. 4 and E.O. 19 are next, at 1.9 and 1.8, respectively. E.O. 7 is the weakest in an absolute sense, with only eight total parallels, while E.O. 14, 6 and 8 have the lowest "score per line" at 0.7, 0.8, and 0.8, respectively.

Figure 7 summarizes and compares the numbers for all twenty-one poems.

Poem	Lines	Parallels (total)	Parallels (strongest)	Parallels (additional)	Total "Parallel Score"	"Parallel Score" per line
E.O. 1	26	16	4	12	24	0.9
E. O. 2	18	15	4	11	23	1.3
E. O. 3	26	19	3	16	25	1.0
E. O. 4	18	19	7	12	33	1.8
E. O. 5	32	20	7	13	34	1.1
E. O. 6	30	19	3	16	25	0.8
E. O. 7	10	8	3	5	14	1.4
E. O. 8	24	16	2	14	20	0.8
E. O. 9	36	27	6	21	39	1.1
E. O. 10	18	23	4	19	31	1.7
E. O. 11	28	15	5	10	25	0.9
E. O. 12	36	31	9	22	49	1.4
E. O. 13	14	13	1	12	15	1.1
E. O. 14	42	16	6	10	28	0.7
E. O. 15	14	13	3	10	19	1.4
E. O. 16	6	11	5	6	21	3.5
E. O. 17	24	24	6	18	36	1.5
E. O. 18	48	33	9	24	51	1.1
E. O. 18b	24	24	3	21	30	1.25
E. O. 19	18	29	3	26	35	1.9
E. O. 20	28	25	5	20	35	1.25
E. O. 21	28	34	7	27	48	1.7
Totals	548	450	105	345	660	1.2

Figure 7. Comparison Chart of Poetic Parallels.

With 450 passages containing significant Shakespearean parallels (divided by a total of 548 lines), there is almost one such passage *for every line* in this early de Vere poetry—and about one *unusually strong parallel* (some of which occur uniquely in Shakespeare and de Vere or very rarely in other contemporaneous writers) for every five lines.

We do, where it may be of special interest, mention specific scholars in relation to certain parallels, but as a general rule we have not tried to credit every parallel noted in previous studies. Doing so would introduce excessive detail and risk unintended omission. We credit the past scholarly commentaries on the parallels to each poem generally, following the text of each poem. We have certainly relied upon those (in some cases building upon them) and are very grateful for them. We welcome information about any additional commentaries we may have missed. Titles for all the poems are suggested in this edition, not necessarily following those in the early manuscript and print sources, where titles may have been crafted or chosen by an editor or transcriber. We also do not generally follow the titles provided in past modern editions like Grosart's or Looney's. May did not suggest any titles, except to note the manuscript titles of E.O. 13 and 18.

While we cannot be confident that de Vere himself chose or intended titles for any of the poems, we feel reasonably confident in assigning the text of each poem to him. Titles are a great convenience, helping readers remember and keep track of the poems. Thus, we use all or part of the first line of text of each poem for the title, or some other line of text that captures its overall theme. We adopt the apt title for E.O. 4 suggested by Prechter (149) but preserve the equally apt manuscript title of E.O. 13 (though it is not found in that poem's text).

Following each poem's number and title as given in this edition, we indicate how the poem was listed by May (from E.O. 1 to E.O. 16) among those he viewed as very likely by Oxford (1980, 25-37, 67-79; 1991, 270-81), or "possibly" so (1980, 38-42, 79-83; 1991, 282-86). We then indicate each poem's basic structure and the title (if any) provided by Looney as well as the original source of publication or MS reference.

The text of the poems used here largely follows Looney's 1921 edition (Miller ed. 1975, 1: 560-96) (hereinafter "Looney" in this appendix; Looney in turn relied heavily on Grosart's 1872 edition, 394-429). We are also guided by the thorough scholarship evident in May's editions (1975, 391-93; 1980, 25-42; 1991, 270-86). Spelling and punctuation are silently modernized and harmonized for the convenience of readers, and brief explanatory notes are provided after the text of each poem to clarify basic linguistic or contextual cues; readers are urged to consult them before tackling a poem.

Insofar as has been possible, line numbers for Shakespeare plays are referenced to the Riverside edition and the Spevack concordance. In this volume, spelling has been modernized to facilitate easier comprehension, unless comparison to original spelling is germane to that argument.

Acquaintance with a large and variegated data set is preferable to assuming that one or another subset of that data affords a reliable basis for comparison. Following the method originated by Fowler in his 1986 study of Oxford's letters, we pursue an inductive, data-based approach to comparison of the writing samples under examination. Shakespeare's career was one of copious invention of literary situations and characters that would enable him to expand his range of dialogical expression; his characters speak in musical Welsh, comically bad French, and pedantic Latin, not to mention a full range of English dialects and linguistic registers. The computer has not yet been invented that can reliably distinguish his voice on the basis of a few pre-selected, arbitrary, stylistic features.

Doubtless the evidence presented in these two volumes will be variously interpreted. Some will question whether parallelisms of single words, especially more common ones, have any evidentiary value at all. Our impression is that there is much more "evidence" in this case than we yet know of, because evidence is always partly a matter of perception, and until our perception of the realities is honed through exposure to "alternative" hypotheses, it is easy to overlook a perception that might under other circumstances deserve greater attention. A single word, used in a functionally parallel context, can indeed have significant value as evidence. In rare places, even an odd element of punctuation in a parallel structure may signify a likelihood of identity. And if that same word happens to be a particularly rare one, and if we have a handful of them, then we have a phenomenon worthy of further exploration. For these reasons, the question of how we classify and make use of evidence is an important one. In our methodology, context is always king. The reader is invited to discover patterns in the evidence which have been partly arranged by the editors, constructed from some truly remarkable raw materials that exhibit multiple indices of common origin. As J. T. Looney considered this question,

> The predominating element in what we call circumstantial evidence is that of coincidence. A few circumstances we may treat as simply interesting; a number of coincidences we regard as remarkable; a vast accumulation of extraordinary coincidences we accept as conclusive proof. (80)

To what extent the materials contained in these two volumes have gone beyond "simply interesting" or transcended being a series of merely "remarkable" coincidences," to reflect a set of "extraordinary coincidences" that may generally be accepted as "conclusive proof" is for every reader to judge; a fresh approach to early modern literary studies based on the already well-reasoned hypothesis positing Oxford's overlooked role as a giant but politically obscured literary figure of his day requires new methods and new forms of comprehension. Carefully examined, the poems assembled here attest to a clear trajectory of artistic development over time, from his earliest productions in the *Paradise of Dainty Devices* in "E.O." lyrics, through the middle period of pseudonymous productions of "Ignoto" and "Shepherd Tony" and the earliest of the Shakespearean works, the *Henry VI* plays and the two narrative poems, and then through to the most mature and pessimistic works like *Hamlet*, *Troilus and Cressida*, or *As You Like It*.

To conclude on a personal note, the editors have, in the compiling of these materials, both experienced many "I can't believe it" moments, when the sudden convergence of evidence provokes a sense of wonder through its elegance as a proof. If the reader has had even one or a few of those in contemplating this introduction, then she or he is prepared for what follows. Echoing the intrinsic intersubjectivity of reading, the transference of meaning between writer and reader, words from "Shepherd Tony" (Volume II) will send us off:

> Through Forrest as I went
>> vpon a Sommer's day,
> I met a Wood-man quaint and gent,
>> yet in a strange array.
> I maruail'd much at his disguise,
>> whom I did know so well:
> But thus in tearmes both graue and wise,
>> his minde he 'gan to tell.
> Friend, muse not at this fond array,
>> but list awhile to me.

E.O. 1: "The Labouring Man That Tills the Fertile Soil"

1	The labouring man that tills the fertile soil
2	And reaps the harvest fruit hath not indeed
3	The gain, but pain, and if for all his toil
4	He gets the straw, the Lord will have the seed.
5	The Manchet fine falls not unto his share,
6	On coarsest cheat his hungry stomach feeds.
7	The Landlord doth possess the finest fare;
8	He pulls the flowers, the other plucks but weeds.
9	The mason poor, that builds the Lordly halls,
10	Dwells not in them, they are for high degree;
11	His Cottage is compact in paper walls,
12	And not with brick or stone as others be.
13	The idle Drone that labours not at all
14	Sucks up the sweet of honey from the Bee.
15	Who worketh most, to their share least doth fall;
16	With due desert reward will never be.
17	The swiftest Hare unto the Mastiff slow
18	Oft times doth fall to him as for a prey;
19	The Greyhound thereby doth miss his game we know
20	For which he made such speedy haste away.
21	So he that takes the pain to pen the book
22	Reaps not the gifts of goodly golden Muse,
23	But those gain that who on the work shall look,
24	And from the sour the sweet by skill doth choose.
25	For he that beats the bush the bird not gets,
26	But who sits still, and holdeth fast the nets.

Structure: Six four-line stanzas rhyming ABAB with terminal couplet.

Textual sources: F.p. *Cardanus Comforte* (1573); Grosart (422-23); Looney (1921, Miller ed. 1975, 1: 572-73); May (1980, 25; 1991, 270-71); May #1 (67-69). Looney's title: "Labour and Its Reward."

Explanatory Notes:

(5-6)   *Manchet* and *cheat* refer respectively to wheat bread of premium and second-rate quality (*OED* 3: 66; 9: 297). See sonnet 125.11, "is not mixed with seconds," where the same metaphor is employed.

(9-11)   *Mason* [who dwells in] . . . *paper walls*. Suggests an early allusion to the practices and doctrines of speculative freemasonry, especially since the bee is a celebrated masonic mascot.

(22)   The nine *Muses*, in Greek mythology, are the inspirational goddesses of poets and other writers, artists, and scholars.

Introduced by the notation "The Earle of Oxenforde to the Reader," this poem was published in 1573, when de Vere was only twenty-three, as part of the preface to Thomas Bedingfield's translation of *Cardanus Comforte* (1573, rev. 1576), which was dedicated to de Vere (see Figure 8, facing page). *Comforte* is a philosophical work by the Italian mathematician Girolamo Cardano (1501–76), originally published in Venice as *De Consolatione* (1542).

The book's influence on the philosophical dimensions of *Hamlet* has been widely acknowledged. As discussed by Miller (1975, "Cardanus"), Ogburn (525-28), Sobran (279-86), Stritmatter (1998), and others, orthodox scholars including Hardin Craig have long documented an intimate connection between *Cardanus* and *Hamlet*. In a 1934 article (which avoided even mentioning de Vere), the strictly orthodox Craig termed it "Hamlet's Book," believing it to be the one from which the prince reads in act 2, scene 2. Thomas Churchyard, de Vere's long-time literary associate at least since 1567, contributed dedicatory verses to the volume.

De Vere's separate prose letter to Bedingfield, introducing *Cardanus*, was reprinted and praised by Grosart as "extremely interesting and characteristic, graceful and gracious" (423-24). Oxfordian scholars have documented the letter's literary, philosophical, and linguistic connections to Shakespeare at least since Barrell's two 1946 articles, the first of which noted that even then, *Cardanus* had "long been recognized . . . as the source from which the author of *Hamlet* drew inspiration for memorable scenes and striking passages" (35). See also Fowler (118-62).

As Sobran noted (279), de Vere's prefatory letter "unmistakably prefigures the Southampton poems of Shakespeare: the Sonnets, *Venus and Adonis*, and *The Rape of Lucrece*." Sobran observed (279) that "the letter anticipates those poems in spirit, theme, image, and other details . . . borrow[ing], for fig urative use, the languages of law, commerce, horticulture, and medicine. It speaks of publication as a duty and of literary works as tombs and monuments to their authors." Sobran also noted that the letter has echoes in the Shakespeare plays, including striking parallels to *Coriolanus* (279-82). As detailed below, the prefatory poem also has significant parallels to the plays, but only one (that we have seen) to *Hamlet* specifically (see parallels to lines 9-10 & 13-14). This may reflect, as noted by Ogburn (525), that the poem (unlike the letter) appears to have little if any thematic connection to *Comforte*.

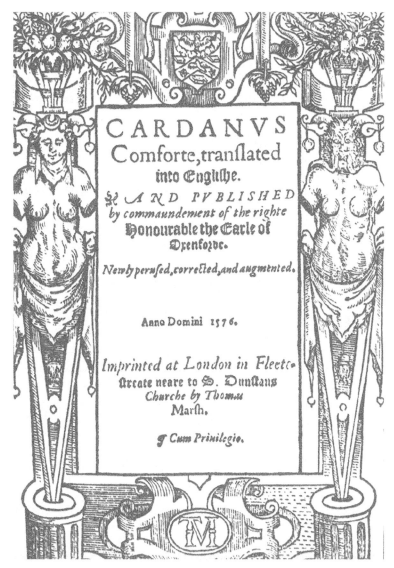

Figure 8. Title page of *Cardanus Comforte* (1573, rev. 1576), published by Thomas Marsh "by the commaundement of" the 17th Earl of Oxford.

Strongest parallels:

(1-3) The *laboring man* that tills the fertile soil,
and *reaps the harvest* hath not indeed
the gain, put *pain. . .*

"And of *our labours* thou shalt *reap the gain*" (*3 Hen. VI* 5.7.20).

(8)   He *pulls the flowers,* the other *plucks but weeds*

> "They bid thee *crop a weed,* thou *pluck'st a flower"* (*Venus* 946); "which I have
> sworn to *weed and pluck* away" (*Rich. II* 2.3.167); "He *weeds* the corn, and
> still *lets grow the weeding"* (*LLL* 1.1.96); "*Weeds* among *weeds,* or *flowers* with
> *flowers* gather'd" (*Sonnets* 124.4). An *EEBO* search (1473-1623) for "*pluck* near
> *weed"* returns only eleven hits in nine records; "*pluck* near *weeds"* thirty-five
> in thirty.

(9-10, 13-14)   The *mason* poor that *builds* the Lordly halls,
>   Dwells not in them . . .

>   . . .

>   The *idle Drone* that *labours* not at all
>   *Sucks up the sweet of honey* from *the Bee*

> "For so work *the honey-bees* . . ./ The singing *masons building* roofs of gold . .
> ./ The *lazy yawning drone"* (*Hen. V* 1.2.187-204); "Not to *eat honey like a drone*
> from *others' labors"* (*Per.* 2. prol. 18-19); "Where *the bee sucks"* (*Tem.* 5.1.88);
> "*Drones suck* not eagles' blood, but rob *beehives"* (*2 Hen. VI* 4.1.109); "Death,
> that *hath sucked the honey* of thy breath" (*R&J* 5.3.92); "That *sucked the honey*
> of his music vows" (*Ham.* 3.1.156); "My *honey* lost, and I, *a drone-like bee* . . . /
> In thy weak hive a wand'ring wasp hath crept/ And *sucked the honey* which thy
> chaste *bee* kept" (*Lucrece* 836-40).

> As these examples illustrate, the idea of *drones* sucking *honey* from *the bees*
> is a characteristic idiom of both samples. See also E.O. 2.7-8 (*The Drone* more
> honey *sucks, that laboureth not at all,/* Than doth *the Bee).*

> Also of interest is how both Oxford and Shakespeare associate *masons* with
> literally unreal or symbolic construction materials (*paper* and *roofs of gold*
> respectively).

> As often happens, the earlier stratum of composition from plays such as
> the *Hen. VI* trilogy ends up supplying what is perhaps the strongest range
> of parallelism in thought and diction to de Vere's juvenilia: "Our thighs with
> wax, our mouths *with honey pack'd,/* We bring it to the hive, and, *like the bees,/*
> Are murd'red for our pains" (*2 Hen. VI* 4.5.76-78), where the same contrast
> between workers and drones critiques the uselessness of the drones.

(17-20)   The *swiftest Hare* unto the *Mastiff slow*
>   . . .
>   The *Greyhound* thereby doth miss his *game* we know

> "Like a brace of *greyhounds,* Having the fearful *flying hare* in sight" (*3 Hen. VI*
> 2.5.130); "like *greyhounds* in the slips . . . The *game's* afoot!" (*Hen. V* 3.1.31);
> "thy *greyhounds* are as *swift"* (*Shrew* ind.2.47).

> The seemingly spontaneous references to the *greyhounds* (or *mastiff*) and the
> *hares* suggest personal experience of such aristocratic hunting sports.

(20) For which he *made such speedy haste*

> "Good lords, *make* all the *speedy haste* you may" (*Rich. III* 3.1.60) *EEBO* (1473-1623) returns only twenty-two hits in twenty records for the phrase *speedy haste*.

Additional parallels:

(1) The *labouring man* that tills the *fertile soil*

> "Let the magistrates be *labouring men*" (*2 Hen. VI* 4.2.18); "I had hope of France,/ Even as I have of *fertile* England's *soil*" (*2 Hen. VI* 1.1.238); I had hope of France/ As firmly as I hope for *fertile England*./ Thus are my blossoms blasted in the bud (*2 Hen. VI* 3.1.87-89). The latter two passages, like de Vere, contrast the *fertility of the soil* with unjust appropriation.

(2-3) *reaps the harvest* fruit . . . for all his *toil*

> "They that *reap* must *sheaf and bind*" (*As You* 3.2.102);"I shall think it a most plenteous crop/ To glean the broken ears after the man/ That the main *harvest reaps*" (*As You* 3.5.101-03); "And *reap the harvest* which that rascal sowed" (*2 Hen. VI* 3.1.381); "We are to *reap the harvest* of his son" (*3 Hen. VI* 2.2.116); "To *reap the harvest* of perpetual peace" (*3 Hen. VI* 5.2.15); "My poor lips, which should *that harvest reap*" (*Sonnets* 128.7); "never *ear so barren a land* for fear it *yield* me so bad a *harvest*" (*Venus* ded.); barren practisers,/ Scarce show a *harvest* of their heavy *toil*" (*LLL* 4.3.322-23).

(3) *gain . . . pain*

> But one must be refused; more mickle was the *pain*
> That nothing could be used to turn them both to *gain*
> > (*Pass. Pilg.* XV.9-10)
> Having no other pleasure of his *gain*
> But torment that it cannot cure his *pain*
> > (*Lucrece* 906)

(10) *dwells not in them*

> "To seek out sorrow *that dwells every where*" (*Rich. II* 1.2.72).

(10) *high degree*

> "Thou wast installed in that *high degree*" (*1 Hen. VI* 4.1.17); cf. "And thou art but of *low degree*" (*Oth.* 2.3.94); "Take but *degree* away, untune that string,/ And hark what discord follows" (*Troil.* 1.3.109).

(15) *Most . . . least*

> "With what I *most* enjoy contented *least*" (*Sonnets* 129.8);
> "*Most* power to do *most* harm, *least* knowing ill" (*LLL* 2.1.58);
> "Love, therefore, and tongue-tied simplicity/ In *least* speak *most*" (*Dream*

5.1.104); "A true soul/ When *most* impeach'd stands *least* in thy control" (*Sonnets* 125.14).

(17) *The swiftest hare* unto the mastiff *slow*

"Thou art so far before/ *That swiftest wing of* recompense *is slow*" (*Mac.* 1.4.17). Note the highly particular pattern of unsymmetrical antithesis (antithesis plus comparison).

(19) doth miss his game *we know*

"And you in every blessed shape *we know*" (*Sonnets* 53.12); "Easy it is/Of a cut loaf to steal a shive, *we know*" (*Titus* 2.1.87).

(20) For which he *made* such speedy *haste away*

"Then let's *make haste away*" (*2 Hen. VI* 1.1.208).

(24) *from the sour the sweet*

"The *sweets* we wish for turn to loathed *sours*" (*Lucrece* 867); "Things *sweet* to taste prove in digestion *sour*" (*Rich. II* 1.3.236); "Speak *sweetly*, man, although thy looks be *sour*" (*Rich. II* 3.2.193); "How *sour sweet* music is/ When time is broke" (*Rich. II* 5.5.42-43); "Touch you the *sourest* points with *sweetest* terms" (*A&C* 2.2.24); "have their palates *both for sweet and sour*" (*Oth.* 4.3.94); "To that *sweet* thief which *sourly* robs from me" (*Sonnets* 35.14); "that thy *sour* leisure gave *sweet* leave" (*Sonnets* 39.10); "For *sweetest* things turn *sourest* by their deeds" (*Sonnets* 94.13); "*Sweetest* nut hath *sourest* rind" (*As You* 3.2.109).

This *sweet/sour* antithesis, while undoubtedly commonplace, is an early indication of the richly patterned use of antithesis in both the de Vere poetry and Shakespeare. Both samples exhibit a marked fondness for antithesis and paradox, with reversal of a given idea (dialectical opposition) being almost a spontaneous mode of thought in both samples.

(25-26) For he that beats the *bush* the *bird* not gets,/ But who sits still, and holdeth fast the *nets*

Compare the apparently earlier version from E.O. 2: "*And he that beats the bush, the wished bird not gets,/ But such I see as sitteth still, and holds the fowling nets*" (5-6).

"Poor *bird*, thou'dst never fear the *net* nor lime" (*Mac.* 4.2.34); "Look how a *bird* lies tangled in a *net*" (*Venus* 67); "Let there *be the same net* spread for her" (*Much* 2.3.213); "*Birds* never *limed* no secret *bushes* fear" (*Lucrece* 88).

(26) *Holdeth fast*

"Let us rather/ *Hold fast* the mortal sword" (*Mac.* 4.3.3).

Previous commentaries: Singleton (162); Sobran (231-34); Brazil & Flues.

E.O. 2: "Even as the Wax Doth Melt"

1	Even as the wax doth melt, or dew consume away
2	Before the Sun, so I, behold, through careful thoughts decay,
3	For my best luck leads me to such sinister state
4	That I do waste with others' love, that hath myself in hate,
5	And he that beats the bush, the wished bird not gets,
6	But such I see as sitteth still, and holds the fowling nets.
7	The Drone more honey sucks, that laboureth not at all,
8	Than doth the Bee, to whose most pain least pleasure doth befall;
9	The Gardener sows the seeds whereof the flowers do grow,
10	And others yet do gather them that took less pain, I know;
11	So I the pleasant grape have pulled from the Vine,
12	And yet I languish in great thirst while others drink the wine.
13	Thus like a woeful wight I wove my web of woe;
14	The more I would weed out my cares, the more they seem to grow.
15	The which betokeneth hope, forsaken is of me,
16	That with the careful culver climbs the worn and withered tree
17	To entertain my thoughts, and there my hap to moan,
18	That never am less idle, lo, than when I am alone.

Structure: Three six-line stanzas in rhyming couplets.

Textual sources: F.p. in *Paradise* (1576) as by "E.O." (77-78), altered in 1578 to "E. Ox." (K2v); Grosart (396-98); Looney (1921, Miller ed. 1975, 1: 589-90); May (1980, 26; 1991, 271). May #2. Looney's title: "Care and Disappointment."

Explanatory Notes:

The poem evidently develops many of the same thematic contrasts as E.O. 1. Although, by evidence of style, it should on a chronological basis come before E.O. 1, we have followed the order established by May (1980).

(2, 16)   *Careful* is used idiomatically here to mean "*full* of *cares* or worries," not "cautious" (*OED* 2: 896). See also E.O. 10.15. *Culver* refers to a dove or pigeon (*OED* 4: 122).

(13)   A *wight* means a person (male or female), with some connotation of commiseration or contempt (*OED* 20: 328).

(18) that never am less idle, lo, than when I am alone

   Invokes Montaigne's ideal of the reflexive self-understanding through contemplative or artistic means as expressed especially in "Of Solitude"

(1572-74): "we have a soul that can be turned upon itself; it can keep itself company" (Frame 177).

Strongest parallels:

(1-2) Even as *the wax* doth *melt*, or *dew consume away*/ Before the Sun, so I, behold, through careful thoughts *decay*

> The image of *wax, dew,* or snow, *melting,* dissolving, *decaying,* or being *consumed,* especially under the influence of *the sun,* occurs frequently in Shakespeare, often related (as here) to the *melting* or *decay* of the self, the body, or of such human attributes as *virtue, willpower,* or *love.*
>
> "let virtue be as *wax*/ And *melt* in her own fire" (*Ham.* 3.4.85); "when *sun* doth *melt* their snow" (*Lucrece* 1218); "As mountain snow *melts with the midday sun*" (*Venus* 750); "Scarce had *the sun* dried up the *dewy* morn" (*Pass. Pilg.* VI.1); "cold snow *melts with the sun's hot beams*" (*2 Hen. VI* 3.1.223); "her *wax* must *melt*" (*3 Hen. VI* 3.2.51); "*melted* away with rotten *dews*" (*Cor.* 2.3.30); "this too too sullied flesh would *melt,*/ Thaw, and resolve itself into a *dew*" (*Ham.* 1.2.129); "As soon *decayed* and done/ As is the morning's *silver-melting dew*/ Against the golden splendor of the sun!" (*Lucrece* 23-25).
>
> The distinctive phrase *consume away* is similarly applied by Shakespeare to the idea of the body being *consumed* by suppressed or overpowering emotion, care, or *thoughts,* e.g., "Therefore let Benedick, like covered fire, *Consume away in sighs,* waste inwardly" (*Much* 3.1.78); cf. "That you *in pity may dissolve to dew*" (*Rich. II* 5.1.9); "*consume away* in rust" (*John* 4.1.65).
>
> The latter quotation from *John* refers to hot irons cooling and dissolving in young Arthur's tears, as if in pity, rather than putting out his eyes.

(4) that *hath myself in hate*

> "*My name,* dear saint, is *hateful to myself*" (*R&J* 2.2.55); "He scowls and *hates himself* for his offence" (*Lucrece* 738); "Whose deed *hath made herself herself detest*" (*Lucrece* 1566).
>
> This theme of *self-hatred* is perhaps explored in most elaborate fashion in *Richard III:*
>
> > What do I fear? myself? there's none else by:
> > Richard loves Richard; that is, I am I.
> > Is there a murderer here? No. Yes, I am:
> > Then fly. What, from myself? Great reason why:
> > Lest I revenge. What, myself upon myself?
> > Alack. I love myself. Wherefore? for any good
> > That I myself have done unto myself?
> > O, no! alas, I rather hate myself
> > For hateful deeds committed by myself!

I am a villain: yet I lie. I am not.　　　　(5.3.198-207)

(7-8) The *Drone* more *honey sucks*, that *laboureth not at all,/* Than doth *the Bee*

> See parallels to E.O. 1 (lines 9-10 & 13-14), especially the latter two lines: "The *idle Drone* that *labours not at all/ Sucks up* the sweet of *honey* from *the Bee*" (9.13-14). Comparison suggests that E.O. 2 was probably written first.

(16-18)　　　　That with the careful culver climbs the worn and withered tree
　　　　　　　　To entertain my thoughts, and there my hap to moan
　　　　　　　　That never am less idle, lo, than when I am alone

> Compare the scene deftly sketched by Shakespeare between the disconsolate teenagers Romeo and Benvolio (perhaps recalling to the mature playwright this lyric written during his own moody youth):

> "*Ben.* Towards him I made, but he was ware of me And *stole into the covert of the wood.* I, measuring his affections by my own,/ Which then most sought where most might not be found [i.e., Benvolio also wanted to be alone],/ *Being one too many by my weary self,/ Pursued my humor,* not pursuing his,/ And gladly shunned who gladly fled from me" (R&J 1.1.122-28).

Side-by-side comparison greatly enhances the impression of a close association of some kind between the two passages (Figure 9):

E.O. 2, lines 16-18	***Romeo and Juliet* (Q1)**
That with the careful culver climbs the worn and withered tree / To entertain my thoughts, and there my hap to moan / That *never am less idle, lo, than when I am alone.*	*Ben.* I drew towards him, but he was ware of me, / And drew into the thicket of the wood: / I noting his affections by mine own, / *That most are busied when th'are most alone* ....

Figure 9: Comparison with *Romeo and Juliet* (Q1).

> Looney (1920, 164) noted this parallel with a quotation of these lines in *Romeo and Juliet* that seemed to blend later versions of the play with its first (so-called "bad") quarto (1597) (the second quarto appeared in 1599, followed by later quarto versions and the 1623 First Folio).

Additional parallels:

(2) *careful* thoughts

> As noted, *careful* is used not to mean "cautious," but in its strict etymological sense as "*full of cares* or worries," as also in line 16 (*careful culver*), E.O. 10.15 (*careful corse*), and in de Vere's letter of October 31, 1572, to his father-in-law,

William Cecil (Lord Burghley): "Your last letters . . . after so many storms passed of your heavy grace towards me, lightened and disburdened my *careful mind*" (Fowler 107).

Likewise in Shakespeare: "By Him that raised me to this *careful* height" (*Rich. III* 1.3.84); "The feast is ready, which the *careful* Titus hath ordained to an honourable end" (*Titus* 5.3.21-22). *Careful* here means not that Titus prepared the feast "with *care*" (i.e., cautiously or with attention to detail), but rather while "*full of cares.*"

(4) that *hath myself in hate*

Self-hatred is a huge theme in the plays, especially in *Rich. II* and *Rich. III*: "He scowls and *hates himself* for his offence" (*Lucrece* 738); "I love myself. Wherefore? for any good/ That I myself have done unto myself?/ O, no! alas, I rather *hate myself*/ For hateful deeds committed by myself!" (*Rich. III* 5.3.189-90).

As, likewise, are many further similar and curious reflexive expressions: "When *he himself himself confounds*" (*Lucrece* 160).

(5-6) And he that beats the bush, the wished bird not gets,/ But such I see as sitteth still, and holds the fowling nets

See parallels given in E.O. 1 (lines 25-26) ("For he that beats the bush the bird not gets, But who sits still, and holdeth fast the nets").

(8) To whose most *pain* least *pleasure* doth befall

"Having no other *pleasure* of his *gain*/ But torment that it cannot cure his *pain*" (*Lucrece* 860-61); "since you make your *pleasure* of your *pains*" (*Twelfth* 3.3.2); "No *pains*, sir. I take *pleasure* in singing, sir" (*Twelfth* 2.4.67). These are all literary antecedents of what would become in time the principle that "*sweet* are the uses of *adversity*" (*As You* 2.1.12).

See also E.O. 8.18 (*What thing did please, and what did pain?*) and E.O. 13.14 (*a pleasure mixed with pain*). On this oxymoron, cf. Sarah Smith, "The Reattribution of Munday's *Pain of Pleasure*" (2002).

(11) So I the *pleasant grape* have pulled from the *vine*

"For one *sweet grape* who will the *vine* destroy?" (*Lucrece* 215).

(13) *Wove* my *web* of woe

"Now she *unweaves the web* that she hath *wrought*" (*Venus* 991).

(14) The more I would *weed* out *my cares*, the more they seem to *grow*

"To *weed my vice* and let his *grow*" (*Meas.* 3.2.70)

(14) *The more* they seem to *grow*

> "For though the camomile, *the more* it is trodden on the faster *it grows*, yet youth, the more it is wasted the sooner it wears" (*1 Hen. IV* 2.4.400); "*The more* we stay, the stronger *grows* our foe" (*3 Hen. VI* 3.3.40); "*the more* she spurns my love,/ *The more it grows*" (*Two Gent.* 4.2.14-15).

(14) The *more* I would weed out my cares, *the more* they seem to grow

> This is a habitual way of forming an isocolonic structure in Shakespeare: "*The more* of you 'twas felt, *the more* it shaped" (*Cym.* 5.5.346); "*The more I* stay, *the more* I'll succor thee" (*3 Hen. VI* 3.3.41); "*The more I* hate, *the more* he follows me" (*Dream* 1.1.198); "*The more I* love, *the more* he hateth me" (*Dream* 1.1.19); "*the more I* give to thee,/ *The more I* have, for both *are infinite*" (*R&J* 2.2.135).

(17) *To entertain* my *thoughts*

> "*To entertain* the time with *thoughts of love*/ Which time and *thoughts* so sweetly doth deceive" (*Sonnets* 39.11-12).

(18) Than when I am alone

> "*When I am alone*" (*Shrew* 1.1.243). *EEBO* (1473-1623) returns only fourteen hits in fourteen records for the phrase *when I am alone*.

Previous commentaries: Sobran (235-36); Brazil & Flues.

E.O. 3: "Forsaken Man"

1   A Crown of Bays shall that man wear
2   That triumphs over me,
3   For Black and Tawny will I wear,
4   Which mourning colours be.

5   The more I followed on, the more she fled away,
6   As Daphne did full long agone, Apollo's wishful prey;
7   The more my plaints resound, the less she pities me;
8   The more I sought, the less I found that mine she meant to be.

9   Melpomene, alas, with doleful tunes help then,
10 And sing (*bis*), woe worth on me, forsaken man.
11 Then Daphne's Bays shall that man wear that triumphs over me,
12 For Black and Tawny will I wear, which mourning colours be.

13 Drown me you trickling tears, you wailful wights of woe;
14 Come help these hands to rent my hairs, my rueful haps to show
15 On whom the scorching flames of love doth feed you see;
16 Ah lalantida, my dear dame hath thus tormented me.

17 Wherefore you Muses nine, with doleful tunes help then,
18 And sing (*bis*), woe worth on me, forsaken man.
19 Then Daphne's Bays shall that man wear that triumphs over me,
20 For Black and Tawny will I wear, which mourning colours be.

21 An Anchor's life to lead, with nails to scratch my grave,
22 Where earthly Worms on me shall feed, is all the joys I crave,
23 And hide myself from shame, sith that mine eyes do see,
24 Ah lalantida, my dear dame hath thus tormented me.

25 And all that present be, with doleful tunes help then,
26 And sing (*bis*), woe worth on me, forsaken man.

Structure: Five stanzas of four lines in rhyming couplets prefaced by four half-lines rhyming ABAB and concluding with a rhyming couplet. Written to be set to music. Many lines of the main stanzas have mid-line rhymes, e.g., *resound/found* (7-8) or *shame/dame* (23-24), perhaps intended to create emphases of various kinds.

Textual sources: F.p. *Paradise* (1576), 70-71; Grosart (403-04); Looney (1921, Miller ed. 1975, 1: 585-86); May (1980, 26-27; 1991, 271-72). May #3. Looney's title: same as above.

Explanatory Notes:

(1)   *Bays* refers to laurel leaves (see also lines 11 & 19).

(6)   *Daphne* is a naiad (water-nymph) in Greek mythology, referenced three times in these de Vere poems (see also lines 11 and 19). She is also referenced three times in canonical Shakespeare (Spevack 263). *Apollo* is the Greco-Roman god of the sun, also known as *Phoebus* (as in 14.31, 17.24, 19.8, and 20.4). *Apollo* is referenced once in these de Vere poems and twenty-nine times in canonical Shakespeare (Spevack 54). There are also twenty-three references to *Phoebus* (including one spelled "Phibbus") in canonical Shakespeare (Spevack 976-77).

On the amours of the gods (a common interest of these de Vere poems and Shakespeare), see also E.O. 6 (7-10, 17-18, and 23-24), E.O. 8.6 and E.O. 4.31-32.

(9)   *Melpomene,* in Greek mythology, is the *Muse* of tragedy. There is no specific reference to her in canonical Shakespeare. The ancient Greek poet Sappho was historically sometimes described as "the tenth Muse," but Shakespeare in Sonnet 38 seems instead to refer to the mysterious beloved youth of the Sonnets as such.

(10, 18, 26) *Bis* is a musical term indicating that the next passage (as in music) should be repeated (*OED* 2: 220), here referring to the refrain ("Woe worth on me, forsaken man . . . mourning colours be"). Like several early de Vere poems, this was evidently composed as a song lyric. This would also explain the lamentation *Ah lalantida* (see below on lines 16 & 24).

(13)   *Wight* (used figuratively here) means a person (male or female), with some connotation of commiseration or contempt (*OED* 20: 328).

(16, 24) *Ah lalantida* is a lamentation of unknown meaning. As Looney suggested, the first and third syllables of *làlantìda* should be stressed to maintain the apparent intended rhythm of the line.

(17)   The *nine Muses*, in Greek mythology, are the inspirational goddesses of poets and other writers, artists, and scholars (see above on line 9).

(23)   The archaic *sith* means "since" (*OED* 15: 563-64).

Strongest parallels:

(5, 7-8) *The more I followed on, the more she fled away*

        . . .

   The more my plaints resound, the less she pities me;
   The more I sought, the less I found that mine she meant to be

   "*Her. The more I hate, the more he follows me. Hel. The more I love, the more he* hateth me" (*Dream* 1.1.198-99); "*Dem.* Hence, get thee gone, and *follow me no more! Hel. You draw me,* you hard-hearted adamant! . . ./ And *even for that do I love you the more*" (*Dream* 2.1.194-95, 202); "*I followed fast, but faster he did fly* " (*Dream* 3.2.416).

See additional parallels below to lines 7-8. Contrasting (e)motions produce paradoxical results, a favorite motif of Shakespeare.

(21-22) to *scratch* my *grave,/ Where earthly worms on me shall feed,/* is all the *joy* I crave

Compare the dying Mercutio: "a *scratch*, a *scratch*. . . ./ Ask for me tomorrow, and you shall find me a *grave man*. . . ./ They have made *worms' meat of me*" (*R&J* 3.1.91, 95-96, 107).

Shakespeare further elaborates the thought in *Ham.*: "Not where he *eats, but where 'a is eaten.* A certain convocation of politic *worms are e'en at him.* Your *worm* is your only emperor for *diet.* We fat all creatures else to fat us, and *we fat ourselves for maggots.* . . ./ A man may fish with *the worm that hath eat of a king,* and eat of the fish that hath *fed of that worm*" (4.3.19-23, 27-28).

See also: "thus chides she *Death—Grim-grinning ghost, earth's worm*" (*Venus* 932-33); "The *mortal worm* might make *the sleep eternal*" (*2 Hen. VI* 3.2.263); "Let's talk of *graves,* of *worms,* and epitaphs" (*Rich. II* 3.2.145); "The *worm* of conscience still *begnaw thy soul!*" (*Rich. III* 1.3.221); "*Percy.* And *food for—* [Dies.] *Prince Hen.* For *worms,* brave Percy" (*1 Hen. IV* 5.4.85-86); "Thou *worms' meat*" (*As You* 3.2.62); "For thou dost fear *the soft and tender fork Of a poor worm*" (*Meas.* 3.1.16-17); "I wish you all *joy* of the *worm*" (*A&C* 5.2.260).

(23) *mine eyes do see*

If ever mortal *eyes do see* (*Oth.* 3.3.399); To *see't mine eyes* are blasted (*A&C* 3.10.4).

EEBO returns thirty hits in twenty-seven records, including both *Oth.* and E.O. 3. for the phrase *eyes do see.*

Additional parallels:

(1) *Crown of Bays*

"An olive branch and *laurel crown*" (*3 Hen. VI* 4.6.34); "*crowns,* sceptres, *laurels*" (*Troil.* 1.3.107). As noted above, *bays* are laurel leaves.

(6) As *Daphne* did full long agone, *Apollo's* wishful prey

"*Apollo* flies, and *Daphne* holds the chase" (*Dream* 2.1.231); "Tell me, *Apollo,* for thy *Daphne's* love" (*Troil.* 1.1.98); "Or *Daphne* roaming through a thorny wood,/ Scratching her legs that one shall swear she bleeds, And at that sight shall sad *Apollo* weep" (*Shrew* ind.2.55-57).

(6) did full *long agone*

> "For *long agone* I have forgot to court" (*Two Gent.* 3.1.85).

> The expression is surprisingly commonplace.

(7-8) *The more* my plaints resound, *the less* she pities me; *The more* I sought, *the less* I found that mine she meant to be

> In a variation on the *more/more* paradox (see parallels above to lines 5 & 7-8), the *more/less* antithesis is another figure commonly evident in both samples, e.g.: "by hoping *more* they have but *less*" (*Lucrece* 137); "That moves in him *more rage and lesser pity*" (*Lucrece* 468); "The *lesser* thing should not the *greater* hide" (*Lucrece* 663); "The repetition cannot make it *less, For more* it is than I can well express" (*Lucrece* 1285); "*More* than I seem, and *less* than I was born to" (*3 Hen. VI* 3.1.56); "Not that I loved Caesar *less,* but that I loved Rome *more*" (*Caes.* 3.2.22); "The *more* my prayer, the *lesser* is my grace" (*Dream* 2.2.89); "A little *more* than kin, and *less* than kind" (*Ham.* 1.2.65); "An eye *more* bright than theirs, *less* false in rolling" (*Sonnets* 20.5).

(7) The more *my plaints* resound, the less *she pities me*

> Looney noted (1920, 161) "the recurrence of what seems . . . a curious appeal for *pity*" in these de Vere poems and the works of Shakespeare. *Pity* (and its variants) appears more than 300 times in the Shakespeare canon (Spevack 980-81). In addition to line 7, see E.O. 9.36 (*pity me*) and E.O. 17.8 (*some pity in the rocks*), and compare, e.g.:

> "Melt at my tears, and be compassionate; Soft *pity* enters at an *iron gate*" (*Lucrece* 593); "This you should *pity* rather than despise" (*Dream* 3.2.235); "May move your hearts to *pity*" (*Rich. III* 1.3.348); "*Pity*, you *ancient stones*, those tender babes" (*Rich. III* 4.1.98); "*Pity me* then" (*Sonnets* 111.8, 13); "Thine eyes I love, and they as *pitying me*. . . ./ And suit *thy pity* like in every part" (*Sonnets* 132.1, 12); "*my pity-wanting pain*" (*Sonnets* 140.4).

(7) The more *my plaints resound*

> "Hearing how *our plaints* and prayers *do pierce*" (*Rich. II* 5.3.127). The lines not only share the word *plaint* coupled with a first person pronoun, but in both cases the plaints have some characteristic agency ("resound" and "do pierce").

(7) The more my plaints *resound*

> Whose hollow womb *resounds* like heaven's thunder (*Venus* 268).

(9, 17, 25) *Melpomene*, alas, with *doleful tunes* help then,

> . . .

> Wherefore you *Muses* nine, with *doleful tunes* help then,

> . . .

> And all that present be, with *doleful tunes* help then

"A very *doleful tune*" (*Win.* 4.4.262); cf. "Be thou the tenth *muse*" (*Sonnets* 38.9).

(13) *Drown me you trickling tears*

Both these de Vere poems and Shakespeare place great emphasis on *tears* and weeping, signifying a fascination with states of human emotion, including weeping as an outward expression of various emotional states. Comments Eric Sams: in Shakespeare "tears . . . resemble rivers or the sea in their drowning capacity, at least in the poetic imagination. Further, both elements are salt" (313, 1985).

In his St. Bartholomew's Day massacre letter of 1572 Oxford's elaborate *descriptio* of the horrific event uses weeping as a powerful indicator of emotional tone: "your news which doth here ring dolefully in the ears of every man, of the murder of the Admiral of France, and a number of noble men and worthy gentlemen, and such as greatly have in their lifetimes honoured the Queen's Majesty our mistress, on whose tragedies we have an number of French Aeneases in this city, that tell of their own overthrows *with tears falling from their eyes*, a *piteous thing* to hear but a cruel and far more grievous thing we must deem it them to see" (Fowler 55). On *trickling tears*, see also E.O. 9.1. On the broader theme of *tears* and weeping, see also E.O. 4.10, 5.12, 6.26. and 17.8–9.

"Floods of *tears* will *drown* my oratory" (*Titus* 5.3.90); "*drowned* their enmity in my true *tears*" (*Titus* 5.3.107); "Lest with my sighs or *tears* I blast or *drown* King Edward's fruit" (*3 Hen. VI* 4.4.23-24); "Weep not, sweet queen; for *trickling tears* are vain" (*1 Hen. IV* 2.4.391); "*drown* me in thy sister's flood of *tears*" (*Errors* 3.2.46); "*drown* our gains in *tears*" (*All's Well* 4.3.68); "*tears* shall *drown* the wind" (*Mac.* 1.7.25); "*drown* the stage with *tears*" (*Ham.* 2.2.562); "burns Worse than *tears drown*" (*Win.* 2.1.112); cf. "My heart is *drowned* with grief, Whose flood begins to flow within mine eyes" (*2 Hen. VI* 3.1.198); "Then can I *drown* an eye unused to flow" (*Sonnets* 30.5).

(14) help *these hands* to *rent* [i.e., rend or *tear*] my *hairs*

"Let him have time *to tear* his curled *hair*" (*Lucrece* 981); "*These hands shall tear* her" (*Much* 4.1.191); "this mouth should *tear* this *hand* for lifting food to 't?" (*Lear* 3.4.15).

(15) On whom *the scorching flames of love* doth *feed*

"Whom *flaming* war doth *scorch*" (*Kins.* 1.1.91); "*feed'st* thy *light's flame*" (*Sonnets* 1.6); "to *feed* for aye her lamp and *flames of love*" (*Troil.* 3.2.160).

(21) An *Anchor's* life to lead, with nails to scratch my grave

"An *anchor's* cheer in prison be my scope!" (*Ham.* 3.2.219).

(23) And *hide myself* from *shame*

> "Canst thou now find out *to hide thee from* this open and apparent *shame*?" (*1 Hen. IV* 2.4.264); "The *shame* hereof will make *me hide my head*" (*1 Hen. VI* 1.5.39); "O, that which *I would hide* from heaven's eye,/ *Our empress' shame*, and stately Rome's disgrace!" (*Titus* 4.2.59-60).

(23) *Sith that* mine eyes do see

> "*Sith that* the justice of your title to him/ Doth flourish the deceit" (*Meas.* 4.1.73-74); "*Sith that* both charge and danger/ Speak 'gainst so great a number" (*Lear* 2.4.239-40).

(25) with *doleful tunes* help then

> This pale faint swan,/ Who chants *a doleful hymn* to his own death (*John* 5.7.22); And there sung the *dolefull'st ditty* (*Pass. Pilg.* 20.11); And *doleful dumps* the mind oppress (*R&J* 4.5.127).

(26) woe worth *on me, forsaken man*

> Of him, myself, and thee, *I am forsaken* (*Sonnets* 133.7)

Previous commentaries: Sobran (237-38); Brazil & Flues.

E.O. 4: "The Loss of My Good Name"

1	Framed in the front of forlorn hope, past all recovery,
2	I stayless stand t'abide the shock of shame and infamy.
3	My life, through lingering long, is lodged in lair of loathsome ways,
4	My death delayed to keep from life the harm of hapless days.
5	My sprites, my heart, my wit and force in deep distress are drowned;
6	The only loss of my good name is of these griefs the ground.
7	And since my mind, my wit, my head, my voice and tongue are weak
8	To utter, move, devise, conceive, sound forth, declare and speak
9	Such piercing plaints as answer might, or would, my woeful case,
10	Help crave I must, and crave I will, with tears upon my face
11	Of all that may in heaven or hell, in earth or air, be found
12	To wail with me this loss of mine, as of these griefs the ground.
13	Help gods, help saints, help sprites and powers that in the heaven do dwell,
14	Help ye that are to wail, ay wont, ye howling hounds of hell,
15	Help man, help beasts, help birds and worms that on the earth doth toil,
16	Help fish, help fowl that flocks and feeds upon the salt sea soil,
17	Help echo that in air doth flee, shrill voices to resound
18	To wail this loss of my good name, as of these griefs the ground.

Structure: Three six-line stanzas in rhyming couplets.

Textual sources: F.p. *Paradise* (1576), 24 [where, however, the text of l. 1 reads "fraud is the front of fortune past all recovery"; this is corrected in 1578 (poem 33, Fol. 15) to the present reading]. Grosart (401-02); Looney (1921, Miller ed. 1975, 1: 580-81); May (1980, 27-28; 1991, 272-73). Looney's title: "Loss of Good Name." *Paradise* title: "His Good name being blemished, he bewayleth."

Explanatory Notes:

(5, 13) *Sprites* is an archaic usage (meaning "spirits") that may confuse modern readers (*OED* 16: 361). The archaic meaning survives to some extent in modern usage (e.g., *sprite*ly = "spirited," meaning one's "spirit" or mood). *Sprites,* in the context of this imprecation, is used in a distinct yet related sense (more readily comprehensible today), referring to elves or "spirit" creatures.

(5, 7) The term *wit* as used here refers to intelligence or mental sharpness, not humor (*OED* 20: 432-34).

This presentation of the parallels to this poem draws on Robert Prechter's 2012 article. As a general rule, we generally make no attempt to credit specific scholars with regard to every cited parallel, instead only identifying them as needed for specific purposes.

Strongest parallels:

(3) My *life*, through *lingering long*, is lodged in *lair of loathsome* ways

> Theme, diction, and alliteration all link the following: "*life,/* Which false hope *lingers in extremity*" (*Rich. II* 2.2.71-72); "by the minute feed on *life* and, *ling'ring,/ By inches* waste you" (*Cym.* 5.5.51-52); "*lean*-faced Envy in her *loathsome cave*" (i.e., *lair*) (*2 Hen. VI* 3.2.315); "This *loathsome sequestration* have I had . . . detained me *all my flow'ring youth/ Within a loathsome dungeon, there to pine*" (*1 Hen. VI* 2.5.25, 57); "O, let him *keep* his *loathsome cabin still*" (*Venus* 637).

(5) *my* sprites, *my* heart, *my* wit and force

> "a letter to *my* lord, *my* love, *my* dear" (*Lucrece* 1293); "*my* tears, *my* sighs, *my* groans" (*Lucrece* 588); "*My* mind, *my* thought, *my* busy care" (*Venus* 383).

(6, 18) *loss of my good name*

> Shakespeare may fairly be described as obsessed with the theme of *good name* and *loss of* same (see Looney 1920, 157-60; Spevack 866-67). The phrase *good name* occurs at least twelve times in the Shakespeare canon, including three uses of the phrase *my good name*. Perhaps best known is Iago's rumination on *loss of good name*: "*Good name* in man and woman. . .Is the immediate jewel of their souls. Who steals my purse steals trash . . ./ But he that *filches from me my good name/ Robs me* of that which not enriches him/ And makes me poor indeed" (*Oth.* 3.3.155-61).

> See also: "*Let my good name . . . be kept unspotted*" (*Lucrece* 820-21); "an excellent *good name*" (*Much* 3.1.98); "a *good name*" (*Much* 3.3.14); "your great deservings and *good name*" (*1 Hen. IV* 4.3.35); "well bred and of *good name*" (*2 Hen. IV* 1.1.26); "in *good name* and fame" (*2 Hen. IV* 2.4.75); "keep that *good name*" (*Hen. V* 3.7.102); "thy *good name*" (*Timon* 5.1.160); "[Cloten:] Sell me your *good report*. [Lady:] How? *My good name?*" (*Cym.* 2.3.83-84); "Some part of a *good name*" (*Kins.* 5.3.27).

> We should pursue the theme one step further. Looney noted in particular (158) the expectation or desire expressed in *Shake-speare's Sonnets* that the poet's name, due to some mysterious disgrace, should be "buried with his body" and would remain unknown to posterity—a point, as Looney noted, "quite inconsistent with either the Stratfordian or the Baconian theory of authorship," but strongly consistent with the Oxfordian one. Looney quoted at length from Sonnets 29, 71, 72, 81, 110, 111, 112, and 121.

> When *in disgrace with* Fortune *and men's eyes,*
> I all alone beweep *my outcast state,*
> And trouble deaf heaven with my bootless cries,
> And look upon myself and curse my fate.

> (*Sonnets* 29.1-4)

See also: "*The shame,/ Which like a canker in the fragrant Rose,/ Doth spot the beauty of thy budding name?*" (*Sonnets* 95.1-3); "*my name receives a brand*" (*Sonnets* 111.5); "*dishonor not her honorable name*" (*1 Hen. VI* 4.5.14); "hath dishonored Gloucester's honest name" (*2 Hen. VI* 2.1.193); "So shall *my name* with *slander's tongue be wounded*" (*2 Hen. VI* 3.2.68); "Never yet did base *dishonor blur our name*" (*2 Hen. VI* 4.1.39); "wrong the reputation of *your name*" (*LLL* 2.1.154); "who can *blot that name?*" (*Much* 4.1.80); "She *robs thee of thy name*" (*As You* 1.3.76); "*my land*[,]/ *Legitimation, name*, and all is gone" (*John* 1.1.247-48); "but *my fair name,/* Despite of death that lives upon my grave,/ To dark dishonor's use thou shalt not have" (*Rich. II* 1.1.167-69); "thou dost seek to *kill my name*" (*Rich. II* 2.1.86); "I love/ *The name of honor* more than I fear death" (*Caes.* 1.2.88-89); "To keep *my name* ungored" (*Ham.* 5.2.239); "O God, Horatio, *what a wounded name,/* Things standing thus unknown, shall live behind me!" (*Ham.* 5.2.333-34).

(7) *my voice* and *tongue* are *weak*

"To *beg the voice* and utterance of *my tongue*" (*Caes.* 3.1.261)

(7-8, 10-11) my mind, my wit, my head, my voice and tongue are *weak*
> To *utter, move,* devise, conceive, *sound forth, declare and speak*
> . . . Help crave I must . . .
> *Of all that may in heaven or hell,* in earth or air, be found

Compare the force of two verbs above (though the samples use *move* in different senses) in a similar rapid-fire list of verbs: "they . . . do muster true gait, eat, *speak,* and *move* under the *influence of the most received star; and though the devil lead* the measure [i.e., the dance], such are to be followed" (*All's Well* 2.1.52-56).

Both samples involve the subject seeking help from, or acting under the influence of, both *heavenly* and *hellish* forces. See also the parallels to lines 10-11 & 13-15, especially line 11.

Later, in the same scene of *All's Well*, *weak/speak* is echoed by *speak/weak*: "Methinks in thee some blessed spirit doth *speak/* His powerful *sound* within an organ *weak*" (*All's Well* 2.1.175-76). It would be unremarkable if each sample merely used the same two common words to create a rhyme, but both also present the same image of a *weak* vessel with a powerful message *to declare and speak.*

There's more: The latter Shakespearean lines are spoken by the King in response to Helena wagering—yes—the *loss of (her) good name* (see parallels to lines 6 & 18; see also line 2, *shame and infamy*), if she proves unable to cure the King's malady.

"*King.* What dar'st thou venture? *Helena.* Tax of [i.e., charge me with] impudence,/ A strumpet's boldness, a divulged *shame*/ Traduced by odious ballads; *my maiden's name Seared otherwise*" (2.1.170-73).

(10) *Help crave* I must, and *crave I will*

"*I crave* no more than hath your Highness offer'd,/ Nor *will* you *tender* less" (*Lear* 1.1.195).

(10-11, 13-15) *Help crave* I must . . .
   Of all that may *in heaven or hell, in earth or air,* be found

   . . .

   Help gods, help saints, help sprites and powers that in the heaven do dwell,
   Help ye that are to *wail,* ay wont, *ye howling hounds of hell,*
   Help man, *help* beasts, *help* birds and worms that on the
   earth doth toil

Echoing the young de Vere, Shakespeare's *Lucrece,* Joan of Arc in *I Hen. VI,* Prospero in *Tem.* and Queen Margaret in *Rich. III* all call upon various supernatural forces and entities for *help*:

"She conjures him by *high almighty Jove* . . ./ By *heaven and earth, and all the power of both* . . ./ To *all the host of heaven* I complain me" (*Lucrece* 568, 572, 598).

"Now *help, ye* charming *spells and periapts* [i.e., amulets, objects with supernatural *powers*]; And *ye choice spirits* that *admonish* me" (*1 Hen. VI* 5.3.2-3).

"*Ye elves* [i.e., *sprites or spirits*] of hills, brooks, standing lakes, and groves,/ And *ye that* on the sands with printless foot/ Do chase the ebbing Neptune . . . *you demi-puppets* [i.e., *elves or sprites or spirits*] . . . *by whose aid* . . . I have bedimmed/ The noontide sun, called forth mutinous winds" (*Tem.* 5.1.33-36, 40-42).

"A *hellhound* that doth hunt us all to death . . . *Earth* gapes, *hell* burns, *fiends roar, saints pray,*/ To have him suddenly conveyed from hence./ Cancel his bond of life, *dear God, I pray*" (*Rich. III* 4.4.48, 75-77).

Compare, in the last quotation above, the tersely rhythmic two-syllable clauses in de Vere's lines 13-15 with six similar clauses in the second part of that quotation — five of which use de Vere's very words.

Expanding on Prechter's astute observation (150), these four short

Shakespearean passages quoted above— each conveying the theme of desperately invoking supernatural *help*—use *fifteen words or phrases* a total of *nineteen times* that are identical or closely interchangeable with *fifteen words or phrases used twenty-four times* by the teenage de Vere *in just the five lines* quoted above, conveying the very same theme:

de Vere	**Shakespeare**
help ye	*help ye*
all that may in heaven or ... earth ... be found	*powers that in the heaven do dwell / heaven and earth, and all the power of both / all the host of heaven.*
sprites	*elves / demi-puppets*
hounds of hell	*hellhound / fiends / spirits*
gods	*God, Jove*
saints	*saints*
howling	*roar*
wail	*roar*
powers	*power*
heaven (twice)	*heaven* (twice)
hell and *hounds of hell*	*hell* and *hellhound*
help (eight times)	*help*
earth (twice)	*earth* (twice)
ye (twice)	*ye* (four times)
ye that	*ye that*

The modern pronoun "you" was becoming common in Shakespeare's time, and is used well over 14,000 times in the Shakespeare canon (Spevack 1566). The archaic *ye* (*OED* 20: 707-08), already starting to go out of fashion, occurs far less often—just 409 times in the canon (including all sixty-three instances of the contraction y" on the assumption *ye* was meant), i.e., less than 0.05% (<1 in 2,000) of all 880,000-plus words in the canon (Spevack 1555-56).

Here are the total counts in canonical Shakespeare for the other parallel words:

Help (339), *heaven(s)* (855), *hell* (171), *hound(s)* (42), *hellhound(s)* (3), *fiend(s)* (82), *earth* (332), *god(s)* (1,325), *Jove(s)* (102), *saint(s)* (131), *sprite(s)* (18), *spirit(s)* (396), *elf(ves)* (10), *demi-puppet(s)* (1) ("puppet(s)" alone appears another 10 times), *power(s)* (380), *wail(ed/ing/s)* (39), *howl(ed/ing/s)* (36), *roar(ed/ing/s)* (77) (Spevack 284, 339-40, 346-47, 410, 488-92, 564-66, 570-72, 604, 614, 651-52, 998-99, 1024, 1066, 1079-80, 1194-96, 1198, 1437).

Thus, the concentrated conjunction of all these words in just five lines of de Vere's poetry and four short Shakespearean scenes—*all five samples involving the very same motif of seeking supernatural assistance*—cannot plausibly be dismissed as an artifact of common usage. Most of these words are not rare in Shakespeare (though some are, as indicated above)—certainly not in such striking conjunction, matching de Vere's parallel concentrated usage.

Shakespeare also refers specifically elsewhere to *hounds of hell*:

"A pair of cursed *hell-hounds* and their dam" (*Titus* 5.2.144); "Turn, *hellhound*, turn!" (*Mac.* 5.8.3).

(12, 14) On the conjunction of *wail* and *howling*, see: "my father *wailing*, my sister crying, our maid *howling*" (*Two Gent.* 2.3.6-7).

(12, 18) To *wail with me this loss of mine . . ./*To *wail this loss of my* good name

"*Wailing our losses*" (*3 Hen. VI* 2.3.26); "Wise men ne'er sit and *wail their loss*" (*3 Hen. VI* 5.4.1); cf. "That she hath thee is *of my wailing* chief,/ A *loss* in love that touches *me* more dearly" (*Sonnets* 42.3).

Again we see in each sample, in strikingly similar words, the common interest in extreme states of emotion. Does the second parallel to *3 Hen. VI* suggest perhaps some wisdom that with age had come to the poet?

(16) fowl that flocks and feeds upon the *salt sea* soil

"*Salt-sea* shark" (*Mac.* 4.1.24).

Sobran observed this parallel (154), and some have suggested that the compound adjective *salt-sea* is rare. However, *EEBO* returns 164 hits on "salt sea" in ninety-two records before 1623, many of them compound adjectives modifying nouns. *Sea-salt*, on the other hand, as in "Drown the lamenting fool in *sea-salt tears*" (*Titus* 3.2.20), is rare, returning only ten hits in eight records (1473-1623).

See also: "Drown the lamenting fool [thy heart] in *sea-salt* tears" (*Titus* 3.2.20); "As many fresh streams meet in one *salt sea*" (*Hen. V* 1.2.210); "the eastern gate, all fiery red,/ Opening on Neptune . . ./ Turns into yellow gold *his salt green streams*" (*Dream* 3.2.391-93); cf. "With tears *as salt as sea*" (*2 Hen. VI* 3.2.96); "For still thy eyes, which I may call the sea,/ Do ebb and flow with tears; the bark thy body is,/ Sailing in this *salt flood*" (*R&J* 3.5.133-35); "*Neptune's salt wash*" (*Ham.* 3.2.147).

Additional parallels:

(1) forlorn *hope, past all recovery*

> "For grief that they are *past recovery;* For were there *hope* to conquer them again" (*2 Hen. VI* 1.1.114-15).

(2) *shame* and infamy

> "*Shame* and trouble" (*Errors* 5.1.14)

(4) *death delayed* to keep from life the harm of *hapless days*

> "His *days may finish* ere that *hapless time*" (*2 Hen. VI* 3.1.200); "In the *delaying death*" (*Meas.* 4.2.164).

(5) in *deep distress* are *drowned*

> Ophelia, *drowning,* is "incapable of her own *distress*" (*Ham.* 4.7.178); "And homeward through the dark laund runs apace;/ Leaves Love upon her back *deeply distress'd.*" (*Venus* 813-14); "When I do tell thee, there *my hopes* lie *drown'd,*/ Reply not in how many fathoms *deep*/ They lie indrench'd" (*Troil.* 1.1.); "And *deeper* than did *ever* plummet sound/ I'll *drown* my book" (*Tem.* 5.1.56).

(6, 12, 18) of these *griefs* the *ground*

> "Any *ground* To build a *grief* on" (*2 Hen. IV* 4.1.109-10).

> In addition to the alliterative word parallel, note the similar usage of the less common singular *ground,* in atypical relation to emotions as opposed to cognitive or rational matters (contrast, e.g., "grounds for a claim"). See also: "We see *the ground* whereon these *woes* do lie,/ But the *true ground* of all these piteous *woes*/ We cannot without circumstance descry" (*R&J* 5.3.179-80); "A reverend man . . . desires to know/ In brief the *grounds* and motives of her *woe*" (*Lover's Comp.* 63).

(9) Such *piercing plaints* as answer might

> "Hearing how our *plaints* and prayers do *pierce*" (*Rich. II* 5.3.127);

(9) or would, my *woeful case*

> "the traitor /Stands in *worse case of woe*" (*Cym.* 3.4.86-87).

(10) *Help crave I* must, and crave I will

> "Hence *will I* to my ghostly father's cell, His *help* to *crave*" (*R&J* 2.2.189-90).

(10) *with tears* upon my *face*

> "Cooling his hot *face* in the chastest *tears*" (*Lucrece* 682); "Poor soul, thy *face* is much abused *with tears*" (*R&J* 4.1.29).

On the theme of *tears* and weeping, see also 3.13, 5.12, 6.26, 9.1, and 17.8-9.

(11) *in heaven or hell, in earth or air*

Yet more parallels to this line in particular (see also those to lines 7-8 & 10-11, and to lines 10-11 & 13-15):

"Whether *in sea or fire, in earth or air,*/ Th' extravagant and erring spirit hies/ To his confine" (*Ham.* 1.1.153); "Bring with thee airs from *heaven* or blasts from *hell*" (*Ham.* 1.4.41); "Am I *in earth, in heaven, or in hell?*" (*Errors* 2.2.211); "*I' th' air or th' earth?*" (*Tem.* 1.2.388).

(17) *echo that in air doth flee, shrill voices* to resound

"*Shrill echoes* from the hollow earth" (*Shrew* ind.2.46); "What *shrill-voiced* suppliant makes this eager cry?" (*Rich. II* 5.3.75); cf. "thy small pipe/ Is as the maiden's organ, *shrill* and sound" (*Twelfth* 1.4.31-32).

(18) To *wail this loss* of my good name, as of these *griefs* the ground

"Long mayst thou live *to wail thy children's loss*" (*Rich. III* 1.3.203); "It were *lost sorrow* to wail one that's *lost*" (*Rich. III* 2.2.11)

(18) as of these *griefs the ground*

"It not appears to me . . ./ That you should have an inch of *any ground*/ To build *a grief on*" (*2 Hen. IV* 4.1.107-110).

Previous commentaries: Looney (1920, 157-60); Prechter (2012).

E.O. 5: "I Am Not as I Seem to Be"

1   I am not as I seem to be,
2   Nor when I smile I am not glad,
3   A thrall although you count me free
4   I, most in mirth, most pensive-sad;
5   I smile to shade my bitter spite,
6   As Hannibal, that saw in sight
7   His country soil, with Carthage town,
8   By Roman force defaced down.

9   And Caesar, that presented was
10 With noble Pompey's princely head,
11 As 'twere some judge to rule the case,
12 A flood of tears he seemed to shed;
13 Although indeed it sprung of joy,
14 Yet others thought it was annoy;
15 Thus contraries be used, I find,
16 Of wise to cloak the covert mind.

17 I Hannibal, that smiles for grief,
18 And let you Caesar's tears suffice,
19 The one that laughs at his mischief,
20 The other all for joy that cries;
21 I smile to see me scorned so,
22 You weep for joy to see me woe,
23 And I a heart by love slain dead
24 Presents, in place of Pompey's head.

25 O cruel hap and hard estate
26 That forceth me to love my foe,
27 Accursed by so foul a fate
28 My choice for to prefix it so,
29 So long to fight with secret sore,
30 And find no secret salve therefor;
31 Some purge their pain by plaint, I find,
32 But I in vain do breathe my wind.

Structure: Four eight-line stanzas of iambic tetrameter.

Textual sources: F.p. *Paradise* (1576), 76-77 as by "E.O.," attribution altered to "E.Ox." in 1578 (K2v) and 1585 (K4r); Grosart (395-96); Looney (1921, Miller ed. 1975, 1: 587-88); May (1980, 28-29; 1991, 273-74). May #5. Looney's title: same as above. *Paradise* title: "Not attaining his desire, he complaineth."

Explanatory Notes:

(10, 24) *Pompey* refers to the ancient Roman consul (106-48 BCE).

(30)   *Therefor,* modernized from *therefore,* does not mean "for that reason" or "it follows that," but rather, simply "*for* (something)" (i.e., the *salve* is *for* the *sore*) (*OED* 17: 909).

Strongest parallels:

(1) *I am not as I seem to be*

> "*I am not what I am*" (*Twelfth* 3.1.140, and *Oth.* 1.1.65); "*I am not I,* if there be such" (*R&J* 3.2.50); "Richard loves Richard; that is, *I am I*" (*Rich. III* 5.3.199); "*I'll seem* the fool *I am not*" (*A&C* 1.1.42).

> De Vere and Shakespeare very distinctively ring variations on the Biblical phrase "*I am* that *I am*" (Exodus 3.14) (meaning "*I am* that [which] *I am*").

> See also de Vere's defiant letter of October 30, 1584, to his father-in-law, William Cecil (Lord Burghley): "I mean not to be your ward nor your child, I serve Her Majesty, and *I am* that *I am*" (Fowler 321).

> See also, with the same meaning: "*I am* that *I am*" (*Sonnets* 121.9). Compare, indeed, the entire theme of Sonnet 121, best known by its memorable first line: "'Tis better *to be vile* than *vile esteemed,*" where the same contrast between *being* and *appearance* is fundamental.

> This entire de Vere poem (see also, e.g., line 2, *when I smile I am not glad,* and line 16, *to cloak the covert mind*), and numerous Shakespearean passages (those quoted above being merely a few examples), explore the ancient philosophical dichotomy between appearance and being.

> This *topos* of *dissimulatio*—the purposeful obscuring of an internal mental state, used by various characters, especially in the histories and tragedies for the sake of Machiavellian advantage (often imitated from Seneca)—is immensely important to Shakespearean studies and strongly imprinted on both bodies of work compared here. On this leitmotif of *dissimulation,* see also E.O. 6.4, 9.2, 10.9-10, 12.16, and 18.40.

(2) Nor *when I smile I am not glad*

> "Not a courtier,/ Although they wear their faces to the bent/ Of *the king's looks,* hath a heart that *is not/ Glad at* the thing *they scowl* at" (*Cym.* 1.1.13-15); "I am *not merry*; but *I do beguile/The thing I am,* by *seeming* otherwise" (*Oth.* 2.1.122); "*Buried this sigh* in wrinkle of *a smile:/* But *sorrow,* that is couch'd in *seeming gladness,/* Is like that *mirth* fate turns to *sudden sadness*" (*Troil.* 1.1.38-40).

(2) *I am not glad*

> "*I am not glad* that such a sore of time/ Should seek a plaster by contemn'd revolt" (*John* 5.2.13). The phrase *I am not glad* returns only two hits in *EEBO* (1473-1623): to Oxford's poem and the *John* passage.

(4) I, most in *mirth,* most *pensive-sad*

> "*I show more mirth* than I am mistress of" (*As You* 1.2.3); "With *mirth* in funeral, and with *dirge* in marriage" (*Ham.* 1.2.12); "So mingled as if *mirth* did make him *sad*" (*Kins.* 5.3.52); "But *sorrow* that is couched in *seeming gladness* is like that *mirth* fate turns to *sudden sadness*" (*Troil.* 1.1.40); "*sad* tales doth tell/ To pencilled *pensiveness*" (*Lucrece* 1496-97).

> Beyond *dissimulation,* the line invokes the related but distinct Shakespearean motif of antithetical states of emotion, discussed further in connection with lines 17-22 and E.O. 12.5-6. Looney commented perceptively (1920, 168, and generally 167-70) on the vivid duality and contrast reflected in line 4 (among others in these poems) between light humor and stark grief: these lines foreshadow Shakespeare's "striking combination" and "startling contrast" between "high comedy and profound tragedy" (167). It is worth noticing in this context that although Oxford was honored and remembered as a writer of comedies, the dominant tone of the poetry published under his own name is of loss, unrequited secret love for a powerful woman, and shame, just like *Shake-speare's Sonnets.*

(4, 12, 14, 17, 18) *mirth,* most *pensive-sad . . . flood of tears . . . annoy . . . grief . . . tears suffice*

> Compare two passages from *Lucrece*:

>> For *mirth* doth search the bottom of *annoy;*
>> *Sad* souls are slain in *merry* company;
>> *Grief* best is pleased with *grief's* society.
>> True *sorrow* then is feelingly *sufficed*
>> When with like semblance it is sympathized.
>>> (1109-13)

>> Dear lord, thy *sorrow* to my *sorrow* lendeth
>> Another power; no *flood* by raining slaketh.
>> My *woe* too sensible thy passion maketh,
>> More *feeling-painful.* Let it then *suffice*
>> To drown one *woe,* one pair of *weeping eyes.*
>>> (1676-80)

(15) *These contraries* be used, I find

> *These contraries* such unity do hold (*Lucrece* 1558); I' the commonwealth I would *by contraries*/ Execute all things (*Tem.* 2.1.148)

(17-22) *I Hannibal,* that *smiles for grief,*
  And let you *Caesar's tears* suffice,
  The one that *laughs* at his *mischief,*
  The other all for *joy* that *cries;*
  I *smile* to see me *scorned* so,
  You *weep* for *joy* to see me *woe*

> "Then they for sudden *joy* did *weep,* And I for *sorrow* sung, That *such a king* should play bo-peep, And go the fools among" (*Lear* 1.4.175); "*weeping joys*" (*2 Hen. VI* 1.1.34); "how much better is it to *weep at joy than to joy at weeping!*" (*Much* 1.1.28).

> The antithetical states of emotion continue the common thread seen in other parallels, revealing the Shakespearean tendency to treat ostensibly opposing emotions as instead paradoxically correlative. See also line 4 (*most in mirth, most pensive-sad*) and E.O. 12.5-6.

> The example above from *King Lear,* when contrasted with the Oxford lines, gives a nice snapshot of the developmental patterns of the artist. The *weeping* and *joy* motifs are handled with considerably greater naturalism in the mature work—and yet the connectedness in diction and thought of one with the other is quite evident on careful inspection.

Additional parallels:

(2) when I smile *I am not glad*

> "*I am not merry*; but I do beguile/ The thing I am by seeming otherwise" (*Oth.* 2.1.125).

(6-7) As *Hannibal,* that saw in sight
 His country soil, with *Carthage town*

> Four references to *Hannibal* and seven to *Carthage* occur in Shakespeare (Spevack 184, 536), e.g., "My thoughts are whirled like a potter's wheel;/ I know not where I am, nor what I do;/ A witch, by fear, not force, *like Hannibal,*/ Drives back our troops and conquers as she lists" (*1 Hen. VI* 1.5.19-22).

(8) By Roman force *defaced* down

> "And see *the cities and the towns defaced*" (*1 Hen. VI* 3.3.45).

> In Shakespeare the idea of *deface*ment is closely connected to the related notions of *erasure* or "deformation," and the manner in which "the line between the 'psychological' and the 'historical' is blurred" (Garber 1987 32-38).

> See also E.O. 10.16 (*raze the ground*).

(10) *Pompey's* princely head

> The name *Pompey* appears twice in this poem (see also line 24). Two of Shakespeare's Roman plays (*Julius Caesar* and *Anthony and Cleopatra*), and three others (*Hen. V*; *2 Hen. VI*; and *LLL* [act 5 of the latter is largely devoted to a scene in which a character plays *Pompey*]), make a total of sixty-five references to *Pompey*, the Roman consul (not counting twenty-six references to the clownish pimp "Pompey" in *Meas.*) (Spevack 992-93).

(10) *Noble* Pompey's *princely head*

> "When as the *noble* Duke of York *was slain*,/ Your *princely father* and my loving lord!" (*3 Hen. VI* 2.1.47-47); "The aweless lion could not wage the fight,/ Nor keep his *princely heart* from Richard's *hand*" (*John* 1.1.267); "And, *princely peers*, a happy time of day!" (*Rich. III* 2.1.48).

(12) *A flood of tears he seemed to shed*

> "Return thee therefore with *a flood of tears*" (*1 Hen. VI* 3.3.56); "My heart is drowned with grief, Whose *flood begins to flow within mine eyes*" (*2 Hen. VI* 3.1.198-99); "*floods of tears* will drown my oratory" (*Titus* 5.3.90); "drown me in thy sister's *flood of tears!*" (*Errors* 3.2.46); "till *the tears that she hath shed* for thee *Like envious floods o'er-run* her lovely face" (*Shrew* ind.2.62-63).

> On the theme of *tears* and weeping, see also lines 17-22, and E. O. 3.13, 4.10, 6.26, 9.1, and 17.8-9.

(13-14) Although indeed it sprung of *joy*,/ Yet others thought it was *annoy*

> A characteristic Shakespearean rhyme scheme, occurring seven times in Shakespeare, e.g., "But now I lived, and life was *death's annoy*;/ But now I died, and death was *lively joy*" (*Venus* 497-98).

(16) *to cloak* the *covert mind*

> "*To cloak* offenses with a *cunning brow*" (*Lucrece* 749).

> On the leitmotif of *dissimulation*, see also line 1, and E.O. 6.4, 9.2, 10.9-10, 12.16, and (again using the word *cloak*) 18.40.

(23) *a heart by love slain dead*

> "Number there in *love* was *slain*" (*P&T* 28); "Presume not on thy *heart* when mine *is slain*" (*Sonnets* 22.13).

(25) O cruel *hap* and *hard estate*

> "Our *hap is loss*, our hope but sad despair" (*3 Hen. VI* 2.3.9); "'twere *hard* luck, being in so preposterous *estate* as we are" (*Win.* 5.2.147-48).

(26) *That forceth me to love my foe*

> "*My only love, sprung from my only hate!* . . ./ Prodigious birth of *love* it is to me

> *That I must love a loathed enemy!"* (*R&J* 1.5.138 140-41).

(29-30) So long to fight with secret *sore*, And find no secret *salve* therefor

> "A *salve* for any *sore* that may betide" (*3 Hen. VI* 4.6.88).

> See also parallels to E.O. 9.22 (*She is my salve, she is my wounded sore*) and E.O. 18.9 (*No wily wit to salve a sore*). The *salve/sore* motif (like some others) was echoed by many other Elizabethan poets and writers (*EEBO* returns 424 hits in 267 records for the search "*salve* near *sore*"). As with the vast majority of these parallels, their significance lies in their cumulative force when considered in light of the rarer "coincidences" documented here.

(32) But I *in vain* do *breathe my wind*

> "You *breathe in vain*" (*Timon* 3.5.59); "no *wind* of blame shall *breathe*" (*Ham.* 4.7.65).

The more mature thought has gained clarity and energy through compression, but the idiom is preserved. The locution *in vain*, which occurs three times in these de Vere poems (see also E.O. 9.26 and 18b.11), appears another forty times in canonical Shakespeare (Spevack 1421).

Previous commentaries: Looney (1920, 168-70); Singleton (84-87); Sobran (240-41); Brazil & Flues; Goldstein (2016, 55-58).

E.O. 6: "If Care or Skill Could Conquer Vain Desire"

1   If care or skill could conquer vain desire,
2   Or reason's reins my strong affection stay,
3   Then should my sighs to quiet breast retire,
4   And shun such signs as secret thoughts bewray;
5   Uncomely love, which now lurks in my breast,
6   Should cease my grief, through wisdom's power oppressed.

7   But who can leave to look on Venus' face,
8   Or yieldeth not to Juno's high estate?
9   What wit so wise as gives not Pallas place?
10   These virtues rare each God did yield a mate,
11   Save her alone who yet on earth doth reign,
12   Whose beauty's string no Gods can well distrain.

13   What worldly wight can hope for heavenly hire
14   When only sighs must make his secret moan?
15   A silent suit doth seld to Grace aspire;
16   My hapless hap doth roll the restless stone;
17   Yet Phoebe fair disdained the heavens above,
18   To joy on earth her poor Endymion's love.

19   Rare is reward where none can justly crave,
20   For chance is choice where reason makes no claim;
21   Yet luck sometimes despairing souls doth save:
22   A happy star made Gyges joy attain;
23   A slavish smith of rude and rascal race
24   Found means in time to gain a Goddess' grace.

25   Then lofty Love thy sacred sails advance;
26   My seething seas shall flow with streams of tears.
27   Amidst disdain drive forth my doleful chance;
28   A valiant mind no deadly danger fears.
29   Who loves aloft and sets his heart on high,
30   Deserves no pain, though he do pine and die.

Structure: Five six-line stanzas of iambic pentameter.

Textual sources: F.p. *Paradise* (1576), 74-75, where it is originally attributed to "M.B."; attribution corrected to "E.O." in 1578, R1v. Grosart (399-400); Looney (1921, Miller ed. 1975, 1: 592-93); May (1980, 29-30; 1991, 274-75). May #6. Looney's title: "Reason and Affection." *Paradise* title: "Being in Love, he Complaineth."

Explanatory Notes:

(7)   *Venus* is the Roman goddess of love (Aphrodite to the Greeks), married to Vulcan.

(8)   *Juno* refers to the Roman goddess, wife of Jupiter and equivalent to the Greek queen of the gods, Hera (wife of Zeus).

        Venus . . . Juno . . . Pallas together suggest the contemporary allegorization of Elizabeth I as the actual winner of the ancient mythic contest of female aspects, as displayed for example in the 1569 mythological portrait by Hans Eworth of her defeating Venus, Pallas, and Hera to carry away the apple of feminine dominance.

        There are thirty-three references to the Roman goddess *Venus* (Aphrodite to the Greeks) in canonical Shakespeare, along with two to Minerva (one quoted above) and four to the Greek goddess *Pallas* (Spevack 826, 956, 1425). Minerva is the Roman name of *Pallas* (also known to the Greeks as Athena).

        Interestingly, there are no canonical Shakespearean references (nor by de Vere in the poems studied here) to Aphrodite or Athena. Thus, both de Vere and canonical Shakespeare seem to prefer *Venus* (in place of Aphrodite) and *Pallas* (instead of Athena or Minerva, the latter being also not mentioned in these de Vere poems).

        Lines 7-10 refer glancingly to the amours of the gods (a common interest of these de Vere poems and Shakespeare), also referenced in lines 17-18 and 23-24, and in E.O. 3.6, 8.6, and 14.31-32.

(9) *Pallas Athena* (known to the Romans by the Latin name Minerva), the goddess of political prudence, warfare, and the arts; the patron saint of Athens and all things Athenian; in statecraft an advisor and strategist, as to Odysseus in the final chapters of *The Odyssey*; in philosophy the patroness of wisdom, and in the arts, of the theatre as well as handicraft, as exemplified by the Aventine temple of Minerva, from its earliest records in the 3rd c. BCE not only a temple but a theatrical guild including both actors and writers. Line 9 is the only reference to *Pallas* in these de Vere poems.

(9)   The term *wit* as used here refers to intelligence or mental sharpness, not humor (*OED* 20: 432-34).

(13)   A *wight* is a person (male or female), with some connotation of commiseration or contempt (OED 20: 328).

(17)   *Phoebe*, a Greek goddess associated with the moon, is referred to three times by Shakespeare (Spevack 977).

(18)   *Endymion*, a handsome young shepherd/astronomer in Greek tradition (Apollodorus and Pausanius, among others) who fell in love with the

moon, is the title character of John Lyly's (c. 1586) *Endymion*, a court allegory featuring a protagonist based on Lyly's patron, Oxford. The only Shakespearean reference to him (Spevack 353) is quoted below.

(22) *Gyges*, in Greek mythology, is a shepherd who seizes the throne of Lydia and is said to possess a magic ring rendering him invisible.

(23-24) The "slavish smith" refers to Vulcan, Roman god of metallurgy and crafts, married to *Venus* (see above on line 7).

Strongest parallels:

(3) *to quiet breast* retire

> "*Into the quiet closure of my breast*" (*Venus* 782); cf. "Truth hath a *quiet breast*" (*Rich. II* 1.3.96). *EEBO* (1473-1623) returns only ten hits in ten records for the search *quiet breast,* including both E.O. 6 and *Rich. II.*

(16) My hapless hap doth *roll the restless stone*

> "Giddy Fortune's furious fickle wheel—That goddess blind, That stands upon *the rolling restless stone*" (*Hen. V* 3.6.26-28); cf. "I told ye all, When we first put this dangerous *stone a-rolling,* 'Twould fall upon ourselves" (*Hen. VIII* 5.3.103-05). *EEBO* confirms the rarity of the two closely related phrases, *roll the restless stone* (de Vere) and *rolling restless stone* (Shakespeare): the former phrase returns only five hits (1473-1623), including to de Vere's *Paradise* poem; *rolling restless stone* returns only two hits, both to *Henry V.*

(26) *My seething seas shall flow with streams of tears*

> Eric Sams notes that Shakespeare spontaneously associates tears with dynamic bodies of water: "*Tears* . . . resemble rivers or the *sea* in their drowning capacity. . . . Further, both elements are salt" (313).

> Perhaps most telling parallel to de Vere's lyric (among many others) is *Romeo & Juliet*: "For still thy eyes, which I may call *the sea,/ Do* ebb and *flow with tears;* the bark thy body is,/ Sailing in this *salt flood*" (*R&J* 3.5.133-35).

> See also E.O. 4.16, 12.19 and 18.33 (associating motions of the *sea*, or objects on the *sea*, with emotions). On the general theme of *tears* and weeping, see also E.O. 3.13, 4.10, 5.12, 9.1, and 17.8-9.

> Compare also: "Mine eyes. . . As from a mountain *stream*. . ./ Shall *gush* pure *streams*" (*Lucrece* 1076-78); "And about her *tear-distained* eye blue circles *streamed*" (*Lucrece* 1587-88); "*My heart is drowned* with grief,/ *Whose flood begins to flow* within mine eyes" (*2 Hen. VI* 3.1.198-99); "Fain would I . . . *drain* Upon his face *an ocean of salt tears*" (*2 Hen. VI* 3.2.141-43); "just against thy heart make thou a hole,/ That *all the tears that thy poor eyes let fall/ May run* into that sink, and soaking in,/ *Drown* the lamenting fool in *sea-salt tears*" (*Titus* 3.2.17-20); "my eye shall be *the stream*" (*Merch.* 3.2.46); "Had I

as many eyes as thou hast wounds,/ *Weeping* as fast as they *stream forth* thy blood" (*Caes.* 3.1.200-01).

Aside from the parallels, surely line 26 exhibits some proto-Shakespearean power and beauty. Instead of the more predictably structured metaphor one might expect (e.g., "*my tears flow* like the *seas*"—a model actually followed by two Shakespearean samples above: "mine eyes . . . gush pure *streams*" and "drain upon his face an ocean"), the young de Vere deftly inverts this to suggest *seas* of emotion within that are revealed through the external sign of tears.

Shakespeare, and originally the young de Vere, may deserve credit for influencing the signature lyric of the extraordinarily popular and durable lute song ("Flow, My Tears"), written after 1596 by John Dowland (1563-1626).

Additional parallels:

(1) *conquer* vain *desire*

> "Therefore, brave *conquerors*—for so you are,/ That *war against your own affections*/ And the huge army of the world's *desires*" (*LLL* 1.1.8-10).

(2) *reason's reins my strong affection stay*

> "Curb *his heat*, or *rein his rash desire*" (*Lucrece* 706); "for now I give *my sensual race the rein*" (*Meas.* 2.4.160); "What *rein* can hold *licentious wickedness*" (*Hen. V* 3.3.22); "he cannot/ Be *reined* again to *temperance*" (*Cor.* 3.3.28).

> The image, found often in Shakespeare, is of emotion being *reined* in. The danger posed by emotion is construed in equestrian terms, as if one might relax or tighten the *reins*. Cf. "Let wisedome *bridle* brainsicke wit ("In Prayse of the Snayle").

> See also: "in all *reason,* we must *stay* the time" (*Dream* 5.1.248); "*Stay* yet; hear *reason*" (*Lear* 5.3.82); "*Stay,* my lord,/ And *let your reason with your choler question*" (*Hen. VIII* 1.1.129-30).

(4) *secret thoughts*

> The history of all her *secret thoughts*" (*Rich. II* 3.5.28); "Nor shall he smile at thee in *secret thought*" (*Lucrece* 1065); on the dissimulation leitmotif, a common pattern in both samples, see also E.O. 5 (*passim*) and E.O. 9.2, 10.9-10, 12.16, and 18.40 as well as further discussion in volume II, appendix E. Index of Motifs.

(5) Uncomely love, which now *lurks in my breast*

> "Tyrant folly *lurk in gentle breasts*" (*Lucrece* 851).

(6) my *grief,* through wisdom's power *oppressed*

> "To counterfeit *oppression* of such *grief*" (*Rich. II* 1.4.14).

(7, 9) *Venus'* face . . . *Pallas* place?

> "Laming the shrine of *Venus*, or straight-pight [erect] *Minerva*" (*Cym.* 5.5.164).

(9) What *wit* so *wise* as gives not Pallas place?

> As noted above, *wit* refers here to intelligence or mental sharpness, not humor. The juxtaposition of *wise* (176 canonical references) and *wit* (268) (see Spevack 1521, 1523) is typically Shakespearean, e.g.: "Your *wit* makes *wise* things foolish . . ./ *Wise* things seem foolish and rich things but poor (*LLL* 5.2.374-78); "This fellow is *wise* enough to play the fool;/ And to do that well craves a kind of *wit*" (*Twelfth* 3.1.60-61); "For though it have holp madmen to their *wits*, In me it seems it will make *wise* men mad" (*Rich. II* 5.5.62-63).

> See also E.O. 9.16 (*wisest wit*), E.O. 10.12 (*wit ... will*), and E.O. 18.9 (*wily wit*).

(13) What *worldly wight* can hope for *heavenly* hire?

> The antithesis between *worldly* (or "earthly") and *heavenly* is another pattern found in both samples, e.g., "My vow was *earthly*, thou a *heavenly love*" (*LLL* 4.3.64); "a *heavenly effect* in an *earthly actor*" (*All's Well* 2.3.23); "heaven's praise with such an *earthly tongue*" (*LLL* 4.2.118); "Between this *heavenly* and this *earthly* sun" (*Venus* 198); "Such *heavenly* touches ne'er touched *earthly* faces" (*Sonnets* 17.8).

(13) can *hope for* heavenly hire?

> "How shalt thou *hope for* mercy, rendering none?" (*Merch.* 4.1.88).

(17-18) *Phoebe* fair disdained the heavens above,/ *To joy on earth her poor Endymion's love*

> "A title to *Phoebe*, to *Luna*, to *the moon*" (*LLL* 4.2.37); "And *the moon sleeps with Endymion*" (*Merch.* 5.1.109).

> On the amours of the gods (a common interest of these de Vere poems and Shakespeare), see also lines 7-10 and 23-24, and E.O. 3.6, 8.6, and 14.31-32.

(22) *A happy star* made Gyges joy obtain

> "*A happy star*/ Led us to Rome" (*Titus* 4.2.32-33); cf. "my thwarting *stars*" (3 *Hen. VI* 4.6.22); "no comfortable *star*" (*Lucrece* 164); "constant *stars*" (*Sonnets* 14.1). An *EEBO* search for the phrase *happy star* (1473-1623) returns only twenty-four hits in twenty records.

> Adjectives used to personify *stars* are common in canonical Shakespeare. *Star* (and related variants and compounds) occurs 147 times in the canon (Spevack 1203-04). Variants from de Vere's letters include "I know not by what unfortunate *star*" (Fowler 652).

As noted above, *Gyges* is a mythological Greek shepherd-king who obtained power by using a magic ring of invisibility. Fletcher in *Fair Maid of the Inn* (1647) exposes the early modern association of Gyges's ring with the popular belief that fern seed could confer invisibility. That fern seed, like Gyges's ring, could confer invisibility, is also the basis for the conversation between Gadshill and the Chamberlain in *1 Hen. IV*:

"Gadshill. . . . We steal as in a castle, cocksure; we have *the receipt of fern-seed, we walk invisible. Chamberlain.* Nay, by my faith, I think you are more beholding to the night than to *fern-seed* for your *walking invisible.*"

(2.1.86-90)

(23-24) *A slavish smith* of rude and rascal race/ Found means in time to *gain a Goddess' grace*

The references are to Vulcan, Roman god of metallurgy and craft, and his wife *Venus* (see line 7). Vulcan is referred to six times in canonical Shakespeare (Spevack 1436), e.g., "as like as *Vulcan and his wife*" (*Troil.*1.3.168).

On the amours of the gods (a common theme of these de Vere poems and Shakespeare), see also lines 7-10 and 17-18, and E.O. 3.6, 8.6, and 14.31-32.

(23) of *rude and rascal race*

"Like *a rude and savage man* of Inde" (*LLL* 4.3.218); "too *rude and bold* of voice" (*Merch.* 2.2.181).

(25) lofty *Love* thy *sacred sails* advance

"*Purple the sails*, and so perfumed that/ The winds were *love-sick* with them" (*A&C* 2.2.193-94). Shakespeare is one of only four poets who spontaneously associates *sails* and *love;* E.O. 6 (1576) is the first recorded instance in *EEBO*.

(29-30) Who loves aloft and sets *his heart on high*

"Just *as high as my heart*" (*As You* 3.2.96).

(29-30) Who *loves* aloft and sets his heart on high, /Deserves no pain, though *he do pine and die*

"To *love*, to wealth, to pomp, *I pine and die*" (*LLL* 1.1.31).

Previous commentaries: Ogburn (588); Sobran (242-43); Brazil & Flues.

E.O. 7: "What Wonders Love Hath Wrought"

1   To work what wonders love hath wrought,
2   Wherewith I muse why men of wit have love so dearly bought;
3   For love is worse than hate, and eke more harm hath done:
4   Record I take of those that rede of Paris, Priam's son.
5   It seemed the God of sleep had mazed so much his wits
6   When he refused wit for love, which cometh but by fits;
7   But why accuse I him, whom earth hath covered long?
8   There be of his posterity alive, I do him wrong.
9   Whom I might well condemn to be a cruel judge
10   Unto myself, who hath the crime in others that I grudge.

Structure: Two stanzas of four lines each of rhyming couplets, with terminal rhyming couplet.

Textual sources: F.p. *Paradise* (1576), 78. Grosart (410); Looney (1921, Miller ed. 1975, 1: 594); May (1980, 30; 1991, 275). May #7. Looney's title: "Love and Wit."

Explanatory notes:

(2, 5-6) *Wit* or *wits*, mental acuity, not humor (*OED* 20: 432-34).

(3)   *Eke*, an archaic synonym for "also" or "in addition" (*OED* 5: 105).

(4)   *Rede,* an archaic verb meaning to advise or counsel (*OED* 13: 409). *Paris*, in Greek mythology, is the son of King *Priam* of Troy.

(5)   In modern English, *mazed* has fairly mild connotations of amazement, dazedness, confusion, or bewilderment, but into the 16th century could include more severe mental derangement—to be crazed or delirious (*OED* 9: 507-08). See also E.O. 10.3 (*My mazed mind in malice so is set*).

Strongest Parallels:

(2) *I muse why* men of wit

> "*I muse why* she's at liberty" (*Rich. III* 1.3.304). *EEBO* returns only twelve hits in eleven records from 1473 to 1623 for the locution *I muse why,* including the *Rich. III* passage, but not E.O. 7.

(5) *the God of sleep*

> "On your eyelids crown *the god of sleep,/ Charming* your blood with pleasing heaviness" (*1 Hen. IV* 3.1.214). The phrase "god of sleep" is rare in early modern documents; *EEBO* (1473-1623) returns only twenty-four hits in twenty records where it appears.

An interest in the curative powers of *sleep* (and here, the bewitching powers of this deity) is another motif in Shakespeare's variegated study of psychology. Neither Shakespeare nor this de Vere poem uses the god's proper name, *Hypnos* or *Somnus*.

(6) love, which *cometh but by fits*

"'Tis said a woman's fitness *comes by fits*" (*Cym.* 4.1.6). Like "god of sleep," variants of the phrase *come by fits* (*came, commeth,* and *comes*) appear in only fifteen hits in fifteen *EEBO* records (1473-1623), including this *Cym.* quote from the 1623 F1. The "wits"/"fits" rhyme is also attested in Shakespeare: "The consequence is then thy jealous *fits*/ Have scared thy husband from the use of *wits*" (*Errors* 5.1.85-86)

Additional Parallels:

(1) what *wonders love hath wrought*

"*Love wrought* these *miracles*" (*Shrew* 5.1.124).

The locution *hath wrought* occurs five times in Shakespeare (Spevack 1555), e.g., "Now she unweaves the web that she hath wrought;/ Adonis lives, and Death is not to blame" (*Venus* 991-92).

(2) have love so *dearly bought*

"The pound of flesh, which I demand of him, Is *dearly bought*" (*Merch.* 4.1.99-100).

(4) *Paris, Priam's son*

This is a common mythological point of reference throughout the Shakespeare canon, e.g.:

"Had doting *Priam* checked his *son's* desire" (*Lucrece* 1490); "As *Priam* was for all his valiant *sons*" (*3 Hen. VI* 2.5.120); "*sons*,/ Half of the number *that King Priam had*" (*Titus* 1.1.80); "all *Priam's sons*" (*Troil.* 2.2.126); "You valiant *offspring of great Priamus*" (*Troil.* 2.2.207); "*a son of Priam*" (*Troil.* 3.3.26); "the youngest *son of Priam*" (*Troil.* 4.5.96); "*great Priam's seed*" (*Troil.* 4.5.121); "A bastard *son of Priam's*" (*Troil.* 5.7.15).

(8) I *do him wrong*

"You *do him wrong*, surely" (*Meas.* 3.2.129); "*I* never *do him wrong*,/ But he does buy my injuries, to be friends" (*Cym.* 1.1.101-03).

(10) who hath *the crime* in others that *I grudge*

"*My blood is mingled* with *the crime* of lust" (*Errors* 2.2.141); "My noble queen, let *former grudges* pass" (*3 Hen. VI* 3.3.195).

Previous commentary: Sobran (244-45).

E.O. 8: "The Lively Lark Stretched Forth Her Wing"

1   The lively lark stretched forth her wing,
2   The messenger of morning bright,
3   And with her cheerful voice did sing
4   The day's approach, discharging night,
5   When that Aurora, blushing red,
6   Descried the guilt of Thetis' bed.

7   I went abroad to take the air,
8   And in the meads I met a knight,
9   Clad in carnation colour fair;
10   I did salute this gentle wight,
11   Of him I did his name inquire.
12   He sighed, and said he was desire.

13   Desire I did desire to stay,
14   Awhile with him I craved to talk;
15   The courteous knight said me no nay,
16   But hand in hand with me did walk.
17   Then of desire I asked again
18   What thing did please and what did pain?

19   He smiled, and thus he answered then,
20   "Desire can have no greater pain
21   "Than for to see another man
22   "That he desireth to obtain;
23   "Nor greater joy can be than this,
24   "Than to enjoy that others miss."
25   Laridon, tan tan

Structure: Four stanzas of six lines of iambic tetrameter with "nonsense" song refrain concluding short line.

Textual sources: F.p. *Paradise* (1576) 69, but omitted from 1578 and subsequent editions. Grosart (405-06); Looney (1921, Miller ed. 1975, 1: 565); May (1980, 30-31; 1991, 275-76). May #8. Looney's title: "Desire."

Explanatory notes:

(5-6)   *Aurora*, the dawning sun, twice in Shakespeare (Spevack 78). *Thetis*, a Greek sea-nymph, six times in Shakespeare (Spevack 1310). See also E.O. 14.31-33 (*When Phoebus from the bed of Thetis doth arise, The morning, blushing red*). *Phoebus* is an epithet for *Apollo*, Greco-Roman god of the sun. See lines 1-2, 6.

(10)   A *wight* is a person (male or female), with some connotation of commiseration or contempt (*OED* 20: 328).

(20-24) May used quotation marks (kept here for clarity), though Looney did not. The evident meaning (lines 21-22) is *to see another man . . . obtain . . . [t]hat [which] he [the other man] desireth* and (line 24) *to enjoy that [which] others miss.*

(25) *Laridon, tan tan.* The apparently unique nonce-phrase returns no hits in *EEBO*.

Strongest Parallels:

Caroline Spurgeon notes that "the spectacle of the rising sun seems ever peculiarly to inspire and delight Shakespeare . . . [his] great fondness for the picture of changing colour, though not confined solely to the human face or to the sunrise, is very rarely found applied to anything else" (63).

(1-2) *The lively lark* stretched forth her wing, *The messenger of morning* bright

> "Lo here *the gentle lark*, weary of rest,/ From his moist cabinet mounts up on high,/ And *wakes the morning*" (*Venus* 853-55); *"the morning lark"* (*Dream* 4.1.94, and *Shrew* ind.2.44); *"the lark, the herald of the morn"* (*R&J* 3.5.6); "Hark! Hark! *The lark at heaven's gate sings, And Phoebus 'gins arise*" (*Cym.* 2.3.19-20); *"Like to the Lark at break of day arising, From sullen earth sings hymns at Heaven's gate"* (*Sonnets* 29.11-12).

> The *Cym.* passage is one of twenty-three references to *Phoebus* (including one spelled "Phibbus") in canonical Shakespeare (Spevack 976-77). *Apollo* is referenced once in these de Vere poems (E.O. 3.6) and twenty-nine times in canonical Shakespeare (Spevack 54).

(9) *Clad in carnation colour fair*

> "'A could never abide *carnation*; 'twas a *colour* he never liked" (*Hen. V* 2.3.33). *EEBO* returns thirty hits in twenty-four records for the search *"carnation near colour,"* including two to *Hen. V* and three to editions of Thomas Elyot's *Dictionary* (1538, 1542), the earliest uses and a probable source for the others, but no hit for E.O. 8.

Additional Parallels:

(2) The *messenger of morning* bright

> "As glorious to this night, being o'er my head/ As is a *winged messenger of heaven*" (*R&J* 2.2.27-28).

(3) and *with her* cheerful voice *did* sing

> "*And with her* breath she *did* perfume the air" (*Shrew* 1.1.175).

(3) *cheerful voice*

"With one *cheerful voice* welcome my love" (*2 Hen. VI* 1.1.36); cf. "This general applause and *cheerful shout*" (*Rich. III* 3.7.39). EEBO (1473-1623) returns sixty-six hits in fifty-four records for the phrase *cheerful voice*, including the *2 Hen. VI* passage, several editions of Sternhold & Hopkins psalms, "George Gascoigne" (1573), and an anonymous poem (twice), "The Louer compareth him self to the painful Falconer" published in Clement Robinson's 1584 *A handefull of pleasant delites,* but not de Vere's *Paradise* lyric.

(4) *The day's approach*

"The approach of day" (*Hen. V* 4.1.86); "The vaporous night approaches" (*Meas.* 4.1.57); "The time approaches" (*Mac.* 5.4.16); "Approach, thou beacon [the sun] to this under globe" (*Lear* 2.2.159).

(5-6) When that *Aurora, blushing red,* Descried the guilt of *Thetis' bed*

"Many a *morning* hath he there been seen . . . as the all-cheering *sun/ Should in the farthest East begin to draw/* The shady curtains from *Aurora's bed*" (*R&J* 1.1.129, 132-34); "And yonder *shines Aurora's harbinger,/* At whose approach, ghosts, wandering here and there,/ Troop home to churchyards" (*Dream* 3.2.380-82); cf. "When lo *the blushing morrow/ Lends light* to all" (*Lucrece* 1082-83); "King Richard doth himself appear,/ As doth *the blushing discontented sun/* From out *the fiery portal of the east*" (*Rich. II* 3.3.62-64); "a *blush* modest as *morning*" (*Troil.* 1.3.229); "Yet do thy cheeks look *red as Titan's face/ Blushing* to be encountered with a cloud" (*Titus* 2.4.31-32).

(6) *Thetis' bed*

"*Juno's* crown, O blessed bond of board and *bed!*" (*As You* 5.4.142); "*Hymen's purest bed*" (*Timon* 4.3.383); "*Cytherea,* how bravely thou becom'st *thy bed!*" (*Cym.* 2.2.15); "Whom *Jove* hath marked The honour of *your bed*" (*Kins.* 1.1.30).

See also parallels to lines 5-6 above.

The Ovidian conjunction of mythological figures and *bed*-play is another motif common to these de Vere poems and the works of Shakespeare. The amours of the gods are a conspicuous point of curiosity in both. See also E.O. 3.6, E.O. 6 (lines 7-10, 17-18, and 23-24), and E.O. 14.31-32.

(12) *He sighed, and said* he was desire

"With that *she sighed* as she stood,/ And *gave this sentence* then" (*All's Well* 1.3.75-76).

(13) Desire *I did desire to* stay

"Last night *you did desire it*" (*A&C* 1.1.55); "And never *did desire to see thee more*" (*Dream* 3.2.278); "*I do not desire you to* please me; *I do desire you to* sing" (*As You* 2.5.17-18). *EEBO* returns thirty-two hits in twenty-six records for the search *I did desire*, and 149 hits in 79 records for *I do desire*.

(15) The *courteous knight*

"You are right *courteous knights*" (*Per.* 2.3.27).

(16) *hand in hand* with me *did walk*

The phrase *hand in hand* occurs ten times in Shakespeare, e.g., "Let me embrace thee, good old chronicle,/ That hast so long *walk'd hand in hand* with time" (*Troil.* 4.5.202-03).

(18) What thing did *please* and what did *pain?*

"Having no other *pleasure* of his *gain*/ But torment that it cannot cure his *pain*" (*Lucrece* 860-61); "since you make your *pleasure* of your *pains*" (*Twelfth* 3.3.2); "No *pains*, sir. I take *pleasure* in singing, sir" (*Twelfth* 2.4.67).

See also E.O. 2.8 (*to whose most pain least pleasure doth befall*) and E.O. 13.14 (*a pleasure mixed with pain*).

(20) Desire *can have no greater pain*

"Therein false struck, *can take no greater wound*" (*Cym.* 3.4.119).

(22) That he *desireth to obtain*

"Such hazard now must doting Tarquin make,/ Pawning his honour *to obtain his lust*" (*Lucrece* 205-06); "As I wooed for thee *to obtain her*, I will join with thee to disgrace her" (*Much* 3.2.126-27).

(23-24) Nor greater joy can be than *this,*/Than to *enjoy what others miss*

"O, though *I love what others do abhor,*/ With others thou shouldst not abhor my state" (*Sonnets* 150.11-12); "Be gone to-morrow, and be sure of *this,*/ What I can help thee to thou shalt not *miss*" (*All's Well* 1.3.255-56).

Previous commentaries: Looney (1920, 165); Ogburn (586); Sobran (244-45); Eagan-Donovan.

E.O. 9: "The Trickling Tears That Fall Along My Cheeks"

1	The trickling tears that fall along my cheeks,
2	The secret sighs that show my inward grief,
3	The present pains perforce that love ay seeks,
4	Bid me renew my cares without relief
5	In woeful song, in dole display,
6	My pensive heart for to bewray.
7	Bewray thy grief, thou woeful heart, with speed,
8	Resign thy voice to her that caused thy woe;
9	With irksome cries bewail thy late-done deed,
10	For she thou lovest is sure thy mortal foe,
11	And help for thee there is none sure,
12	But still in pain thou must endure.
13	The stricken Deer hath help to heal his wound,
14	The haggard hawk with toil is made full tame,
15	The strongest tower the Cannon lays on ground,
16	The wisest wit that ever had the fame
17	Was thrall to Love by Cupid's sleights;
18	Then weigh my case with equal weights.
19	She is my joy, she is my care and woe,
20	She is my pain, she is my ease therefor,
21	She is my death, she is my life also,
22	She is my salve, she is my wounded sore;
23	In fine, she hath the hand and knife
24	That may both save and end my life.
25	And shall I live on earth to be her thrall?
26	And shall I sue and serve her all in vain?
27	And shall I kiss the steps that she lets fall?
28	And shall I pray the gods to keep the pain
29	From her, that is so cruel still?
30	No, no, on her work all your will.
31	And let her feel the power of all your might,
32	And let her have her most desire with speed,
33	And let her pine away both day and night,
34	And let her moan, and none lament her need,
35	And let all those that shall her see
36	Despise her state, and pity me.

Structure: Six stanzas of six lines; four of iambic pentameter and two of iambic tetrameter in each stanza.

Textual sources: F.p. *Paradise* (1576), 75-76. Grosart (394-95); Looney (1921, Miller ed. 1975, 1: 583-84); May (1980, 31-32; 1991, 276-77). May #9. Looney's title: "Love and Antagonism."

Explanatory notes:

(1-2, 4) The spellings of *fall, show,* and *Bid* are corrected from the original *tears that falls, sighs that shows,* and *Bids me renew,* consistently with our general approach to modernizing spelling (see Methodological Afterword), and because otherwise the grammatical mismatches (according to modern usage) could trip up readers.

(14) A *haggard* (a term of art in falconry) refers to a wild adult *hawk* (typically female) caught for training; it is thus mainly a noun in this context (not to be confused with the adjective indicating an exhausted appearance) (*OED* 6: 1013).

(16) *Wit* as used here refers to intelligence or mental sharpness, not humor (*OED* 20: 432-34).

(17) *Cupid,* in classical mythology, is the god of love and desire. His *sleights* refers to his use of cunning or deception.

(20) The spelling of *therefor* is modernized from *therefore,* again consistently with our general approach to spelling, and also with the meaning here, which is not "*therefore*" as in modern usage ("for that reason" or "it follows that"), but rather, simply "*for* (something)" (i.e., *she* is the poet's *ease . . . for* his *pain*; the very point seems to be to highlight this as a paradox, *not* what one would expect "*therefore*" to follow) (*OED* 17: 909).

Strongest parallels:

(10) *thy mortal foe*

> "I return his sworn and *mortal foe*" (*3 Hen. VI* 3.3.257); "I here proclaim myself *thy mortal foe*" (*3 Hen. VI* 5.1.94). *Thy mortal foe* returns only sixteen hits in fourteen *EEBO* records (1473-1623), including both *3 Hen. VI* and E.O. 9.

(13) *The stricken Deer* hath help *to heal his wound*

> "Why, let *the stricken deer* go weep" (*Ham.* 3.2.287); "My pity hath been balm *to heal their wounds*" (*3 Hen. VI* 4.8.41). Indicating the extreme rarity of the phrase *stricken deer, EEBO* (1473-1623) returns no hits for it, or for the variant spelling *strucken deer.*

(14) The *haggard hawk* with toil *is made full tame*

"*My falcon* now is sharp and passing empty, And till she stoop she must not be full-gorged, For then she never looks upon her lure. Another way I have *to man my haggard, To make her come and know her keeper's call*" (*Shrew* 4.1.177-81); cf. "If I do prove her *haggard,/* Though that her jesses were my dear heartstrings,/ I'd whistle her off and let her down the wind/ To prey at fortune" (*Oth.* 3.3.260-63); "I know her spirits are as coy and *wild/ As haggards* of the rock" (*Much* 3.1.35-36).

Note that line 14 is explicitly echoed by the very title of *The Taming of the Shrew.* See also E.O. 19, lines 9 (*like haggards wild they [women] range*) and 15 (*train them [women] to our lure*). See the Methodological Afterword for more discussion of the *haggard hawk* parallels.

Falconry was a distinctly aristocratic sport and status symbol in medieval and early modern Europe (and other parts of the world). In early English falconry literature, *hawk* or "falcon" usually refers to a female (a male *hawk* is known to falconers as a "tiercel"). A *haggard*, as noted above, refers to a wild adult *hawk* caught for training.

The *haggard hawk* in line 14 thus suggestively represents *her that caused thy* (the poet's *woeful heart's*) *woe* (lines 7-8) and *she thou lovest* (line 10), whom lines 30-36 urge the *love*lorn male to *tame*. But in an interesting duality, other lines, e.g., lines 8 (*Resign thy voice to her*) and 12 (*still in pain thou must endure*), suggest that *haggard hawk* may also refer to the *love*lorn poet himself (*made full tame by* his female *love*).

Such gender-bending is very typically Shakespearean. Indeed, a fourth canonical Shakespeare reference to *haggard* explicitly uses it as a metaphor for male behavior: "This fellow is wise enough to play the fool ... And like the *haggard,* check at every feather/ That comes before his eye" (*Twelfth* 3.1.58, 62-63).

There are at least five canonical Shakespearean references to *haggards* (Spevack 528)—the four quoted above, plus another in *Shrew.* There is also a sixth passage which, though not explicitly invoking a *haggard* by name, flips the expected gender roles (as in *Twelfth*) to depict Juliet as a falconer trying to *lure* a flighty Romeo (see Looney 1920, 163-64): "this proud disdainful *haggard*" (*Shrew* 4.2.39); "*Juliet.* Hist! Romeo, hist! O for a *falc'ner's voice/ To lure this tassel-gentle* back again!" (*R&J* 2.2.159-60).

Edward III, which many scholars now view as a canonical Shakespeare play, also explicitly refers to a female *haggard*, but again (as in *Twelfth* and *R&J*) deploys the term as a metaphor for *male* behavior: "*King Ed.* dare a *falcon* when she's in her flight/ And ever after *she'll be haggard-like.* Let [Prince] Edward be delivered by our hands/ And still in danger he'll expect the like"

(*Edw. III* 8.46-49, Proudfoot & Bennett 275).

By far the most intriguing set of parallelisms, reaching in both directions — into both Shakespeare and de Vere's treatment of the haggard theme — is the anonymous "The Louer compareth him self to the painful Falconer," published as the concluding poem in Clement Robinson's 1584 anthology *A handefull of pleasant delites* (c4r-c4v).

(15) The *strongest tower* the Cannon lays on ground

"Who in a moment *even with the earth Shall lay* your *stately and air-braving towers*" (*1 Hen. VI* 4.2.12); "When sometime *lofty towers* I see *down rased*" (*Sonnets* 64.3); cf. "the teeming [i.e., quaking] earth . . . *topples down Steeples and mossgrown towers*" (*1 Hen. IV* 3.1.28, 32-33); "the king's name is a *tower of strength*" (*Rich. III* 5.3.12).

See also, in "When as Thine Eye" (additional parallels to line 4 below): "*The strongest* castle, *tower*, and towne/ *The golden bullet beats it down.*"

(18) *weigh* my case *with equal weights*

"I have *in equal balance justly weighed*" (*2 Hen. IV* 4.1.67); cf. "Commit my cause *in balance to be weighed*" (*Titus* 1.1.55); "*Weigh*, oath with oath, and you will nothing *weigh./* Your vows to her and me, *put in two scales,/* Will *even weigh*" (*Dream* 3.2.131-33); "*equalities* are so *weighed*" (*Lear* 1.1.6); "In *equal scale weighing* delight and dole" (*Ham.* 1.2.13).

This strikingly Shakespearean sentiment of equipoised justice becomes, of course, the title and theme of an entire canonical play, *Measure for Measure*. See, e.g.: "you *weigh equally;* a feather will turn the scale" (*Meas.* 4.2.26-27).

(34-36) And *let her moan, and none lament her need,*
And *let all* those that shall her *see*
Despise *her state,* and *pity me.*

> Compare *Lucrece:*
>
> *Let him* have time to *tear his curled hair,*
> *Let him* have time *against himself to rave,*
> *Let him* have time of Time's help to despair,
> *Let him* have time to live a loathed slave,
> *Let him* have time a beggar's orts to crave,
> And time to *see one that by alms doth live*
> *Disdain to him disdained scraps to give.* (981-87)

The parallel above was first identified by Looney (1920, 155-56; 1921, Miller ed. 1975, 1: 584), and further discussed by Sobran in 1997 (246-47) and Eagan-Donovan in 2017.

Compare especially these eight words in line 34—*let her moan, and none lament her need*—with the following eight words in *Lucrece*:

"make him moan, but pity not his moans" (977).

Note the identical comma placement after the first three words, *let/make her/ him moan*, which we double-checked to make sure the original versions were not affected by modern emendation or harmonization of punctuation—as to E.O. 9, May 1980, 32, 68-69; 1991, 277; as to *Lucrece*, a facsimile of the original 1594 edition).

Additional parallels:

(1) The *trickling tears* that fall along my *cheeks*

"Weep not, sweet queen; for *trickling tears* are vain" (*1 Hen. IV* 2.4.391); "*tears fret channels* in her *cheeks*" (*Lear* 1.4.285).

Tears and *cheeks* often occur together in Shakespeare. On *trickling tears*, see also E.O. 3.13. On the broader motif of *tears* and *weeping*, see also 4.10, 5.12, 6.26, and 17.8-9.

(2) The *secret sighs* that show *my inward grief*

"*My grief lies all within*" (*Rich. II* 4.1.295); "A plague of *sighing* and *grief!*" (*1 Hen. IV* 2.4.332); "Consume away in *sighs*, waste *inwardly*" (*Much* 3.1.78).

On the broader theme of *tears* and *sighs* (linked by lines 1-2), see also E.O. 17.8-9. Line 2 is a strong example of the topos of emotional dissimulation.

On the leitmotif of dissimulation, a suggestive common interest seen in both samples, see also E.O. 5 (*passim*) and E.O. 6.4, 10.9-10, 12.16, and 18.40.

(3) *present pains*

"Put me to *present pain*" (*Per.* 5.1.222); "Tis good for men to love their *present pains*" (*Hen. V* 4.1.18).

(4) Bid me *renew my cares* without relief

"And by her presence still *renew his sorrows*" (*Titus* 5.3.82).

A version of this line is found in the "apocryphal" Shakespeare poem "When as Thine Eye Had Chose the Dame" (Rollins 1938, 308-09) (i.e., "and stalde *the deare* that thou shouldst *strike*"). The earliest text of "When as Thine Eye" is the Cornwallis manuscript (Folger 1.112, c. 1585–90), with a spine labeled "Poems by the Earl of Oxford and Others." Among the thirty-three poems contained in the manuscript are de Vere's "echo" verses (E.O. 17) and a number of anonymous poems, several apparently in the handwriting of King's Men actor John Bentley, who died in 1585 (see Miller, "Cornwallis").

(16) The wisest wit

> See also E.O. 6.9 (*wit so wise*), E.O. 10.12 (*wit . . . will*), and E.O. 18.9 (*wily wit*).

(17-25) Was *thrall to Love* by Cupid's sleights;

> . . .
>
> And shall I live on earth *to be her thrall?*
>
> "How *love* makes young men *thrall,* and old men dote" (*Venus* 837); cf. "*my mistress' thrall*" (*Sonnets* 154.12).

(19) She is my *joy,* she is my *care and woe*

> "Your tributary drops belong to *woe,*/ Which you, mistaking, offer up to *joy*" (*R&J* 3.2.103).

(20) She is my *pain,* she is *my ease* therefor

> "Give physic to the sick, *ease to the pained*" (*Lucrece* 901).

(21) She is my *death,* she is my *life* also

> "Showing *life's* triumph in the map of *death* . . . *life lived in death, and death in life*" (*Lucrece* 402, 406); "*life* imprisoned in a *body dead*" (*Lucrece* 1456); "Yet in this *life*/ Lie hid more thousand *deaths*" (*Meas.* 3.1.39-40); "*seeking death, find life*" (*Meas.* 3.1.44); "That *life is better life,* past fearing *death*" (*Meas.* 5.1.397).

(22) She is my *salve,* she is my *wounded sore*

> "To see the *salve* doth make the *wound* ache more" (*Lucrece* 1116); "A *salve* for any *sore* that may betide" (*3 Hen. VI* 4.6.88); "*salve*/ The long-grown *wounds* of my intemperance" (*1 Hen. IV* 3.2.155-56); "For no man well of such a *salve* can speak/ That heals the *wound,* and cures not the disgrace" (*Sonnets* 34.7-8); "The humble *salve* which *wounded bosoms* fits!" (*Sonnets* 120.12).

> See also E.O. 5.29-30 (*So long to fight with secret sore, And find no secret salve therefor*) and E.O. 18.9 (*No wily wit to salve a sore*).

> As the *salve/sore* motif (like many others) was often echoed by other Elizabethan poets and writers, these parallels are not telling in and of themselves (see May 2004, 229), but as with many of the additional parallels noted, their significance instead lies in the cumulative force of the assembled parallelisms.

(25) *And shall I live on earth to be her thrall?*

> "*And shall I* stand, and thou sit in *my throne?*" (*3 Hen. VI* 1.1.84).

(26) And *shall I sue* and serve her all in vain?

> "What love, think'st thou, *I sue* so much to get?" (*3 Hen. VI* 3.2.61); "*I sue* for exiled majesty's repeal" (*Lucrece* 640); "I love! *I sue!* I seek a wife!" (*LLL* 3.1.189).

(26) And shall I sue and serve her *all in vain*?

> The phrase occurs six times in Shakespeare, e.g., "But *all in vain*; good queen, it will not be" (*3 Hen. VI* 2.1.135).

(28) *I pray the gods* to keep the pain

> "*I pray the gods* make me honest" (*As You* 3.3.33); "*I pray the gods* she may, with all my heart" (*Shrew* 4.4.67).

(28-30) *And shall I* pray the gods to keep the pain. . ./ *No, no, on her* work all your will

> "*And shall I* now give o'er the yielded set?
> *No, no, on my soul*, it never shall be said." (*John* 5.2.108)

Additionally, Looney (1920, 153-54) pointed out structural similarities between these lines and passages in *3 Hen. VI* and *Lucrece*. May (2004, 228) dismissed this point without fully engaging Looney's argument or quoting the Shakespearean parallels:

> *Did I* forget that by the House of York
> My father came untimely to his death?
> *Did I* let pass th' abuse done to my niece?
> *Did I* impale him with the regal crown?
> *Did I* put Henry from his native right?
> *And am I* guerdoned [i.e., rewarded] at the last with shame?
> (*3 Hen. VI* 3.3.186-91)

> What's worse than murderer, that I may name it?
> *No, no,* my heart will burst an if I speak.
> (*3 Hen. VI* 5.5.58-59)

> Why should the worm intrude the maiden bud?
> *Or* hateful cuckoos hatch in sparrow's nests?
> *Or* toads infect fair founts with venom mud?
> *Or* tyrant folly lurk in gentle breasts?
> *Or* kings be breakers of their own behests?
> *But no* perfection is so absolute
> That some impurity doth not pollute.
> (*Lucrece* 848-54)

(29) From her, that is *so cruel still*?

> "*Still so cruel?*" (*Twelfth* 5.1.110)

(31) let her feel the *power* of all your *might*

> "O, from what *power* hast *thou this powerful might*" (*Sonnets* 150.1).

(32) *let her have* her most desire

> *Let her have* your voice (*Oth.* 1.3.260).

> "There is a vice that *most* I do *abhor,*/ And *most desire* should meet the blow of justice" (*Meas.* 2.2.29-30); cf. "our *most* just and right *desires*" (*2 Hen. IV* 4.2.40).

(33) let her *pine away*

> "Go to Flint Castle: There I'll *pine away*" (*Rich. II* 3.2.209); "the fool hath much *pined away*" (*Lear* 1.4.71).

(36) *pity me*

> Looney noted "the recurrence of what seems . . . a curious appeal for *pity*" (1920, 161) in these de Vere poems and the works of Shakespeare; *pity* (and its variants) appear more than 300 times in the Shakespeare canon (Spevack 980-81). See also 3.7 (*the less she pities me*) and 17.8 (*some pity in the rocks*), and compare, e.g.: "Melt at my tears, and be compassionate;/ Soft *pity* enters at *an iron gate*" (*Lucrece* 594-95); "This you should *pity* rather than despise" (*Dream* 3.2.235); "May *move your* hearts to *pity*" (*Rich. III* 1.3.348); "*Pity*, you *ancient stones*, those tender babes" (*Rich. III* 4.1.98); "*Pity me* then" (*Sonnets* 111.8, 13); "Thine eyes I love, and they as *pitying me* . . ./ And suit *thy pity* like in every part" (*Sonnets* 132.1, 12).

Previous commentaries: Looney (1920, 139-40, 153-56, 161, 163-64); Sobran (244-47); Brazil & Flues; May (2004, 223-24, 228); Eagan-Donovan.

E.O. 10: "Fain Would I Sing But Fury Makes Me Fret"

1   Fain would I sing but fury makes me fret,
2   And rage hath sworn to seek revenge of wrong;
3   My mazed mind in malice so is set
4   As death shall daunt my deadly dolours long.
5   Patience perforce is such a pinching pain,
6   As die I will or suffer wrong again.

7   I am no sot to suffer such abuse
8   As doth bereave my heart of his delight,
9   Nor will I frame myself to such as use
10   With calm consent to suffer such despite.
11   No quiet sleep shall once possess mine eye,
12   Till wit have wrought his will on injury.

13   My heart shall fail and hand shall lose his force,
14   But some device shall pay despite his due;
15   And fury shall consume my careful corse,
16   Or raze the ground whereon my sorrow grew.
17   Lo, thus in rage of ruthful mind refused,
18   I rest revenged of whom I am abused.

Structure: Three six-line stanzas of iambic pentameter in ABABCC rhyme scheme.

Textual sources: Grosart (421-22); Looney (1921, Miller ed. 1975, 1: 582); May (1980, 32-33; 1991, 277). May #10. Looney's title: "Revenge, of Wrong."

Explanatory notes:

(1)   The archaic word *fain* means "gladly" (*OED* 5: 667-68). See also E.O. 18b.14.

(3)   In modern English, *mazed* has fairly mild connotations of being amazed, dazed, confused, or bewildered, but a meaning it bore into the 16th century included more severe mental derangement—to be crazed or delirious (*OED* 9: 507-08). See also E.O. 7.5 (*mazed so much his wits*).

(4)   *Dolours* refers to pain (*OED* 4: 941).

(12)   The term *wit* as used here refers to intelligence or mental sharpness, not humor (*OED* 20: 432-34).

(15)   *Corse* means a living body (*OED* 3: 975). Here as elsewhere, *careful* is used idiomatically here to mean "*full* of *cares* or worries," not "cautious" (*OED* 2: 896). See also E.O. 2, lines 2 and 16-18.

Strongest parallels:

(6-7) As die *I* will or *suffer wrong* again. *I am no sot to suffer such abuse*

"What *wrongs we suffer*" (*2 Hen. VI* 4.1.68); "the *wrongs I suffer*" (*Errors* 3.1.16); "Shall tender duty *make me suffer wrong?*" (*Rich. II* 2.1.164); "such *suffering* souls/ That welcome *wrongs*" (*Caes.* 2.1.130-31); "he shall *not suffer indignity*" (*Tem.* 3.2.37); "*Malvolio.* Why have you *suffered* me to be imprisoned . . . And made the most notorious geck and gull . . . ? . . . *Olivia.* He hath been *most notoriously abused*" (*Twelfth* 5.1.331, 333, 368).

See also line 10 (*suffer such despite*).

(9-10) Nor will I *frame myself* . . . to *suffer such despite*

"She *framed* thee in high heaven's *despite*" (*Venus* 731); "And *frame my face* to all occasions" (*3 Hen. VI* 3.2.185); "she preparedly may *frame herself*/ To the way she's forced to" (*A&C* 5.1.55-56); "*Frame yourself* to orderly soliciting" (*Cym.* 2.3.46).

See also lines 6-7 (*suffer wrong . . . abuse*).

The idea of *fram(ing) (one)self* for a particular social expectation belongs to the dissimulation topos, a suggestive common interest seen in both samples, see also E.O. 5 (*passim*) and E.O. 6.4, 9.2, 12.16, and 18.40, where we also find a closely similar idea expressed in what appears to be idiomatic language.

On the leitmotif of dissimulation, (12) Till *wit* have wrought his *will*

"What *wit* sets down is blotted straight with *will*" (*Lucrece* 1299); "he wants *wit* that wants resolved *will*/ To learn his *wit*" (*Two Gent.* 2.6.12-13); "a sharp *wit* matched with too blunt a *will*,/ Whose edge, hath power to cut, whose *will* still *wills*" (*LLL* 2.1.49-50); "*Wit*, an 't be thy *will*, put me into good fooling. Those *wits* that think they have thee do very oft prove fools, and I that am sure I lack thee may pass for a wise man. For what says Quinapalus? Better a *witty* fool than a foolish *wit*" (*Twelfth* 1.5.32-36); "your *wit* will not so soon out as another man's *will*" (*Cor.* 2.3.25).

See also E.O. 6.9 (*wit so wise*), E.O. 9.16 (*wisest wit*), and E.O. 18.9 (*wily wit*). As noted above, the term *wit* as used here generally refers to intelligence or mental sharpness rather than humor, but there are overtones of the humorous meaning in the quotations from *LLL* and especially from *Twelfth*.

(17) Of whom *I am abused*

I am abused (*Oth.* 3.3.257); *I am abused* (*Twelfth* 5.1.20). *EEBO* (1473-1623) returns only fifteen hits in fifteen records for the search, including the *Twelfth Night* line, *London Prodigal* (1605), and Golding's 1574 translation of Calvin's sermons on Job.

Additional parallels:

(1) *Fain would I* sing *but*

> "*Fain would I* woo her, *yet* I dare not speak" (*1 Hen. VI* 5.3.65); "*Fain would I* have Canutus win and he is weak" (*Iron.* 1838). On Shakespeare's authorship of *Ironside*, see Sams 1986.

(1) *fury* makes me *fret*

> "And with the wind in greater *fury fret*" (*Lucrece* 648); The phrase *fury. . .fret* is not only another instance of the wide range of emotional expression in both samples, but seems curiously idiomatic. Of four instances in *EEBO* from 1497-1900, two are to editions of *Lucrece*.

(2) *rage hath sworn to seek revenge, of wrong*

> "You both *have vowed revenge* on him" (*3 Hen. VI* 1.1.55); "I will *revenge, his wrong*" (*3 Hen. VI* 3.3.197); "seek not/ T'allay my *rages and revenges*" (*Cor.* 5.3.84-85).

(3) *My mazed mind in malice so is set*

> "The venomous *malice of my swelling heart!*" (*Titus* 5.3.13); cf. "Nor *set down aught in malice*" (*Oth.* 5.2.343); "Who can be wise, *amazed*, temp' rate and *furious*/ Loyal and neutral, in a moment?" (*Mac.* 2.3.104).

> See also parallels to line 1 (*fury*). Looney (1920, 151-52) and Eagan-Donovan suggested a broad thematic linkage between E.O. 10 and Sonnets 140 and 147 (see also parallels to line 5), e.g.:

> "Past care I am, *now reason is past cure,/ And frantic-mad with evermore unrest;/ My thoughts and my discourse as madmen's are*" (*Sonnets* 147.9-11).

(4) As *death* shall *daunt my deadly dolours long*

> "Think you a little din can *daunt mine ears?*" (*Shrew* 1.2.196); "let not discontent/ *Daunt all your hopes*" (*Titus* 1.1.270-71); "To think *their dolour* others have *endured*" (*Lucrece* 1582); "As *ending* anthem of *my endless dolour*" (*Two Gent.* 3.1.242).

(5) *Patience perforce is such a pinching pain*

> "*Patience perforce* with willful choler meeting/ *Makes my flesh tremble*" (*R&J* 1.5.89); cf. "do not press/ My tongue-tied *patience* with too much *disdain*" (*Sonnets* 140.1-2).

> As noted above (see parallels to line 3), Looney and Eagan-Donovan suggested a broad thematic linkage to Sonnets 140 and 147.

> May has argued that phrases like *patience perforce* and *pinching pain* were "ubiquitous in contemporary verse" (2004, 229), and it is true that *patience*

perforce appears fifty-four times in forty-eight pre-1623 *EEBO* documents (giving a 0.192% chance of its co-occurrence in both Shakespeare and de Vere), and *pinching pain* in sixty hits in thirty-four records (0.136% chance of co-occurrence). While this particular parallel may therefore statistically be considerably less compelling than many other, rarer, coincidences of phraseology, scholarly honesty requires considering the overall cumulative weight and context of all the parallels and assessing the evidence in its totality.

As Looney noted (1920), these poems contain many "minor points of similarity, which though insignificant in themselves, help to make up that general impression of common authorship which comes only with a close familiarity with [them] as a whole" (161).

(10) With calm *consent to suffer* such despite

"I did *consent*,/ And often did beguile her of her tears,/ When I did speak of some distressful stroke/ That my youth *suffer'd*" (*Oth.* 1.3.155-58).

(10) to suffer *such despite*

"Alas, Iago, my lord hath so bewhored her./ Thrown *such despite* and heavy terms upon her,/ As true hearts cannot bear" (*Oth.* 4.2.115-17).

(11) No *quiet sleep* shall once *possess mine eye*

"What a strange *drowsiness possesses them!*" (*Tem.* 2.1.199); "Sin of self-love *possesseth all mine eye*" (*Sonnets* 62.1).

There are two distinct ideas in de Vere's lyric, that of something *possess(ing)* the *eye* and that *sleep possess(es)* a person. The speaker, however, complains of sleeplessness. The theme is well developed in Shakespeare. According to Franklin H. Head's study of insomnia in the plays, Shakespeare "constantly contrasts the troubled sleep of those burdened with anxieties and cares, with the happy lot of the laborer whose physical weariness insures him a tranquil night's repose" (12).

(13) My *heart* shall fail and *hand* shall lose his force

The juxtaposition of these two body parts, often personified, is ubiquitous in Shakespeare: "*My hand* would free her, but *my heart* says no" (1 *Hen. VI* 5.3.61); "this *the hand* that slew thy brother Rutland;/ And here's *the heart* that triumphs in their death" (3 *Hen. VI* 2.4.7-8); "The very firstlings of *my heart* shall be/ The firstlings of *my hand*" (*Mac.* 4.1.147-48); "It is *his hand*, my lord; but I hope *his heart* is not in the contents" (*Lear* 1.2.66-67).

(13) hand *shall lose his force*

Rebellion in this land *shall lose his sway* (1 *Hen. IV* 5.5.41).

(14) *some device*

"Plot *some device* of further misery" (*Titus* 3.1.134); "I think by *some odd gimmors or device*" (*1 Hen. VI* 1.2.41); "by *some device* or other" (*Errors* 1.2.95); "entrap thee by *some treacherous device*" (*As You* 1.1.151); "Every day thou daff'st me with *some device*" (*Oth.* 4.2.175).

(14) *pay* despite *his due*

"*Pay him* the *due* of honey-tongued Boyet" (*LLL* 5.2.334); "More is *thy due* than more than all can *pay*" (*Mac.* 1.4.21); "And yet to times in hope my verse shall stand,/ Praising thy worth, *despite his* cruel hand" (*Sonnets* 60.13-14).

(15) And *fury* shall *consume* my careful corse.

"They do *consume* the thing that feeds their *fury*" (*Shrew* 2.1.153).

(16) *raze* the ground

"*Raze the sanctuary*" (*Meas.* 2.2.170); "*Raze* out the written troubles of the brain" (*Mac.* 5.3.49); "To *raze* one title of your honour out" (*Rich. II* 2.3.76); "Till each to *razed oblivion* yield his part/ Of thee, thy record never can be miss'd" (*Sonnets* 122.7-8).

Once again the Shakespearean equivalents are figurative elaborations of their lyric antecedent in de Vere, illustrating the Bloomian principle that Shakespeare grew by "overhearing himself." See also E.O. 5.6-8 (*As Hannibal, that saw . . . defaced down*).

(16) *the ground whereon* my *sorrow* grew.

"We see *the ground whereon* these *woes* do lie,/ But *the true ground* of all these piteous *woes*" (*R&J* 5.3.179-80); "Come, my queen, take hands with me,/ And rock *the ground whereon* these sleepers be" (*Dream* 4.1.85-86).

In addition to the alliterative word parallel (*ground/grew*) in conjunction with *woes* or *sorrows*, note the similar usage of the less common singular *ground*, in atypical relation to emotions as opposed to cognitive or rational matters (contrast, e.g., "grounds for a claim"); "any *ground* To build a *grief* on" (*2 Hen. IV* 4.1.109-10); "*grounds* and motives of her *woe*" (*Lover's Comp.* 63).

(17) *in rage* of *ruthful* mind *refused*

"*In rage*/ With their *refusal*" (*Cor.* 2.3.259); cf. "Complots of mischief, treason, villainies/ *Ruthful* to hear" (*Titus* 5.1.65-66).

(17) *ruthful* mind

"*Ruthful* deeds" (*3 Hen. VI* 2.5.95); "*ruthful* work" (*Troil.* 5.3.48).

Previous commentaries: Looney (1920, 151-52, 164); Sobran (248-49); Brazil & Flues; Goldstein (2016, 58-60); Eagan-Donovan.

E.O. 11: "When Wert Thou Born, Desire?"

1   Come hither, shepherd's swaine!
2   Sir, what do you require?
3   I pray thee shew to me thy name!
4   My name is Fond Desire.
5   When wert thou born, desire?
6   In pomp and prime of May.
7   By whom, sweet boy, wert thou begot?
8   By good conceit, men say.
9   Tell me, who was thy nurse?
10   Fresh youth in sugared joy.
11   What was thy meat and daily food?
12   Sad sighs with great annoy.
13   What hadst thou then to drink?
14   Unfeigned lovers' tears.
15   What cradle wert thou rocked in?
16   In hope devoid of fears.
17   What brought thee then asleep?
18   Sweet speech, that liked me best.
19   And where is now thy dwelling-place?
20   In gentle hearts I rest.
21   Doth company displease?
22   It doth in many a one.
23   Where would desire then choose to be?
24   He likes to muse alone.
25   What feedeth most your sight?
26   To gaze on favour still.
27   What findest thou most to be thy foe?
28   Disdain of my goodwill.
29   Will ever age or death
30   Bring thee unto decay?
31   No, no, desire both lives and dies
32   Ten thousand times a day.
33   Then, fond desire, farewell,
34   Thou art no mate for me;
35   I should be loath, methinks to dwell
36   With such a one as thee.

Structure: Thirty-six lines of question and answer iambic trimeters in which answers rhyme in alternating pairs.

Textual sources: Grosart (407-09); Looney (1921, Miller ed. 1975, 1: 568-69); May (1980, 33; 1991, 277-78) (first four and last four lines in Grosart and Looney editions —omitted by May—are here reproduced). May #11. Looney's title: "Fond Desire." Originally published in *Brittons Bowre of Delights* (1597), as attributed to "E. of Ox." (E3).

Strongest parallels:

(1) *When wert thou*

> *When wert thou* wont to walk alone (*Titus* 1.1.339). The phrase *when wert thou* is surprisingly rare, returning only nine hits in eight *EEBO* records (1473-1623).

(5) *thy nurse*

> *Thy nurse* occurs three times in Shakespeare, e.g., "And if I were *thy nurse*,/ thy tongue to teach,/ 'Pardon' should be the first word of thy speech" (*Rich.* II 5.3.113-14). Surprisingly, the phrase is moderately rare, returning only twenty-eight hits in twenty-five *EEBO* records (1473-1623).

(9-10) What had'st thou then to *drink? Unfeigned lovers' tears*

> "*Drink my tears*" (*John* 4.1.62); "Ye see I *drink the water of my eye*" (*3 Hen. VI* 5.4.75); "Thy napkin cannot *drink a tear of mine*" (*Titus* 3.1.140); cf. "I come in kindness and *unfeigned love*" (*Shrew* 4.2.32); "as *lovers* they do *feign*" (*As You* 3.3.22); "Dismiss your vows, your *feigned tears*" (*Venus* 425).

(16) *gentle hearts*

> "*Gentle hearts*" (*John* 5.2.157); "*gentle hearts*" (*Dream* 5.1.219).

> Surprisingly, the phrase *gentle hearts* returns only twenty-eight hits in twenty-seven *EEBO* records (1473-1623).

(21-22) *What feedeth most your sight?/ To gaze on favour still*

> "With *gazing fed*" (*Merch.* 3.2.68); "I have *fed mine eyes* on thee" (*Troil.* 4.5.231); "Her *eye must be fed*" (*Oth.* 2.1.225); "That makes me *see*, and *cannot feed mine eye?*" (*All's Well* 1.1.221); "I *feed most hungerly* on *your sight*" (*Timon* 1.1.252); cf. "all eyes saw *his eyes enchanted with gazes*" (*LLL* 2.1.245); "youth with comeliness *plucked all gaze his way*" (*Cor.* 1.3.6-7); "all *full with feasting on your sight* (*Sonnets* 75.9).

> See also E.O. 18.10 (*to feed each gazing eye*), and compare these lines in *Venus*:

> But, when *his glutton eye so full hath fed* (399)

> Alas, he naught esteems that face of thine,
> *To which Love's eyes pay tributary gazes* (631-32)

Fold in the object that did *feed her sight* (822)

He *fed* them with his *sight* [i.e., his beauty], they him with berries (1104)

Additional parallels:

(3-4) *By whom, sweet boy* [i.e., desire], *wert thou begot? By good conceit, men say*

> "Tell me *where is fancy bred, Or in the heart,* or in the head? *How begot,* how nourished?" (*Merch.* 3.2.63-64); cf. "*sweet boy*" (*Venus* 155, 583, 613); "*sweet boy*" (*Sonnets* 108.5).

> No less an orthodox Shakespeare scholar than Sir Sidney Lee, notes Goldstein (2016, 50-51; 2017, 23), prophetically compared these lines with the song from *Merch.* a decade before de Vere was proposed as the true Shakespeare in 1920, and thus before he became a threat to be disparaged by devout Stratfordians. In 1910 Lee observed that this passage in E.O. 11, as compared to the lines in *Merch.* "is in a kindred key" (227). See also Lee's praise for de Vere at the turn of the 20th century (quoted in Goldstein 2016, 47).

> Lee added (1910) (seemingly by way of excusing this parallel): "There are indeed few lyrical topics to which the French and English writers failed to apply on some occasion or other much the same language." No doubt, but de Vere and Shakespeare use the same words and concepts far more often than "on some occasion or other" (227) and frequently do so in strikingly similar linguistic or narrative contexts.

> That this parallel caught Lee's attention, and prompted his inclusion of it as a telling example, is significant as yet one more piece of the dense and cumulative network of intertextuality explored here—of which Lee was of course as innocent as a cherub (writing, as noted, ten years before the first publication of the Oxfordian hypothesis).

(6) *Fresh youth*

> "Whose *youth* and *freshness* wrinkles Apollo's" (*Troil.* 2.2.78).

(8) *Sad sighs*

> "*Sad sighs*, deep groans" (*Two Gent.* 3.1.232).

(11) What *cradle* wert thou *rocked* in?

> "And *rock* his brains In *cradle* of the rude" (*1 Hen. IV* 3.1.19); "If drink *rock* not his *cradle*" (*Oth.* 4.4.28).

(14) *Sweet speech*, that liked me best

> "Slow in *speech*, yet *sweet* as springtime flowers" (*Shrew* 2.1.246).

(15) thy *dwelling-place*

"Their assign'd and native *dwelling-place*" (*As You* 2.1.63); "repair to your several *dwelling-places*" (*1 Hen. VI* 1.3.77); "his pure brain,/ Which some suppose the soul's frail *dwelling-house*" (*John* 5.7.3).

(25-26) Will ever *age* or *death*

"*Death*, desolation, ruin, and *decay*" (*Rich. III* 4.4.409); "folly, *age*, and cold *decay*" (*Sonnets* 11.6).

(26) Bring thee unto *decay?*

"Shall I *bring thee on* the way?" (*Win.* 4.3.114)

(27) desire both *lives and dies*

"earthlier happy is the rose distill'd,/ Than that which withering on the virgin thorn/ Grows, *lives and dies* in single blessedness" (*Dream* 1.1.76-78).

(28) *Ten thousand times* a day

"I would be trebled twenty times myself;
A thousand times more fair, *ten thousand times* more rich."
(Merch. 3.2.153-54)

Previous commentaries: Lee (1910, 227); Ogburn (587-88); Sobran (250-51); Goldstein (2016, 50-51; 2017, 23). Sir Sidney Lee, the leading Stratfordian Shakespeare biographer and scholar, deserves credit for the earliest known commentary on any of the parallels between this early de Vere poem and Shakespeare.

E.O. 12: "Winged With Desire"

1   Winged with desire, I seek to mount on high,
2   Clogged with mishap yet am I kept full low;
3   Who seeks to live and finds the way to die,
4   Sith comfort ebbs, and cares do daily flow,
5   But sad despair would have me to retire,
6   When smiling hope sets forward my desire.

7   I still do toil and never am at rest,
8   Enjoying least when I do covet most;
9   With weary thoughts are my green years oppressed,
10   To danger drawn from my desired coast;
11   Now crazed with Care, then haled up with Hope,
12   With world at will yet wanting wished scope.

13   I like in heart, yet dare not say I love,
14   And looks alone do lend me chief relief.
15   I dwelt sometimes at rest yet must remove,
16   With feigned joy I hide my secret grief.
17   I would possess yet needs must flee the place
18   Where I do seek to win my chiefest grace.

19   Lo, thus I live twixt fear and comfort tossed,
20   With least abode where best I feel content;
21   I seld resort where I should settle most,
22   My sliding times too soon with her are spent;
23   I hover high and soar where Hope doth tower,
24   Yet froward Fate defers my happy hour.

25   I live abroad but still in secret grief,
26   Then least alone when most I seem to lurk;
27   I speak of peace, and live in endless strife,
28   And when I play then are my thoughts at work;
29   In person far that am in mind full near,
30   Making light show where I esteem most dear.

31   A malcontent yet seem I pleased still,
32   Bragging of heaven yet feeling pains of hell.
33   But Time shall frame a time unto my will,
34   Whenas in sport this earnest will I tell;
35   Till then, sweet friend, abide these storms with me,
36   Which shall in joys of either fortunes be.

Structure: Six stanzas of six lines of iambic pentameter rhyming ABABCC.

Textual sources: May (1980, 34-35; 1991, 278-79) (not in Grosart or Looney). May #12. The poem contains numerous parallelisms of situation and language to "Though I Seem Strange" (Volume II, E.5).

Explanatory notes:

(4)   *Sith* is an archaic word meaning "since" (*OED* 15: 563-64).

(24)   The term *froward*, no longer in common use, means perverse, obstinate, or contrary (*OED* 6: 225), the etymological opposite of "toward" (as in "to and fro").

(34)   *Whenas*, also out of common use, is equivalent to "when," "whereas," or "inasmuch as" (*OED* 20: 210).

Strongest parallels:

(1) *Winged with desire*

> "Whose haughty spirit, *winged with desire*" (*3 Hen. VI* 1.1.267); "Unable to support this lump of clay/ *Swift-winged with desire* to get a grave" (*1 Hen. VI* 2.5.15) ; "Borne by the trustless *wings* of false *desire*" (*Lucrece* 2). EEBO (1473-1623) returns only two hits in one record — the 1623 F1 texts of *1 & 3 Hen. VI* — for the phrase "winged with desire."

(1) *I seek to mount on high*

> "The gentle lark, weary of rest, From his moist cabinet *mounts up on high*" (*Venus* 854); "*To mount aloft* with thy imperial mistress,/ And *mount* her *pitch,* whom thou in triumph long/ Hast prisoner held" (*Titus* 2.1.13-15); "*Mount, mount, my soul!* thy seat is *up on high*" (*Rich. II* 5.5.112); "a base ignoble mind/ That *mounts no higher* than a bird can soar" (*2 Hen. VI* 2.1.14). EEBO (1473-1623) returns forty-nine hits in thirty-five records on the search *mount on high*.

(8) *Enjoying least when I do covet most*

> "With *what I most enjoy contented least*" (*Sonnets* 29.8).
>
> The slight variations in syntax and word choice cannot obscure this parallel expression of an almost identical complex and subtle point, a profound insight into a paradox of human nature: Sometimes the more we *covet* or *enjoy* something, the less satisfied we are in hindsight. The thought is expressed in each case as a self-aware first-person insight, in remarkably similar turns of phrase. See also lines 20 & 26.

(9) my *green years*

> "The promise of his *greener days*" (*Hen. V* 2.4.136); "my *salad days*, when I was *green in judgement*" (*A&C* 1.5.74). Cf., in the de Vere letters: "both you and

myself from *our greenest years* have been in a manner brought up" (Fowler 739). The use of the color green to indicate immaturity is a characteristic Shakespearean color metaphor that occurs only infrequently in other writers. *EEBO* (1473-1623) returns the following comparative data: *green years* (twenty-seven hits in twenty-six records), *greener years* (nine/seven), *greenest years* (four/four), *green days* (none), *greener days* (one/one, *Hen. V*).

(13) I like in heart, yet *dare not say I* love

"Thou hast beguiled *my hopes*; nought but mine eye/ Could have persuaded me: now I *dare not say/ I* have one friend alive" (*Two Gent.* 5.4.64-66).

EEBO returns only ten hits in nine records (1473-1623) for the phrase *dare not say I*, including *Two Gent.* but not E.O. 12.

(20, 26) With *least* abode where *best* I feel *content* . . . . Then *least* alone when *most* I *seem to* lurk

"*Seeming to* be *most* which we indeed *least* are" (*Shrew* 5.2.175); "In *least* speak *most*" (*Dream* 5.1.105); "The true soul, when *most* impeached stands *least* in thy control" (*Sonnets* 125.14).

See also line 8.

(23) soar where *Hope* doth *tower*

"*Strong* as a *tower* in *hope*, I cry amen" (*Rich. II* 1.3.102). Both lines reflect the influence of Psalm 61.3: "For thou hast been *my hope*, and a *strong towre* for me against the enemie" (Geneva).

(28) and *when I play* then are *my thoughts at work*

"That never am *less idle*, lo, than *when I am alone*" (*E.O. 2.18*); "That *most are busied* when th'are *most alone*" (*R&J* Q1 1.1.122-28). See the extensive commentary on E.O. 2.18.

(31) *Malcontent*

One of the earliest uses of this word, which becomes so much of a cultural leitmotif during the late Elizabethan period, not only as the title character of John Marston's play, *The Malcontent* (c. 1603), but also as a popular character type of the early Jacobean drama, perhaps based in part on the melancholy misanthrope Jaques in *As You Like It*.

EEBO returns the following data for *malcontent* 1) before 1623, 255 hits in 128 records; 2) before 1600, ninety-three hits/ sixty-three records; 3) before 1580, one hit, John Stubbes's *Discovery of a Gaping Gulf* (1579). The word appears four times in Shakespeare: "loiterers and *malcontents*" (*LLL* 3.1.83); "is it for a wife/ That thou art *malcontent*?" (*3 Hen. VI* 4.1.60); "how like you our choice,/ That you stand pensive, as half *malcontent*?" (*3 Hen. VI* 4.1.10); "Then, like a *melancholy malcontent*,/ He veils his tail" (*Venus* 313-14).

Additional parallels:

(3) Who *seeks* to live and *finds* the way to die

> The warm effects which she in him *finds* missing
> She *seeks* to kindle with continual kissing (*Venus* 605-06)

(3) finds *the way to die*

> "All our yesterdays have lighted fools/ *The way to dusty death* (*Mac.* 5.5.22).

(4) *comfort ebbs* and *cares* do daily *flow*

> The linguistic parallelism of *ebb(ing) and flow(ing)* is by itself commonplace, e.g., "The sea will *ebb and flow*" (*LLL* 4.3.212); "*ebb* and *flow* like the sea" (*1 Hen. IV* 1.2.31); "great ones,/ That *ebb* and *flow* by th' moon" (*Lear* 5.3.18-19).

> More characteristically Shakespearean are parallels associating *ebb(ing) and flow(ing)* with fluctuating emotions: "And *sorrow ebbs*, being *blown* with *wind* of *words*" (*Lucrece* 1330); "Thus *ebbs and flows* the *current* of her *sorrow*" (*Lucrece* 1569); "For still thy eyes . . ./ Do *ebb and flow with tears*" (*R&J* 3.5.133-34).

> The broader linkages are between fluctuating or *flow(ing)* emotions (*comfort* and *cares*) and tears, and with motions of the sea (another salty medium). See also line 19 and E. O. 6.26 and 18.33.

(5-6) But sad *despair* would have me to retire, When smiling *hope* sets forward my desire

> Another favorite Shakespearean antithesis: "Our *hope* but sad *despair*" (*3 Hen. VI* 2.3.9); "Where *hope* is coldest and *despair* most fits" (*All's Well* 2.1.144); "past *hope*, and in *despair*" (*Cym.* 1.1.137); "*Despair* and *hope* makes thee ridiculous" (*Venus* 988).

> Again, antithetical yet juxtaposed emotions appear in both samples. See also E.O. 5.17-22.

(11) Now *crazed with* Care

> "The *grief* hath *crazed my wits*" (*Lear* 3.4.170).

(12) With *world* at will yet wanting *wished scope*

> "An anchor's cheer in prison be *my scope*" (*Ham.* 3.2.219).

(13) And *looks* alone *do lend me* chief relief

> "Contempt his scornful perspective did *lend me,*/ Which warp'd the line of every other favour" (*All's Well* 5.3.49); "Lose not so noble a friend on vain suppose,/ Nor with *sour looks* afflict his gentle heart" (*Titus* 1.1.441).

(15) *I dwelt sometimes at rest*

"There was a man . . . *dwelt by a churchyard*: I will tell it softly;/ Yond crickets shall not hear it" (*Win.* 2.1.29-31); "the triplex, sir, is a good tripping measure; or *the bells of Saint Bennet*, sir, may put you in mind; one, two, three" (*Twelfth* 5.1.37-40).

(16) With *feigned joy* I hide my secret grief

"And all that poets *feign*, of bliss and *joy*" (*3 Hen. VI* 1.2.31).

On the leitmotif of dissimulation, a suggestive common interest seen in both samples, see also E.O. 5 (*passim*) and E. O. 6.4, 9.2, 10.9-10, and 18.40.

(19) '*twixt fear* and comfort *tossed*

"Is madly *tossed between* desire and *dread*" (*Lucrece* 171); "No midway '*twixt* these extremes at all" (*A&C* 3.4.20); "But O, the noble combat that "'*twixt joy* and *sorrow was fought* in Paulina!" (*Win.* 5.2.73).

The same word, *tossed*—recalling again an underlying association between emotion and the *motions* of the sea or objects on the sea—sums up the divided condition of *fear* juxtaposed with some positive emotion (*comfort* or "desire"). See also line 4 and E.O. 6.26 and 18.33.

(20) With *least* abode where *best* I feel content

"That sport *best* pleases that doth *least* know how" (*LLL* 5.2.516).

(25) Then *least alone* when most I seem to lurk

Compare E.O. 2: "That never am *less idle*, lo, than *when I am alone*" — where even the patterns of alliteration betray the presence of the same writer.

(27) I speak of *peace*, and live in endless *strife*

Again the antithesis is commonplace in Shakespeare: "As thou liv'st in *peace*, die free from *strife*" (*Rich. II* 5.6.27); "And for the *peace* of you I hold such *strife*" (*Sonnets* 75.3). *Endless strife*, a hyperbole characteristic of a young writer, is not otherwise found in Shakespeare.

(32) *pains of hell*

"My comfort is that heaven will take our souls/ And plague injustice with the *pains of hell*" (*Rich. II* 3.1.34).

(33) But *Time shall frame* a time unto my will

"When *time shall serve*, to show in articles" (*2 Hen. IV* 4.1.74); "*Time shall unfold* what plighted cunning hides" (*Lear* 1.1.280); "When *time shall serve*, let but the herald cry,/ And I'll appear again" (*Lear* 5.1.48-49); "I say little; but when/ *time shall serve*, there shall be smiles" (*Hen. V* 2.1.6).

(33) *frame a time unto my will*

> "And therefore *frame the law unto my will*" (*1 Hen. VI* 2.4.9); "And therefore *frame* your manners *to the time*" (*Shrew* 1.1.227).

(34) Whenas *in sport this earnest* will I tell

> "Marry, I prithee, do, to *make sport* withal; but love no man *in good earnest*, nor no further *in sport*" (*As You* 1.2.26-28).

(34) *this* earnest *will I tell*

> "*This will I tell* my master" (*Tem.* 3.2.115); "*This will I tell* my lady straight" (*Twelfth* 4.1.30). *This will I tell* returns only eleven hits in nine *EEBO* records from 1473 to 1623.

(35) *Till* then, sweet friend, *abide* these *storms with me*

> "*Till storms be past* of civil enmity" (*3 Hen. VI* 4.6.98). Shakespeare habitually naturalizes emotional conflict with weather metaphors, as in *Much Ado*, where Spurgeon discovers "repeated use of weather and seasons for purposes of comparison" to emotional states, "as when Beatrice so wounds Benedict's pride by telling him he was 'duller than a great thaw,' or Don Pedro exclaims at his 'February face', 'so full of *frost*, of *storm*, and *cloudiness*'" (265). The habit is also conspicuous in the de Vere letters: "*after so many storms* passed of your heavy grace towards me" (Fowler 107); "she hath left [me] to try my fortune among the alterations of time, and chance, either without sail whereby to take the advantage of any prosperous gale or with anchor to ride *till the storm be overpast*" (Fowler 740).

(*35*) *abide* these storms *with me*/ Which shall *in joys* of either fortunes be.

> "For none *abides with me*: my *joy* is death" (*2 Hen. VI* 2.4.88-89); "The other two, slight air and purging fire,/ Are both with thee, wherever I *abide*;/ The first my thought, the other my desire,/ These present-absent with swift motion slide . . ./ This told, *I joy*; but then *no longer glad*,/ I send them back again and straight *grow sad*" (*Sonnets* 45.1-4, 13-14).

(36) Which shall in *joys of either fortunes* be

> The violence *of either* grief or *joy*
> Their own enactures with themselves destroy.
> Where *joy* most revels, grief doth most lament;
> Grief *joys, joy* grieves, on slender accident.
> This world is not for aye, nor 'tis not strange
> That even our loves should with our *fortunes* change;
> For 'tis a question left us yet to prove,
> Whether love lead *fortune*, or else *fortune* love (*Ham.* 3.2.196-203).

Previous commentaries: Sobran (250-53); Goldstein (2016, 60-62).

E.O. 13: "Love Compared to a Tennis-Play"

1	Whenas the heart at tennis plays, and men to gaming fall,
2	Love is the court, hope is the house, and favour serves the ball.
3	The ball itself is true desert; the line, which measure shows,
4	Is reason, whereon judgment looks how players win or lose.
5	The jetty is deceitful guile, the stopper, jealousy,
6	Which hath Sir Argus' hundred eyes wherewith to watch and pry.
7	The fault, wherewith fifteen is lost, is want of wit and sense,
8	And he that brings the racket in is double diligence.
9	And lo, the racket is freewill, which makes the ball rebound;
10	And noble beauty is the chase, of every game the ground.
11	But rashness strikes the ball awry, and where is oversight?
12	"A bandy ho," the people cry, and so the ball takes flight.
13	Now in the end, good-liking proves content the game and gain.
14	Thus in a tennis knit I love, a pleasure mixed with pain.

Structure: Fourteen lines of rhyming couplet "fourteeners" (fourteen-beat iambic lines, a form popularized in the "Golding" translation of Ovid's *Metamorphoses*).

Textual sources: May (1980, 35; 1991, 279-80) (not in Grosart or Looney). May #13.

Explanatory notes:

(1) Shakespeare refers often and with seemingly spontaneous naturalism to the early modern aristocratic sport of *tennis* and its terms of art. De Vere devoted all of E.O. 13 to an extended metaphor on the subject.

Shakespeare's reference in *Hamlet* (2.1.59) to "falling out at tennis" has been seen by many scholars, including Chambers (1895, 142), as a possible topical reference to the famous 1579 London "tennis court quarrel" between de Vere and Sir Philip Sidney—which, of course, occurred many years before the orthodox dating of the play.

Shakspere of Stratford was a fifteen-year-old boy in 1579, still growing up in that provincial town. The incident was about a decade past by the time conventional wisdom holds he arrived in London, and still further in the past when he is conventionally thought to have written *Hamlet*. Of course, any playwright might write about an incident in which he himself was not involved—but decades later, when it was old and stale news? Sidney died of battle wounds in 1586 at age thirty-one and was revered as an English national hero. Would a commoner, writing after that, dredge up an unsavory incident from many years before?

(3-10) *house . . . jetty . . . stopper . . . fifteen . . . chase*. Technical tennis terms.

(6) *Argus* Panoptes is a multi-*eyed* giant in Greek mythology, according to which some of his *eyes* always remain *watch*fully awake while others sleep.

(7) The term *wit* as used here refers to intelligence or mental sharpness, not humor (*OED* 20: 432-34).

(14) See also E.O. 2.8 (*to whose most pain least pleasure doth befall*) and E.O. 8.18 (*What thing did please, and what did pain?*) and Smith (2002) on Munday's *Pain of Pleasure*.

Strongest parallels:

(1) Whenas the heart *at tennis plays,* and *men to gaming fall*

"There *[he] was* "*a gaming* . . . here *falling out at tennis*" (*Ham.* 2.1.58-59).

As noted above, the *Ham.* connection undermines the Stratfordian authorship theory and suggests a significant linkage to de Vere.

See also: "*to play at tennis*" (*Kins.* 5.2.56)

Additional parallels:

(2, 10) *court . . . chase*

"That all the *courts* of France will be disturbed /With *chases*" (*Hen. V* 1.2.266).

(3) *the ball* itself

"A man whom both the waters and the wind,/ In *that vast tennis-court*, have *made the ball*/ For them to play upon, entreats you pity him:/ He asks of you, that never used to beg" (*Per.* 2.1.59-62).

(5) The jetty is *deceitful guile*

"Such false *dissembling guile*" (*1 Hen. VI* 4.1.63).

(6) Sir *Argus'* hundred *eyes*

"He is a gouty Briareus, many hands and no use, or *purblind Argus, all eyes* and no sight" (*Troil.* 1.2.28-30).

(6) wherewith *to watch and pry*

"*To pry into* the secrets of the state" (*2 Hen. VI* 1.1.250); "Tut, I can counterfeit the deep tragedian;/ Speak and *look back, and pry* on every side" (*Rich. III* 3.5.5-6).

(7) is *want of wit* and sense

"Some grief shows much of love;/ But much of grief shows still some *want of wit*" (R&J 3.5.72-73); "So then we do neglect/ The thing we have; and, all for *want of wit,*/ Make something nothing by augmenting it" (*Lucrece* 198-200).

"*Watch* thou and *wake when others be asleep, To pry* into the secrets of the state" (2 *Hen. VI* 1.1.247-48); "*Watch* me *like Argus*" (*Merch.* 5.1.230); cf. "one that will do the deed, Though *Argus* were her eunuch and her guard" (*LLL* 3.1.187-88); "purblind *Argus, all eyes* and no sight" (*Troil.* 1.2.29).

(8) *is* double *diligence*

"Accustom'd *diligence*" (1 *Hen. VI* 5.3.9); "due *diligence*" (*Per.* 3.0.19); "speedy *diligence* "(*Lucrece* 1853); "true *diligence*" (*Shrew* ind. 170); "and the best of me *is diligence*" (*Lear* 1.4.35).

(9) the *racket* is *freewill*

"The *tennis-court-keeper* knows better than I, for it is a low ebb of linen with thee when thou keepest not *racket* there" (2 *Hen. IV* 2.2.18); "To come thus was I not constrain'd, but did/ On my *free will*" (*A&C* 3.6.56).

(9) which makes *the ball* rebound

"Stuffed *tennis-balls*" (*Much* 3.2.46).

(9) the ball *rebound*

"I do feel,/ By the *rebound* of yours, a grief that smites/ My very heart at root" (*A&C* 5.2.103-05).

(12) A "*bandy* ho," *the people cry*

Bandy occurs nine times in Shakespeare, e.g., "will not *bandy with thee* word for word" (3 *Hen. VI* 1.4.49); "Hark! do you not hear *the people cry*" (*Troil.* 1.2.225).

(14) Thus in a tennis knit I love

"*Exeter. Tennis-balls*, my liege. *King Hen.* We are glad the Dauphin is so pleasant with us;/ His present and your pains we thank you for:/ When we have matched our *rackets* to these *balls*/ We will, in France, by God's grace, *play a set*/ Shall strike his father's crown into *the hazard.*/ Tell him he hath made a match with such a wrangler/ That all *the courts of France* will be disturb'd/ With *chaces*" (*Hen. V* 1.2.258-66).

(14) a *pleasure* mixed with *pain*

"Having no other *pleasure* of his *gain*/ But torment that it cannot cure his *pain*" (*Lucrece* 860-61); "since you make your *pleasure* of your *pains*" (*Twelfth* 3.3.2); cf. "No *pains*, sir. I take *pleasure* in singing, sir" (*Twelfth* 2.4.67).

Previous commentary: Sobran (254-55).

E.O. 14: "These Beauties Make Me Die"

1	What cunning can express
2	The favour of her face,
3	To whom in this distress
4	I do appeal for grace?
5	A thousand Cupids fly
6	About her gentle eye.
7	From whence each throws a dart,
8	That kindleth soft sweet fire,
9	Within my sighing heart,
10	Possessed by desire;
11	No sweeter life I try,
12	Than in her love to die.
13	The Lily in the field,
14	That glories in his white,
15	For pureness now must yield
16	And render up his right;
17	Heaven pictured in her face
18	Doth promise joy and grace.
19	Fair Cynthia's silver light,
20	That beats on running streams,
21	Compares not with her white,
22	Whose hairs are all sunbeams;
23	Her virtues so do shine,
24	As day unto mine eyne.
25	With this there is a Red
26	Exceeds the Damask Rose,
27	Which in her cheeks is spread,
28	Whence every favour grows;
29	In sky there is no star
30	That she surmounts not far.
31	When Phoebus from the bed
32	Of Thetis doth arise,
33	The morning, blushing red,
34	In fair carnation wise,
35	He shows it in her face
36	As Queen of every grace.
37	This pleasant Lily white,
38	This taint of roseate red,

39	This Cynthia's silver light,
40	This sweet fair Dea spread,
41	These sunbeams in mine eye,
42	These beauties make me die.

Structure: Seven stanzas of six-line iambic trimeters.

Textual sources: Grosart (417-19); Looney (1921, Miller ed. 1975, 1: 563-64); May (1980, 35-37; 1991, 280-81). May #14. Looney's title: "What Cunning Can Express." Published as by Oxford in *Phoenix* (1593) and later in *Eng. Hel.* (1600), where the first line has been altered to "What Sheepheard can expresse . . . ?" in *Phoenix* (62-63).

Explanatory notes:

(5)   *Cupid*, in classical mythology, is the god of love and desire.

(19, 39) *Cynthia* refers to the moon. The name is sometimes used as an epithet for Selene, the Greek goddess of the moon (or her Roman counterpart, Diana).

(24)   *mine eyne*, "my eyes."

(31-32) *Phoebus* is an epithet for *Apollo*, Greco-Roman god of the sun. *Thetis* is a Greek sea-nymph.

(40)   *Dea* is a general Latin term for "goddess."

Strongest parallels:

(5) A *thousand Cupids*

> "Armed with *thousand Cupids*" (*Kins.* 2.2.31). The phrase *thousand cupids* is surprisingly rare: *EEBO* (1473-1623) returns only thirteen hits in eight records. The phrase subsequently became more popular, and a more complete search (1473-1900) draws thirty-three hits in thirty-one records.

(21, 23, 25-27) Compares not with *her white*,

> . . . .
>
> *Her virtues* so do shine
>
> . . . .
>
> With this there is a *Red*
> Exceeds the *Damask Rose*,
> *Which in her cheeks is spread*

> This play of *red* and *white* imagery, comparing the *blush* to a *rose* (specifically the *damask rose*), becomes a leitmotif in Shakespeare. See also parallels below to lines 13-14. See the Methodological Afterword for further and more detailed discussion of the *damask rose* parallels (see also E.O. 17.5-6).

Compare, e.g., these lines in *Lucrece*:

To praise the clear unmatched *red and white*
Which triumphed in that sky of his delight (11-12)

When Beauty boasted *blushes*, in despite
Virtue would stain that o'er with *silver white* (55-56)

This heraldry in Lucrece' face was seen,
Argued by *Beauty's red and Virtue's white.*
Of either's colour was the other queen (64-66)

This silent war of *lilies and roses*
Which Tarquin viewed in her fair face's field (71-72)

Her lily hand *her rosy cheek* lies under (386)

Cheeks neither *red* nor pale, but *mingled* so (1510)

Many further examples can be cited, e.g., "Our veiled dames/ Commit the war of *white and damask* in/ Their nicely gawded *cheeks*" (*Cor.* 2.1.204-06); "Such war of *white and red* within her *cheeks*!" (*Shrew* 4.5.30); "the *blushing rose*/ Usurps *her cheek*" (*Venus* 590-91); "The air hath starved the *roses in her cheeks*" (*Two Gent.* 4.4.154); "*Armado.* My love is most immaculate *white and red . . . Moth.* If she be made of *white and red,/* Her faults will ne'er be known, For *blushing cheeks* by faults are bred,/ And fears by *pale white* shown" (*LLL* 1.2.86, 93-96); "Claps her *pale cheek*, till clapping makes it *red*" (*Venus* 484); "Love's not Time's fool, though *rosy lips and cheeks/* Within his bending sickle's compass come" (*Sonnets* 116.9).

On the *damask rose*, see: "as sweet as *damask roses*" (*Win.* 4.4.220); "I have seen roses damasked, *red and white*, But no such *roses* see I in her *cheeks*" (*Sonnets* 130.5-6); "With *cherry* lips and *cheeks of damask roses*" (*Kins.* 4.1.74); cf. "feed on her *damask cheek*" (*Twelfth* 2.4.112).

(33) *The morning, blushing red*

"When lo *the blushing morrow/ Lends light* to all" (*Lucrece* 1082-83); "King Richard doth himself appear,/ As doth *the blushing discontented sun/* From out the fiery portal of the *east*" (*Rich. II* 3.3.62-64); "a *blush* modest as *morning*" (*Troil.* 1.3.229); cf. "To *blush* and beautify the *cheek*" (*2 Hen. VI* 3.2.167); "His treasons will sit *blushing* in his face" (*Rich. II* 3.2.51). EEBO (1473-1623) confirms the rarity of these expressions, returning only sixteen hits in fourteen records for the search "*blushing* near *morning*" and only seven in seven for "*blush* near *morning*."

(37-42) This pleasant *Lily white,*
This taint of *roseate red,*
This Cynthia's *silver light,*
This *sweet* fair Dea spread,

These sunbeams in mine eye,
These beauties make me die

As noted above, *Cynthia* refers to the moon and *Dea* is a general Latin term for "goddess." Recalling that *Thetis* (line 32) is a nymph—and noting that the writer of each passage clearly felt that great human beauty is (in modern parlance) "to die for"—compare these lines from *Venus*:

The field's chief *flower, sweet* above compare,
Stain to all *nymphs,* more lovely than a man,
More *white and red* than doves or *roses* are;
Nature that made thee with herself at strife
Saith that *the world hath ending with thy life.* (8-12)

(42) *These beauties*

"Would root *these beauties* as he roots the mead" (*Venus* 636). EEBO (1473-1623) returns only nineteen hits in seventeen records for the phrase *these beauties.*

(42) *make me die*

Teach thou this sorrow how to *make me die* (*John* 3.1.30). EEBO (1473-1623) returns only thirty hits in nineteen records for the phrase *make me die.*

Additional parallels:

(1) What cunning *can express*

"My tongue *cannot express* my grief" (*Venus* 1069); "more it is than I *can well express*" (*Lucrece* 1286).

(8) That *kindleth* soft sweet *fire*

"his love-*kindling fire*" (*Sonnets* 153.3); "the raging *fire* of fever *bred*" (*Errors* 5.1.75); "Therefore let Benedick, like covered *fire, Consume away* in sighs, waste inwardly" (*Much* 3.1.78); cf. "let virtue be as wax And melt in her own *fire*" (*Ham.* 3.4.85).

According to Eric Sams, "Among Tudor dramatists, it is [Shakespeare] who notices how *fire* behaves and converts that knowledge, into proverbs and sayings of his own" (1986, 297). This parallel suggests that de Vere was in fact the innovator.

(13-14) *The Lily* in the field, That glories in his *white*

The *lily* is one of Shakespeare's favorite flowers, with twenty-five allusions in the canonical plays and poems (Spevack 723), e.g.:

"most *lily-white* of hue" (*Dream* 3.1.84); "Nor did I wonder at *the lily's white,/* Nor praise the deep vermilion in *the rose*" (*Sonnets* 98.9-10); "*The lily* I condemned for thy hand . . . . *The roses* fearfully on thorns did stand,/ One *blushing* shame, another *white* despair" (*Sonnets* 99.6, 8-9).

See also parallels above to lines 21, 23 & 25-27.

(19) *Cynthia's silver light*

"*Cynthia* for shame obscures her *silver shine*" (*Venus* 728); "Tis but the *pale reflex* of *Cynthia's* brow" (*R&J* 3.5.20); "*Cynthia* with her *borrowed light*" (*Kins.* 4.1.153).

(22) Whose hairs are all *sunbeams*

I saw Jove's bird, the Roman eagle, wing'd/ From the spongy south to this part of the west,/ There vanish'd in the *sunbeams* (*Cym.* 4.2.348-50).

(29-30) *there is no star That she surmounts not far*

"*The brightness of her cheek would shame those stars*" (*R&J* 2.2.19).

(31-32) When *Phoebus* from the bed Of *Thetis* doth *arise*

"And *Phoebus 'gins arise*" (*Cym.* 2.3.20).

Shakespeare refers six times to *Thetis*, a Greek sea nymph (Spevack 1310). See also E.O. 8.5-6 (*When that Aurora, blushing red, Descried the guilt of Thetis' bed*). *Aurora* refers to the dawning sun.

Phoebus (also referenced in E.O. 17.24, 19.8, and 20.4) is an epithet for *Apollo*, Greco-Roman god of the sun. The quotation above from *Cym.* is one of twenty-three references to *Phoebus* (including one spelled, satirically, "Phibbus") in canonical Shakespeare (Spevack 976-77). *Apollo* is referenced once in these de Vere poems (E.O. 3.6) and twenty-nine times in canonical Shakespeare (Spevack 54).

On *Thetis* and *Phoebus*, see also the parallels to E.O. 8 (lines 1-2 and 5-6). On the amours of the gods generally (a common interest of these de Vere poems and Shakespeare, see also E.O. 3.6 and E.O. 6 (lines 7-10, 17-18, and 23-24).

See also E.O. 8.5 (*that Aurora* [i.e., dawning sun] *blushing red*).

(34) In fair *carnation* wise

"The *fairest* flowers o' th' season Are our *carnations* and streaked gillyvors" (*Win.* 4.4.81-82); cf. "how much *carnation* ribbon may a man buy . . .?" (*LLL*, 3.1.135-36); "'A could never abide *carnation;* 'twas a color he never liked" (*Hen. V* 2.3.30).

De Vere employs here another flower (in addition to *lilies* and *roses*) referenced by Shakespeare (on the three occasions quoted above, Spevack 183).

(40) This *sweet* fair Dea *spread*

> "Ere he can *spread* his *sweet* leaves to the air" (*R&J* 1.1.152); "*Sweet* mermaid, with thy note . . ./ *Spread* o'er the *silver* waves thy *golden* hairs" (*Errors* 3.2.47-48).

(41) These *sunbeams in mine eye*

> "*I saw* Jove's bird, the Roman eagle, wing'd/ From the spongy south to this part of the west,/ There vanish'd *in the sunbeams* which portends (unless my sins abuse my divination)/ Success to the Roman host" (*Cym.* 4.2.348-52).

> "I have a rheum *in mine eyes* too" (*Troil.* 5.3.104)

Previous commentaries: Looney (1920, 141-45); Sobran (254-57, 586-87); May (2004, 224).

E.O. 15: "Who Taught Thee First to Sigh?"

1	Who taught thee first to sigh, alas, my heart?
2	Who taught thy tongue the woeful words of plaint?
3	Who filled thine eyes with tears of bitter smart?
4	Who gave thee grief and made thy joys so faint?
	Love
5	Who first did print with colours pale thy face?
6	Who first did break thy sleeps of quiet rest?
7	Above the rest in Court, who gave thee Grace?
8	Who made thee strive in virtue to be best?
	Love
9	In constant troth to bide so firm and sure,
10	To scorn the world, regarding but thy friend,
11	With patient mind each passion to endure,
12	In one desire to settle to thy end?
	Love
13	Love then thy choice, wherein such faith doth bind,
14	As nought but death may ever change thy mind.

Structure: Fourteen full lines in three stanzas of four with concluding couplet, in alternating rhyme, with refrain word "love" repeated after each stanza, in iambic pentameter. The form has dynamic balance as the three one-word lines couple with the last two to form a fourth unit, balancing the other three.

Textual sources: Grosart (413); Looney (1921, Miller ed. 1975, 1: 562); May (1980, 37; 1991, 281). May #15. Looney's title: "Love Thy Choice."

Explanatory Note:

(9)   *Troth* is an archaic term for "truth," also signifying solemnly pledged faith, loyalty, or *constancy* (*OED* 17: 587-88).

Strongest parallels:

(1) *Who taught thee* first *to sigh, alas, my heart?*

    "*Who taught thee* how *to make me love* thee more . . .?" (*Sonnets* 150.9).

    Both samples employ an identical interrogative phrase (*Who taught thee?*) in exactly the same context—a rhetorical question asking about the origins of the speaker's love for another. In both there is a kind of sweet chiding over the beloved's responsibility for inspiring the lover's desire. *EEBO* (1473-1900) returns only fourteen hits in fourteen records to the phrase *who taught thee*, two of them to the Shakespearean sonnet.

(2) Who *taught thy tongue* the *woeful* words of plaint?

> "And if I were thy nurse, *thy tongue to teach*" (*Rich. II* 5.3.113); "To *teach my tongue* to be so long" (*Pass. Pilg.* 18.52); cf. "Those eyes that *taught all other eyes* to see" (*Venus* 952); "How angerly I *taught my brow* to frown" (*Two Gent.* 1.2.62); "And *teach your ears* to list me with more heed" (*Errors* 4.1.101); "*Teach* not *thy lip* such scorn" (*Rich. III* 1.2.171); "O, she doth *teach the torches* to burn bright!" (*R&J* 1.5.44); "my *woe-wearied tongue* is still and mute" (*Rich. III* 4.4.18). An *EEBO* search for *taught* near *thy tongue* returns only nine hits in nine records, including to a variant of this poem printed as the final sonnet in a 1593 volume of sonnets, *The tears of fancie. Or, Loue disdained* attributed to T.W. (presumably Thomas Watson, Oxford's literary associate).

(5) Who first *did print*

> "For she *did print* your royal father off/ Conceiving you" (*Win.* 5.1.125-26).

> *EEBO* returns only four hits in four records, including *Win.*, but not E.O. 15, for *did print*. In *Win.* the phrase denotes an exact copy.

> The parallel here is not merely the infinitive *to teach*, but its specific, playful, metaphorical use as applied to the *tongue* or other body parts or inanimate objects.

(8) *Who made thee*

> *Who made thee,* then, a bloody minister (*Richard III* 1.4.x).

(8-9) *strive in virtue to be best?/ In constant troth*

> "I did *strive to prove/ The constancy and virtue* of your love" (*Sonnets* 117.13-14); "Oaths of thy love, *thy truth, thy constancy*" (*Sonnets* 152.10).

(9) *In constant troth to bide so firm and sure*

> "Though *thou stand'st more sure* than I could do,/ Thou art not *firm* enough" (*2 Hen. IV* 4.5.202-03); "so firm, so constant" (*Tem.* 1.2.207).

> One signification of the word *troth*, as noted above, is solemnly pledged faith, loyalty, or *constancy*.

(11) With patient mind *each passion* to endure

> "*Each passion* labours so" (*Venus* 969).

> *EEBO* returns only thirteen hits in twelve records for *each passion*.

Additional parallels:

(2) *woeful words*

> "*Woeful* pageants" (*As You* 2.7.138); "*woeful* ballad" (*As You* 2.7.148); "*woeful* music" (*Per.* 3.2.88); "*woeful* ditty" (*Venus* 836); "*woeful words*" (*Venus* 1126).

(3) *tears of bitter* smart

> "*Bitter tears*" (*Titus* 3.1.6, 129).

(4-5) Who gave thee grief and made thy joys to *faint?*. . ./ Who first did print with colours *pale thy face?*

> "Affection *faints* not like a *pale-faced* coward" (*Venus* 569); cf. "As burning fevers, ague, *pale* and *faint*" (*Venus* 739).

(6) *break* thy *sleeps* of *quiet rest*

> "*Break* not *your sleeps* for that" (*Ham.* 4.7.30); cf. "*broke* their *sleep*" (*2 Hen. IV,* 4.5.68; *Cor.* 4.4.19); "one *quiet* breath of *rest*" (*John* 3.4.134); "God give you *quiet rest* tonight" (*Rich. III* 5.3.43); "Romeo should . . ./ Soon *sleep in quiet*" (*R&J* 3.5.99-100). References to insomnia are common enough in Shakespeare to suggest a psychoanalytic explanation. See also E.O. 18b.15 (*I break no sleep*).

(7) *Above the rest* in court

> "Wherein it finds a joy *above the rest*" (*Sonnets* 91.6); "Therefore, *above the rest*, we parley to you" (*Two Gent.* 4.1.58).

(11) With *patient* mind each *passion to endure*

> "God of his mercy give/ You *patience to endure*" (*Hen. V* 2.2.179-80); "have *patience* and *endure*" (*Much* 4.1.254); "*endure* the toothache *patiently*" (*Much* 5.1.36); "I must have *patience to endure* the load" (*Rich. III* 3.7.230); "I must have *patience to endure* all this" (*Titus* 2.3.88); "I have the *patience to endure* it now" (*Caes.* 4.3.192).

(12) In one desire, to settle to *thy end*

> "Bloody thou art, bloody will *be thy end*" (*Rich. III* 4.4.195).

(14) As *nought but death*

> "Pistol speaks *nought but truth*" (*2 Hen. IV* 5.5.38); "Whose hollow womb inherits *nought but bones*" (*Rich. II* 2.1.83); "This hand was made to handle *naught but gold*" (*2 Hen. VI* 5.1.7).

(14) may ever *change thy mind*

> "You know that I held Epicurus strong/ And his opinion: now *I change my mind,*/ And partly credit things that do presage" (*Caes.* 5.1.75-77); "it would better fit your honour to *change your mind*" (*Much* 3.2.116).

Previous commentaries: Ogburn (512-13); Sobran (258-59); Brazil & Flues.

E.O. 16: "Were I a King"

1   Were I a king I could command content;
2   Were I obscure unknown should be my cares,
3   And were I dead no thought should me torment,
4   Nor words, nor wrongs, nor loves, nor hopes, nor fears;
5   A doubtful choice of these things one to crave,
6   A kingdom, or a cottage, or a grave.

Structure: Six-line epigram in alternating rhyme with concluding couplet. This poem is a relatively early instance of breaking up the line with a list of thematic key terms.

Textual sources: Printed anonymously in John Mundy's 1594 *Songs and Psalms.* Grosart (426-27): Looney (1921, Miller ed. 1975, 1: 596); May (1980, 37; 1991, 281). May #16: epigram. Looney's title: same as above. The poem was widely imitated. Hannah (147-148) reprints three imitations, by Sir Philip Sidney, "F.M.," and anon. See Appendix B for these poems.

E.O. 16 and 18 express several related thoughts, each echoed copiously in Shakespeare. Compare E.O. 18, line 1 (*My mind to me a kingdom is*) and lines 23-24 (Lo, thus I *triumph like a king,/ Content* with what *my mind* doth bring), which express essentially the same idea but from distinctive perspectives. Both poems betray the distinctive influence of Seneca, e.g. *Thyestes* 455-70, which concludes "*immane regnum est posse sine regno pati* (it is a vast kingdom to be able to cope without a kingdom)" (470).

Strongest parallels:

(1) *Were I a king* I could *command content*

> "*Was ever king* that joyed an earthly throne,/ And *could command* no more *content* than *I?*" (*2 Hen. VI* 4.9.1-2); cf. "a *king* crowned with *content*" (*3 Hen. VI* 3.1.66); "She is *content* to be at your *command;/ Command,* I mean, of virtuous chaste intent" (*1 Hen. VI* 5.5.19-20); "*Were the world mine*" (*Dream* 1.1.190). *EEBO* (1473-1900) returns only six hits in five records to the phrase *command content* (including variant spellings and forms). Of these, only two actually join *command* and *content* in a direct verb-object relationship, in the duplicated phrase from a variant of Oxford's lyric, "I might I might commaund content, were I obscure . . . ." They are from John Mundy's 1594 *Songs and Psalmes composed into 3.4. and 5. parts,* with music by William Byrd and dedicated to the Earl of Essex.

(1-2, 6) *Content . . . obscure . . . A kingdom* or a *cottage* or a *grave*

> "When that this body did contain a spirit,/ *A kingdom for it* was too small

a bound;/ But now *two paces of the vilest earth*/ Is room enough" (*1 Hen. IV* 5.4.90-92); "The *king* shall be *contented* . . . I'll give . . . My gorgeous palace for. . . a *hermitage* . . . And my large *kingdom* for a little *grave*, A little little *grave*, an *obscure grave*" (*Rich. II* 3.3.145). The *EEBO* search "*kingdom* near *cottage* near *grave*" returns only eight hits, all to this poem as printed in the 1594 Mundy volume of Byrd's musical psalms.

Additional parallels:

(2) Were I obscure unknown should be *my cares*

> *Your cares* set up do not pluck *my cares* down.
> *My care* is loss of care, by old care done;
> *Your care* is gain of *care*, by *new care* won:
> The *cares I give I have*, though given away;
> They tend *the crown*, yet still with me they stay. (*Rich. II* 4.1.195-99)

(3) no *thought* should *me torment*

> "The *torture of the mind*" (*Mac.* 3.2.21); "the *thought* whereof/ Doth like a poisonous mineral *gnaw my inwards*" (*Oth.* 2.1.296-97); "But ah, *thought kills* me" (*Sonnets* 44.9).

> Here is another characteristic topic in Shakespeare's theory of the mind, found first in de Vere's lyric: the idea that the mind can make itself sick with too much worry. Shakespeare's kings Richard II, Henry IV, Henry V, and Henry VI all lament the *woes of kings*, an improbable emphasis for a middle-class playwright.

(4) *Nor words*, *nor* wrongs, *nor* loves, *nor* hopes, *nor* fears

> "I have *neither* wit, *nor words, nor* worth" (*Caes.* 3.2.221); "*neither* in estate, years, *nor wit*" (*Twelfth* 1.3.110-11); "*Nor* stony tower, *nor* walls of beaten brass,/ *Nor* airless dungeon, *nor* strong links of iron,/ Can be retentive to the strength of spirit" (*Caes.* 1.3.93-95); "*Nor* shall proud Lancaster usurp my right,/ *Nor* hold the sceptre in his childish fist,/ *Nor* wear the diadem upon his head,/ Whose church-like humours fits not for *a crown*" (*2 Hen. VI* 1.1.244-47).

(4) nor *hopes*, nor *fears*

> "Applying *fears to hopes* and *hopes to fears*" (*Sonnets* 119.3).

(5) of these things one *to crave*

> "Let him have time a beggar's orts *to crave* (*Lucrece* 985).

(5-6) *Grave . . . crave*

> "And having thrown him from your watery *grave*,
> Here to have death in peace is all he'll *crave*" (*Per.* 2.1.10-11).

Previous commentaries: Sobran (258-59); Goldstein (2016, 51-52; 2017, 23).

co-written by Anne Vavasour, Mistress (c. 1560 - c. 1650)

E.O. 17: "Sitting Alone Upon My Thought" (The Echo Verses)

1   Sitting alone upon my thought, in melancholy mood,
2   In sight of sea, and at my back an ancient hoary wood,
3   I saw a fair young lady come, her secret fears to wail,
4   Clad all in colour of a nun, and covered with a veil.
5   Yet, for the day was clear and calm, I might discern her face,
6   As one might see a damask rose hid under crystal glass.
7   Three times with her soft hand full hard on her left side she knocks,
8   And sighed so sore as might have moved some pity in the rocks.
9   From sighs, and shedding amber tears, into sweet song she brake,
10   When thus the echo answered her to every word she spake.

11   "O heavens! Who was the first that bred in me this fever?"
                                                    Vere.
12   "Who was the first that gave the wound, whose scar I wear for ever?"
                                                   Vere.
13   "What tyrant Cupid to my harms usurps the golden quiver?"
                                                   Vere.
14   "What wight first caught this heart, and can from bondage it deliver?"
                                                   Vere.
15   "Yet who doth most adore this wight, O hollow caves, tell true?"
                                                   You.
16   "What nymph deserves his liking best, yet doth in sorrow rue?"
                                                   You.
17   "What makes him not regard good will with some remorse or ruth?"
                                                 Youth.
18   "What makes him show, besides his birth, such pride and such untruth?"
                                                 Youth.
19   "May I his beauty match with love, if he my love will try?"
                                                   Aye.
20   "May I requite his birth with faith? Then faithful will I die."
                                                 Aye.

21   And I, that knew this lady well,
22   Said Lord, how great a miracle,
23   To her how echo told the truth,
24   As true as Phoebus' oracle.

Structure: Ten lines of rhyming couplets of iambic "fourteeners" defining a scene of action, followed by ten more lines of questions rhyming with answers punning on the author's name and a concluding coda of four lines of iambic tetrameter playing on the author's heraldic motto as published in multiple sources.

Textual sources: Grosart (411-12); Looney (1921, Miller ed. 1975, 1: 560-61); May (1980, 38-39; 1991, 282-83). May: possibly by Oxford #I. Looney's title: "Echo Verses."

Explanatory notes:

(1)   *Sitting upon.* May terms this "a phrase with decidedly legal connotations (*OED,* to sit in judgment, deliberate on)" (85).

(11-14) As Looney noted (1920, 162-63), *Vere* in the *echoes* to lines 11-14 would be pronounced "Vair." It is plausible that the early modern pronunciation of the name varied between this sound, rhyming with modern "fair," and *Veer,* like our modern verb *veer.*

(11-20) There are no quotation marks around the *fair young lady*'s words in the manuscript sources. May added quotation marks, but Looney did not. They are used here for clarity. See also comment on line 11 in Figure 10.

(13)   *Cupid,* in classical mythology, is the god of love and desire.

(14-15) A *wight* means a person (who can be male or female), with some connotation of commiseration or contempt (*OED* 20: 328).

(24)   *Phoebus* (cf. 14.31, 19.8, and 20.4) is an epithet for *Apollo,* Greco-Roman god of the sun. There are twenty-three references to *Phoebus* (including one spelled "Phibbus") in canonical Shakespeare (Spevack 976-77). The name *Apollo* is referenced once in these de Vere poems (E.O. 3.6) and twenty-nine times in canonical Shakespeare (Spevack 54).

As summarized by Gary Goldstein, in both *Venus* and E.O. 17 "a female pours out her woes and is answered by echoes from caves; in each, the echoing is preceded by three identical conceptions in identical order: She beats her heart, the caves are moved to pity, and she breaks into song, after which comes the echo" (23). Both de Vere and Shakespeare, moreover, deploy the same Ovidian association between *cave* and *echo.*

This poem appears to have been inspired by de Vere's relationship with his mistress Anne Vavasour (c. 1560–c. 1650). The affair began circa 1579, produced a son (Sir Edward Vere) born in March 1581, and apparently ended later that year (see, e.g., Anderson 161-65, 172-73, 178-81).

May (1980, 79-81) acknowledged strong reasons (convincing in our view) to accept de Vere's authorship of E.O. 17, though he also questioned that attribution. May's text relies on the Folger Library's manuscript 1.1112, which has the name "Vavaser" attached to it. Looney's text relies on the Rawlinson manuscript in Oxford University's Bodleian Library, which identifies "the Earl of Oxford" as the author and seems, overall, the preferable version (thus primarily relied upon here). Several passages in the two manuscript versions are compared in Figure 10.

Also by Anne Vavasour? & devere
* "Though I seem strange sweet friend"
"Though I be strange in..."

Rawlinson MS:	Folger MS:	Commentary:
(3) her secret *fears* to wail	her secret *tears* to wail	How can *tears* be secret, much less wailed?
(4) in colour of a *nun*	in colour of a *vow*	Color of a *vow*? What does that mean? It is not comprehensible.
(6) hid *under* crystal glass	*though* hid *with* crystal glass	*Under* seems a superior poetic choice in diction and concision as well as sense. Both versions scan, but the Folger uses the superfluous *though* and less precise *with*, slowing down the vigor of the Rawlinson version.
(7) *on* her *left side* she knocks	*upon* her *heart* she knocks	*Heart* may be a stronger choice than *left side*. But metrically the one syllable *on* is more apt than *upon*, which fails to scan and needlessly takes two syllables. In these early poems, Oxford already understands the force of the one-syllable word and generally prefers it.
(8) moved some *pity* in the rocks	moved some *mercy* in the rocks	To move *mercy* is a cognitive and jurisprudential act. To move *pity* is an emotive act and seems more apt here.
(10) *When* thus the echo answered her	*And* thus the echo answered her	*When* retains the narrative dimension of the poem, lost in the use of *And*, a dead filler conjunction.
(11) O heavens! Who was the first ... ?	"O heavens," *quoth she*, "who was the first ... ?"	As noted on the previous page, there are no quotation marks in either manuscript, but May added them to the Folger text, perhaps to accommodate the superfluous *quoth she* in that version. The previous line in both versions says the echo answered her to every word she spake, rendering *quoth she* most likely a copyist's interpolation.
(24) *As true as* Phoebus' oracle	as 'twere Apollo's oracle	*As true as* reiterates the de Vere motto ("*Nothing Is Truer Than Truth*"), which is central to the meaning of the coda.

Figure 10. Comparison of Manuscripts of No. 17 shows, *pace* May, that the Rawlinson MS 85, on which Looney relied, prints a more authorial form than the Folger Cornwallis MS (V.a.89).

Strongest parallels:

(1-4, 9) *Sitting alone upon my thought, in melancholy mood,*
    In sight of sea, and at my back an ancient hoary wood,
    I saw a fair young *lady come, her secret fears to wail,*
    Clad all in colour of a nun, and *covered with a veil*

    . . .

    From sighs, and shedding amber tears, into sweet song she brake

Compare these opening lines to the those of *A Lover's Complaint*:

    "*From off a hill* whose concave womb re-worded
    A plaintful story from a sist'ring vale" (1-2)

    "*Ere long [I] espied a* fickle *maid* full pale,
    Tearing of papers, breaking rings a-twain,
    Storming her world with sorrow's wind and rain" (5-7)

    "*Upon her head a platted hive of straw,*
    Which fortified her visage from the sun" (8-9)

    "Oft did she *heave her napkin to her eyne*" [eyes] (15)

    "*That seasoned* woe *had pelleted in* tears" (18)

    "As often *shrieking undistinguished woe*" (20)

See also: "*Sitting on a bank,/ Weeping again* the King my father's wrack,/ *This music crept by me upon the waters*" (*Tem.* 1.2.390-92); cf. "Sweet Cytherea, *sitting by a brook/* With young Adonis. . . told him stories to delight his ear" (*Pass. Pilg.* IV.1-2, 5); "Venus, with young Adonis *sitting* by her/ *Under a myrtle shade*, began to woo him" (*Pass. Pilg.* XI.1-2).

The passages all involve *sitting* in evocative wilderness settings, often with a tree or beside a stream (or, as in the Queen's description of Ophelia's death in *Ham.*, both), where some music or story (a *musical story* or *song*) is then overheard by the reader. The situational device is further exemplified in *Two Gent.* where the speaker is, however, male:

    Val. . . . This shadowy *desert, unfrequented woods,*
    I better brook than flourishing peopled towns:
    Here can *I sit* alone, unseen of any,
    And to *the nightingale's complaining notes*
    Tune my distresses and *record my woes*. (5.4.2-6)

The de Vere poem is an early exploration in lyric of an imagination of an essentially dramaturgical and operatic character. Most strikingly, especially in that male-centric era, in both E.O. 17 and *A Lover's Complaint*—and also in *Venus* (see parallels below to lines 7-10 & 15)—we overhear a *female* soliloquy of romantic woe (observed passively by a hidden man in both E.O. 17 and *Lover's Comp.*). Note that the lamenting *lady* in

Lover's Comp. (like Shakespeare's Venus) seems to be significantly older ("carcass of a beauty spent and done [line 11] . . . Some beauty peeped through lattice of seared age [line 14]") than the *fair young lady* of E.O. 17.

Likewise de Vere, when writing *Complaint* as "Shakespeare"—a pseudonym first used in print with the publication of *Venus* when de Vere was forty-three —was probably significantly older than when he wrote E.O. 17, perhaps during his affair with Vavasour when he was about thirty.

More broadly, E.O. 17, *Lover's Comp., Venus,* and the above-cited scene in *Tem.* all unite in presenting a natural setting for solitary anguish and *tears*.

See below three related and additional sets of parallels, to lines 7-10 & 15, to line 8 (*moved some pity in the rocks*) (including another echo of the latter in *Complaint*), and to lines 8-9.

(7-10, 15) . . . full hard *on her left side* she knocks,
>   And *sighed so sore* . . .
>   From *sighs, and . . . tears, into sweet song she brake*
>   *When thus the echo answered her to every word she spake*
>
>   . . .
>   *"O hollow caves, tell true"*

> Folger manuscript V.a.89 line 7 reads *"upon her heart she knocks."* The *heart*, of course, is on the *left side* of the chest.

Now compare, as Looney (1920, 162-63) and Goldstein (2016, 48-49; 2017, 22-23) do, the following thirteen lines (including two full stanzas) from *Venus and Adonis,* the first work published as by "Shakespeare" in 1593, which also depicts a lovelorn female, alone in a wilderness setting (Venus, after Adonis eludes her), who proceeds to lament her woes, *sighing* and groaning *sorely* and *knocking upon her heart*—also *breaking into song*. Most distinctively of all, in *Venus caves* also *echo every word she speaks:*

> And now *she beats her heart, whereat it groans,*
> That *all the neighbor caves,* as seeming troubled,
> *Make verbal repetition of her moans.*
> Passion on passion deeply is *redoubled:*
> *"Ay me!" she cries,* and twenty times, *"Woe, woe!"*
> *And twenty echoes twenty times cry so.*
>
> She, marking them, begins a wailing note
> And *sings extemporally a woeful ditty*—
> How *love* makes young men thrall, and old men dote;
> How *love* is wise in folly, foolish-witty.
> Her heavy *anthem* still concludes in *woe,*
> *And still the choir of echoes answer so.*
> Her *song* was tedious and outwore the night[.]   (829-41)

See also: *"echo replies/* As if another chase were in the skies" (*Venus* 695); "Thy hounds shall make the welkin *answer them/* and fetch shrill *echoes from the hollow earth*" (*Shrew* ind.2.44); "with *heart-sore sighs*" (*Two Gent.* 1.1.30); "With nightly *tears* and daily *heart-sore sighs*" (*Two Gent.* 2.4.129); "*every word* doth almost s/tell my name" (*Sonnets* 76.7).

Pursuing the parallels to lines 10 and 15 in particular, and noting the *fair young lady's* repeated questions in lines 11-20 (*the echo answering "Vere"* in lines 11-14), consider also the following line uttered by yet another Shakespearean female enraptured by the pangs of love, calling out to her beloved (see Looney 1920, 163-64):

"*Juliet.* Bondage is hoarse and may not speak aloud,/ Else would I tear *the cave where Echo lies/* And make her airy tongue more hoarse than mine/ *With repetition of* 'My Romeo!'" (*R&J* 2.2.161-64).

(7) *her soft hand*

"*Her soft hand's* print" (*Venus* 353).

EEBO returns only twelve hits in twelve records (1473-1623) for the phrase *her soft hand*, including two in Sidney's *Arcadia* and two in Spencer's *Fairie Queene*.

(8) *moved some pity* in the *rocks*

Looney noted (1920, 161) in both these de Vere poems and Shakespeare "the recurrence of what seems . . . a curious appeal for *pity.*" *Pity* (and its variants) appears more than 300 times in the Shakespeare canon (Spevack 980-81). In addition to line 8, see also E.O. 3.7 (*the less she pities me*), E.O. 9.36 (*pity me*). This tendency is even visible in de Vere's 1572 letter to his father-in-law William Cecil: "on whose tragedies we have an [sic] number of French Aeneases in this city, that tell of their own overthrows *with tears falling from their eyes*, a *piteous* thing to hear but a cruel and *far more grievous* thing we must deem it them to see" (Fowler 55).

The theme is ubiquitous in Shakespeare, including in many strikingly parallel constructions, e.g., in the antithetical juxtaposition of the softness of pity and the hardness of stone: "O if no harder than a *stone* thou art,/ *Melt at my tears, and be compassionate;/* Soft *pity* enters at an iron gate" (*Lucrece* 593-95); "*Pity*, you ancient *stones*, those tender babes" (*Rich. III* 4.1.98); "What *rocky heart* to water *will not wear?*" (*Lover's Comp.* 291); cf. "Beat at thy *rocky and wrack-threat'ning heart*" (*Lucrece* 590); "hard'ned *hearts*, harder than *stones*" (*Lucrece* 978).

See also: "He is a *stone*, a very *pebble stone*, and has no more *pity* in him than a dog" (*Two Gent.* 2.3.11); "I am not made of *stones*, But *penetrable to your* kind entreats" (*Rich. III* 3.7.224); "*Your sorrow beats so ardently* upon me/ That it shall make a counter-reflect 'gainst/ My brother's *heart* and *warm it to some pity*, Though it were *made of stone*" (*Kins.* 1.1.126-29); cf. "I would to God my *heart* were *flint*, like Edward's,/ Or Edward's soft and *pitiful* like mine" (*Rich. III* 1.3.139-40); "Clarence is well-spoken, and perhaps/ *May move your hearts to pity*" (*Rich. III* 1.3.347-48). The variations in these expressions around a common theme and modality of thought illustrate very well how Shakespeare varies certain core elements over and over again.

The same idea is expressed in different words by Shakespeare: "*To see* sad sights *moves* more than *hear them told*,/ For then the *eye* interprets *to the ear*/ The heavy motion that it doth *behold*" (*Lucrece* 1324-26).

(23-24) told *the truth as true as*

Echoes by clear intent the de Vere motto, *vero nihil verius* ("*nothing truer than the truth*"). Many further echoes, some quite elaborate, occur in the Shakespeare canon, e.g.:

By heaven, that *thou art fair,* is most infallible;
true, that thou art beauteous; *truth itself*, that
thou art lovely. *More fairer than fair*, beautiful
than beauteous, *truer than truth itself*, have
commiseration on thy heroical vassal!
                              (*LLL* 4.1.60-64)

(24) *As true as Phoebus' oracle*

"And in *Apollo's* name, his *oracle*" (*Win.* 3.2.118); "There is *no truth at all i' th' oracle!*" (*Win.* 3.2.138).

Punctuating as it does the series of ten echoes on the words *Vere, You, Youth,* and *Aye*, the play on the de Vere motto establishes in one blow what will become the giant Shakespearean theme of the kinetic power of the echo to transmit a name.

Additional parallels:

(1) *melancholy mood*

"*Moody* and dull *melancholy*" (*Errors* 5.1.79).

(4) *Clad all in colour of a nun, and covered with a veil*

"But *like a cloistress* she will *veiled* walk" (*Twelfth* 1.1.27); cf. "Where beauty's *veil* doth *cover* every blot" (*Sonnets* 95.11).

(5-6) *I might discern her face*

"*I could discern no part of his face* from the window" (*2 Hen. IV* 2.2.74-75)

(5-6) *As one might see a damask rose*

> "*I have seen roses damasked,* red and white, But no such roses *see I in her cheeks*" (*Sonnets* 130.5-6); "feed on *her damask cheek*" (*Twelfth* 2.4.112); "as sweet as *damask roses*" (*Win.* 4.4.220); "With cherry *lips and cheeks of damask roses*" (*Kins.* 4.1.74).

> See also E.O. 14 (lines 21, 23 & 25-27) (*damask rose* and related parallels) and the discussion of those parallels in the Introduction.

(8-9) *sighed so sore . . . sighs, and shedding amber tears*

> On *tears* and *sighs*, see also E.O. 9.1-2, and on the broader theme of *tears* and weeping, 3.13, 4.10, 5.12, and 6.26.

> As discussed above, *Lover's Comp.* and *Tem.* (especially the former) contain significant parallels to line 9 (*sighs . . . tears*), as well as to lines 1-4.

> "*Sighs dry her cheeks, tears make them wet again*" (*Venus* 966); "My *sighs* are blown away, my salt *tears* gone" (*Venus* 1071); "Be moved with *my tears, my sighs,* my groans" (*Lucrece* 588); "*sighs* and groans *and tears*" (*Lucrece* 1319); "With nightly *tears* and daily *heart-sore sighs*" (*Two Gent.* 2.4.129); "upon the altar of her beauty/ You sacrifice *your tears, your sighs, your heart*" (*Two Gent.* 3.2.72-73); "Can you . . . behold My *sighs and tears* and will not once relent?" (*1 Hen. VI* 3.1.107-08); "Lest with my *sighs or tears* I blast or drown King Edward's fruit" (*3 Hen. VI* 4.4.23-24); "what 'tis to love. It is to be all made of *sighs and tears*" (*As You* 5.2.78-79); "*sighs and tears* and groans/ Show minutes, times, and hours" (*Rich. II* 5.5.57-58). (See also on this theme E.O. 3, commentary on line 23, among others).

> See Spevack 1144-45 for many further examples.

(10) *to every word* she *spake*

> *Every word* occurs eleven times in Shakespeare, e.g., "For *every word* you *speak* in his behalf/ Is slander to your royal dignity" (*2 Hen. VI* 3.2.208-09); *every word* doth almost tell my name" (*Sonnets* 76.7)

(11) *bred* in me this *fever*

> "The raging fire of *fever bred*" (*Errors* 5.1.75).

(12) Who was the first that gave the *wound,* whose scar I wear for ever?

> "When griping grief the heart doth *wound,* And doleful dumps the mind oppress" (*R&J* 4.5.126).

> Both samples use and parody *wound* as a metaphorical extravagance.

(12) *whose* scar I wear *for ever?*

> "*Are you* so gospell'd/ To pray for this good man and for his issue,/ Whose

heavy hand hath bow'd you to the grave/ And beggar'd yours *for ever?*" (*Mac.* 3.1.87-90).

(13) What tyrant *Cupid* to my harms usurps the golden *quiver?*

"If *Cupid* have not spent all his *quiver* in Venice" (*Much* 1.1.241-42).

Shakespeare often uses *usurp* and its variants figuratively (Spevack 1420), as here in de Vere's lyric.

(14) can *from bondage it deliver*

"Cassius *from bondage will deliver* Cassius" (*Caes.* 1.3.90).

(15) Yet who doth most adore *this wight*

"I ken *the wight*: he is of substance good" (*Wives* 1.3.37).

(15) who doth . . . *O hollow caves, tell true?*

"All the *neighbour caves*, as seeming troubled,/ Make *verbal repetition of her moans*" (*Venus* 831); "O, once *tell true, tell true*, even for my sake!" (*Dream* 3.2.67-68).

(15) *tell true. . .*

"When rich ones scarce *tell true*" (*Cym.* 3.6.12); "Wherefore? *tell true*" (*All's Well* 1.3.219).

(15-16) tell *true* . . . in sorrow *rue*

"Nought shall make us *rue*,/ If England to itself do rest but *true*" (*John* 5.7.117).

(17) *What makes him* not regard good will with *some remorse* or *ruth?*

"*What makes you* thus exclaim? (*1 Hen.* VI 4.1.83); "'Pity,' she cries, '*some favour, some remorse!*'"(*Venus* 257); "I'll set a bank of rue, sour herb of grace:/ Rue, even for *ruth*, here shortly shall be seen" (*Rich. II* 3.4.105-06).

(19-20) May I his beauty match with *love* . . ./ May I *requite* his birth with faith?

"I will *requite* your *loves*" (*Ham.* 1.2.251).

"I will *requite* you *with as good a thing*" (*Tem.* 5.1.169); "*love* on, I will *requite* thee" (*Much* 3.1.111); "I do with an eye of *love requite* her" (*Much* 5.4.24); "if he *love* me to madness, I shall never *requite* him" (*Merch.* 1.2.59-60); "I thank thee for thy *love* to me, which . . . I will most kindly *requite*" (*As You* 1.1.127-28).

(20) *Then* faithfull *will I die*

"In that I live and *for that will I die*" (*Rich. II* 1.1.185).

(23) To her how *echo* told

> "*Rumour* doth double, *like the voice and echo,*/ The numbers of the feared" (*2 Hen. IV* 3.1.97-98); "'Ay me!' she cries, and twenty times 'Woe, woe!' And *twenty echoes* twenty times cry so" (*Venus* 833-34).

Previous commentaries: Looney (1920, 141-45, 162-64); Ogburn (393); Sobran (260-62); May (2004, 224); Goldstein (2016, 48-49; 2017, 22-23).

E.O. 18: "My Mind to Me a Kingdom Is"

(By Sir Edward
Dyer in
Courtly Poets)

1	My mind to me a kingdom is;
2	Such perfect joy therein I find
3	That it excels all other bliss
4	That world affords or grows by kind.
5	Though much I want which most men have,
6	Yet still my mind forbids to crave.
7	No princely pomp, no wealthy store,
8	No force to win the victory,
9	No wily wit to salve a sore,
10	No shape to feed each gazing eye,
11	To none of these I yield as thrall.
12	For why? My mind doth serve for all.
13	I see how plenty suffers oft,
14	How hasty climbers soon do fall;
15	I see that those that are aloft
16	Mishap doth threaten most of all;
17	They get with toil, they keep with fear.
18	Such cares my mind could never bear.
19	Content I live, this is my stay;
20	I seek no more than may suffice;
21	I press to bear no haughty sway;
22	Look what I lack my mind supplies.
23	Lo, thus I triumph like a king,
24	Content with that my mind doth bring.
25	Some have too much yet still do crave;
26	I little have and seek no more.
27	They are but poor though much they have
28	And I am rich with little store.
29	They poor, I rich; they beg, I give;
30	They lack, I leave; they pine, I live.
31	I laugh not at another's loss,
32	I grudge not at another's gain.
33	No worldly waves my mind can toss;
34	My state at one doth still remain.
35	I fear no foe nor fawning friend,
36	I loathe not life nor dread my end.
37	Some weigh their pleasure by their lust,
38	Their wisdom by their rage of will;

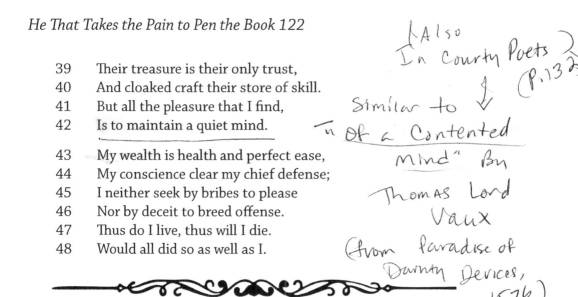

*Also
In Courty Poets
(p. 132)*

*Similar to
" of a Contented
mind" By
Thomas Lord
Vaux
(from Paradise of
Dainty Devices,
1576)*

39   Their treasure is their only trust,
40   And cloaked craft their store of skill.
41   But all the pleasure that I find,
42   Is to maintain a quiet mind.

43   My wealth is health and perfect ease,
44   My conscience clear my chief defense;
45   I neither seek by bribes to please
46   Nor by deceit to breed offense.
47   Thus do I live, thus will I die.
48   Would all did so as well as I.

Structure: Eight stanzas of six lines of iambic tetrameter rhyming ABABCC.

Textual sources: May (1975, 391-92; 1980, 39-40; 1991, 283-84) (not in Grosart or Looney). Printed anonymously, along with E.O. 18b and E.O. 19, in William Byrd's 1588 *Psalmes, Sonets & songs of Sadnes*. A title used for E.O. 18 in the original sources is "In Praise of a Contented Mind." May: Possibly by Oxford #II. See also four additional stanzas in E.O. 18b below. In both the fragment and the whole poem, one can readily detect the intimate influence of both Seneca and Ovid; the poem constitutes a testament to the author's striking capacity to refocus philosophical questions with originality and poetic fluency. It is included here on the strength of May's 1975 attribution as well as on the informed understanding of the editors.

Compare the manuscript title of E.O. 18 ("In Praise of a Contented Mind") with lines 19 and 24 (*Content*), and with E.O. 16.1 (*Were I a king I could command content*). Both 16 and 18 betray the distinctive influence of Seneca, e.g. *Thyestes* 455-70, which concludes "*immane regnum est posse sine regno pati* (it is a vast kingdom to be able to cope without a kingdom)" (470).

These lines from *2 Hen. VI,* spoken by Alexander Iden, esq., the killer of Jack Cade who is royally rewarded by Henry VI with a thousand marks at the close of the play, closely mimic the thought and diction of E.O. 18:

> This small inheritance my father left me
> *Contenteth me, and worth a monarchy.*
> I seek not to wax great by others" waning,
> Or gather wealth, I care not with what envy.
> *Sufficeth that I have maintains my state*
> And send[s] the poor well pleasèd from my gate.
>   (4.10.17-22)

See also E.O. 18b.16-18 (*I wait not at the mighty's gate. / I scorn no poor, nor fear no rich,/ I feel no want nor have too much*).

Explanatory notes:

(9)   The term *wit* as used here refers to intelligence or mental sharpness, not humor (*OED* 20: 432-34).

Orthodox scholars have generally tried to minimize the size of de Vere's canon, though some, like May (1975), have occasionally sought to enlarge it with poems misattributed to other Elizabethan poets, such as E.O. 18.

The correct attribution of E.O. 18 is important. It has long been regarded, in the words of Steven May, as one of "the most popular verses in the English language," exhibiting an "extraordinary and enduring popularity" (May 1975, 385). As May further notes it "has been continuously reprinted since 1588. . . . Of the thousands of lines of moral and philosophical verse turned out during the first half of the Elizabethan age, only this poem seems to have captured the attention of later generations" (1991, 64).

Strongest parallels:

(1) My *mind* to me a *kingdom* is

> The Shakespearean keywords *mind* and *kingdom*, with 393 and 136 references respectively (Spevack 665-66, 821-22), express core concepts in the canon, and Shakespeare is demonstrably intrigued by their juxtaposition and relationship. He employs the phrase *my mind* at least ninety-three times, e.g., "I'll call for pen and ink, and *write my mind*" (*1 Hen. VI* 5.3.66). *Mind* prefigures the playwright's exploration of human psychology, and *kingdom* his study of political organization, especially the contrast between tyranny and legitimate monarchy and problems of governance and law more generally in such plays as *Measure for Measure*. Fused as they are in de Vere's lyric, these terms attest to the fluid nature of the boundary between the psychological and the political—a fluidity that is characteristically Shakespearean.

> "Or whether doth *my mind,* being *crown'd* with you,/ Drink up *the monarch's* plague, this flattery?" (*Sonnets* 114.1-2); "My *library*/ Was *dukedom* large enough" (*Tem.* 1.2.108-09); "O God, I could be *bounded in a nutshell,* and count *myself a king of infinite space,* were it not that I have bad dreams" (*Ham.* 2.2.254-56); "our Caesar tells, *I am conqueror of myself*" (*A&C* 4.14.62); "A *kingdom for a stage*" (*Hen V* pro. 3).

(4) That *world affords*

> "What other *pleasure* can *the world afford?*" (*3 Hen. VI* 3.2.147); "the *sweet degrees* that *this brief world affords*" (*Timon* 4.3.253); "The *world affords* no law to make thee *rich*" (*R&J* 5.1.73); cf. "The spacious *world* cannot again *afford*" (*Rich. III* 1.2.245). EEBO returns only ten hits in ten records (1473-1623) for the search *world afford*; thirty-four in twenty-nine records, for *world affords*.

(10) *No shape to feed each gazing eye*

"*Gaze on* and grovel on *thy face*" (*2 Hen. VI* 1.2.9); "The abject people *gazing on thy face*" (*2 Hen. VI* 2.4.11); "*No shape* but his can *please your dainty eye*" (*3 Hen. VI* 5.3.38); "It is engender'd in *the eyes/* with *gazing fed*" (*Merch.* 3.2.68); "I have *fed mine eyes* on thee" (*Troil.* 4.5.231); "*Her eye* must be *fed*" (*Oth.* 2.1.225); "*That makes me see*, and *cannot feed mine eye?*" (*All's Well* 1.1.221); "I *feed Most* hungerly on *your sight*" (*Timon* 1.1.252); "mine *eyes* have drawn *thy shape*" (*Sonnets* 24.10).

Gaze (and its variants) and *eye(s)* appear together more than a dozen times in the Shakespeare canon (Spevack 468). See also E.O. 11.21 (*What feedeth most your sight?*).

(10-11) *No shape to feed each gazing eye,/ To none of these I yield as thrall*

"Whose sudden *sight hath thralled my wounded eye*" (*Shrew* 1.1.220); "all eyes saw *his eyes enchanted with gazes*" (*LLL* 2.1.245); "So is mine eye enthralled to *thy shape*" (*Dream* 3.1.139).

The line from *LLL* is part of an extended passage on the theme of *enthralled gaze* (2.1.226-51). Compare also, from *Venus:*

But, when *his glutton eye so full hath fed* (399)

Alas, *he naught esteems that face of thine,*
To which Love's eyes pay tributary gazes (631-32)

Fold in the object that did *feed her sight* (822)

He *fed* them with his *sight* [i.e., his beauty], they him with berries (1104)

(14-16) How hasty *climbers soon do fall;*
I see that *those that are aloft*
Mishap doth threaten most of all

"The art o' the court, As hard to leave as keep, *whose top to climb Is certain falling*" (*Cym.* 3.3.46-48).

(20) *I seek no more than may suffice*

"And have *no more* of life *than may suffice*" (*Per.* 2.1.74). The shared phrase is extremely rare. An *EEBO* search *than may suffice* returns only one hit, to Christopher Lever's 1607 *Queene Elizabeths teares*

(23-24) *I triumph like a king*

"To meet at London London's *king in woe./* What, was I born to this, that my sad look/ Should grace *the triumph of* great Bolingbroke?" (*Rich. II* 3.4.98-99); "And now to London *with triumphant march*, There to be crowned England's *royal king*" (*3 Hen. VI* 2.6.88); "Enter *KING EDWARD IV* in *triumph*" (*3 Hen. VI* 5.3.SD).

(24) *Content* with that my *mind* doth bring

> "For 'tis the *mind* that makes the body *rich*" (*Shrew* 4.3.169); "Poor and *content* is *rich and rich enough*" (*Oth.* 3.3.172);

> See also line 19 (*Content I live*), the discussion of the parallels to line 1, and E.O. 16.1 (*Were I a King I could Command Content*).

(27-28) They are *but poor* though much they have And I am *rich* with little store

> The antithesis becomes, again, one of Shakespeare's favorites: "*poorly rich*" (*Lucrece* 97); "My *riches* are these *poor* habiliments" (*Two Gent.* 4.1.13); "Wise things seem foolish and *rich* things *but poor*" (*LLL* 5.2.378); "If thou art *rich*, thou'rt *poor*" (*Meas.* 3.1.25); "Fairest Cordelia, that art *most rich being poor*" (*Lear* 1.1.250); "*Rich* gifts wax *poor*" (*Ham.* 3.1.100).

Indeed, compare not just lines 27-28 but the entire stanza where they appear (lines 25-30) with the stanza in *Lucrece*:

E.O. 18.25-30	***Lucrece***
Some *have too much* yet still do *crave*;	Those that *much covet* are with gain so fond
I *little have* and *seek no more*.	That what *they have* not, *that which they possess*,
They are but *poor* though *much they have*	They scatter and unloose it from their bond,
And I am *rich* with little store.	And so, *by hoping more, they have but less*;
They poor, I rich; they beg, I give;	Or, gaining *more*, the profit of *excess*
They lack, I leave; *they pine, I live*.	Is but to *surfeit*, and such griefs sustain
	That *they prove bankrupt* in this *poor rich* gain.
	(134-40)

Additional parallels:

(2) Such *perfect joy* therein I find

> "The *perfectest* herald of *joy*" (*Much* 2.1.306).

(4) grows *by kind*

> "Your cuckoo sings *by kind*" (*All's Well* 1.3.63); "Fitted *by kind* for rape and villainy" (*Titus* 2.1.116).

(5) I *want* . . . most men *have*

> "I think the meat *wants* that I *have*" (*Errors* 2.2.55); "What you *want* in meat, we'll *have* in drink" (*2 Hen. IV* 5.3.28); "I *have* no way, and therefore *want* no eyes" (*Lear* 4.1.18); "Of that we *have*: so then we do neglect/ The thing we *have*; and, all for *want* of wit" (*Lucrece* 152-53); "What I *have* been I *have* forgot to know; But what I am, *want* teaches me to think on" (*Per.* 2.1.72).

(6) Yet still my *mind* forbids to *crave*

> "The affliction of my *mind* amends, with which, I fear, a madness held me: this must *crave*" (*Tem.* 5.1.122); my lady *craves*/ To know the cause of your abrupt

departure (*1 Hen. VI* 2.3.30).

(7) No princely *pomp*, no *wealthy store*

"To love, to *wealth and pomp*, I pine and die" (*LLL* 1.1.31); "O, him she *stores*, to show what *wealth* she had" (*Sonnets* 67.13).

(8) No force to *win the victory*

"You have *won a happy victory*" (*Cor.* 5.3.186).

(9) No *wily wit*

"Upon my *wit*, to defend my *wiles*" (*Troil.* 1.2.247-48). See also E.O. 6.9 (*wit so wise*), E.O. 9.16 (*wisest wit*), and E.O. 10.12 (*wit . . . will*).

(9) to *salve a sore*

"A *salve* for any *sore* that may betide" (*3 Hen. VI* 4.6.88).

See also parallels to E.O. 9.22 (*She is my salve, she is my wounded sore*) and E.O. 5.29-30 (*So long to fight with secret sore,/ And find no secret salve therefor*). The *salve/sore* motif (like some others) was echoed other Elizabethan poets and these parallels may not be that telling by themselves (see May 2004, 229), but as with many others, their significance lies in the overall cumulative context in which they appear.

(17) *get* with toil, *keep* with fear.

"I'll see if I can *get* my husband's ring,/ Which I did make him swear *to keep* for ever" (*Merch.* 4.2.13).

(18) Such cares *my mind* could *never bear*

The idiom occurs frequently in Shakespeare, e.g., "His letters *bear his mind*, not I, my lord" (*1 Hen. IV* 4.1.20); "Since men prove beasts, let beasts *bear gentle minds*" (*Lucrece* 1148).

(19) Content I live

The phrase *I am content* occurs sixteen times in Shakespeare, e.g., "What you can make her do,/ *I am content* to look on: what to speak,/ *I am content* to hear (*Win.* 5.3.91-93).

(19) this is *my stay*

My stay occurs four times in Shakespeare, e.g., where the structure of the line also echoes the rhythyms and construction of de Vere's "kingdom, or a cottage, or a grave": "God shall be my hope,/ *My stay*, my guide and lantern to my feet" (*2 Hen. VI* 2.3.24-25).

(20) I seek not more

I ask no more (*A&C* 4.2.32); I see no more (*A&C* 4.12.18); I desire no more (*2 Hen. VI* 4.3.9); If ye pinch me like a pasty, I can say no more (*All's Well* 4.3.123).

(21) to bear no *haughty sway*

> My lord, I know a *discontented* gentleman,/ Whose *humble means* match not *his haughty spirit* (*Rich. III* 4.2.37).

(26) I *have little* and *seek no more*

> "*Little joy have I*/ To breathe this news . . . I *speak no more* than every one doth know" (*Rich. II* 3.4.82).

(27) They are *but poor though much* they have

> "O, no! thy love, *though much*, is *not so great*" (*Sonnets* 61.9).

(31-32) I *laugh* not at *another's loss*, I grudge not at *another's gain*

> The *gain/loss* antithesis is another of Shakespeare's linguistic building blocks: "*Laughed at my losses, mocked at my gains*" (*Merch.* 3.1.55); "I earn that I eat, get that I wear, *owe no man hate, envy no man's happiness, glad of other men's good, content* with my harm" (*As You* 3.2.74); "For me to *joy* and *weep* their *gain* and *loss*" (*Rich. III* 2.4.59); "If I lose thee, *my loss* is *my love's gain*" (*Sonnets* 42.8).

> See also lines 19 and 24 (*Content*).

(33, 36) No *worldly waves* my *mind* can *toss* . . . I loathe not life nor *dread my end*

> "Your *mind is tossing on the ocean*" (*Merch.* 1.1.8); "And he, good prince, having all lost,/ By *waves* from coast to coast is *tossed*" (*Per.* 2.0.33-34); "And now this lustful lord . . . is madly *tossed* between desire and *dread*" (*Lucrece* 169-71).

> Once again, using language similar to Shakespeare's, de Vere associates the inner life of the human subject with the motions of the sea. See also E.O. 6.26 and 12.19.

(35) no *foe* nor *fawning friend*

> "How like *a fawning publican* he looks!" (*Merch.* 1.3.41); "Faithfull *friend*, from *flatt'ring foe*" (*Pass. Pilg.* XX.56); "A *foe* to tyrants, and *my country's friend*" (*Caes.* 5.4.5); "That would make good of bad, and *friends of foes*!" (*Mac.* 2.4.41); "Thy *friends are fled* to wait upon thy *foes*" (*Rich. II* 2.4.23); "his despiteful Juno, sent him forth/From *courtly friends*, with *camping foes* to live" (*All's Well* 3.4.13-14).

(36) I loathe not *life* nor *dread my end*

> "*My life's* foul deed, *my life's fair end* shall free it" (*Lucrece* 1208); "The weariest and most *loathed worldly life*/ That age, ache, penury and imprisonment/Can lay on nature is a paradise/ To *what we fear of death*" (*Meas.* 3.1.128-31); "the weariest and most *loathed worldly life*" (*Meas.* 3.1.128); cf. "Why then, though *loath*, yet must I be *content*" (*3 Hen. VI* 4.6.48)

See also lines 19 and 24 (Content).

(38) their *rage of will*

"Dizzy-eyed fury and great *rage of heart*" (*1 Hen. VI* 4.7.11); "*rage of lust*" (*Lucrece* 424).

(40) *cloaked craft*

"To *cloak* offenses with a *cunning* brow" (*Lucrece* 749).

Here again we have the leitmotif of dissimulation, using the word *cloak* in common. See also E.O. 5.16 (*to cloak the covert mind*). On this important topos, a suggestive common interest, see also E.O. 5 (line 1 and *passim*), and also E.O. 6.4, 9.2, 10.9-10, and 12.16.

(43) My *wealth* is health and perfect *ease*

"With honor, *wealth*, and *ease* in waning age" (*Lucrece* 142); "Leaving his *wealth* and *ease*" (*As You* 2.5.52).

(44) *My conscience clear* my chief defense

"'Tis my special hope/ That you will *clear* yourself from all suspect:/ *My conscience* tells me you are innocent" (*2 Hen. VI* 3.1.141).

(44) *my chief defense*

"*My chief care*/ Is to come fairly off from the great debts/ Wherein my time something too prodigal/ Hath left me gaged" (*Merch.* 1.1.127-30).

(45-46) *I neither seek* by bribes to please/*Nor by* deceit to breed offense.

"*I neither lend* nor borrow/ By taking *nor by giving* of excess" (*Merch.* 1.3.61-62).

(46) *breed offense*

"Love *breeds* such *offense*" (*Oth.* 3.3.380).

(47) *Thus do I* live, *thus will I* die

"*Thus do I pine* and *surfeit* day by day" (*Sonnets* 75.13).

(48) *Would* all did *so well as I*

"*As well as I can*, madam" (*A&C* 2.5.7); "*I am not so well as I should be*, but I'll ne'er out" (*A&C* 2.7.30-31); "*Hadst thou* but loved him half *so well as I*" (*3 Hen. VI* 1.1.220).

Previous commentaries: Sobran (262-65); Brazil & Flues; Goldstein (2016, 63-66). Sobran, Brazil & Flues, and Goldstein did not, however, explore the parallels to E.O. 18b.

E.O. 18b: "My Mind to Me a Kingdom Is" (extra stanzas)

1	I joy not in no earthly bliss,
2	I force not Croesus' wealth a straw.
3	For care I know not what it is,
4	I fear not Fortune's fatal law.
5	My mind is such as may not move
6	For beauty bright nor force of love.
7	I wish but what I have at will,
8	I wander not to seek for more.
9	I like the plain, I climb no hill,
10	In greatest storms I sit on shore
11	And laugh at those that toil in vain,
12	To get what must be lost again.
13	I kiss not where I wish to kill,
14	I feign not love where most I hate.
15	I break no sleep to win my will,
16	I wait not at the mighty's gate.
17	I scorn no poor, nor fear no rich,
18	I feel no want nor have too much.
19	The Court ne cart I like ne loathe,
20	Extremes are counted worst of all.
21	The golden mean betwixt them both
22	Doth surest sit and fear no fall.
23	This is my choice, for why I find
24	No wealth is like the quiet mind.

Structure: Four stanzas of six lines of iambic tetrameter additional to those in E.O. 18.

Textual sources: Printed anonymously, along with E.O. 18 and 19, in William Byrd's 1588 *Psalmes, sonets & songs of sadnes;* Rollins (1929, 1: 225-31); May (1975, 391 n. 1, 392-93). Not in Grosart or Looney, and not printed by May (1980).

These four additional stanzas are found in some sources for E.O. 18. Rollins attributed both E.O. 18 and 18b to Edward Dyer, but May (1975, 386-90) leaned in favor de Vere as the author of E.O. 18, while suggesting that no clear attribution was possible for E.O. 18b.

Explanatory notes:

(2)   *Croesus,* in Herodotus and Pausanius, a Lydian monarch of great wealth. Not in Shakespeare.

(19)   *ne,* already an archaic conjunction by the early Elizabethan period) that was sometimes used in place of "nor" in late-15th to mid-16th century English (so *ne . . . ne* essentially means "neither . . . nor") (*OED* 10: 264-65). *Court* and *cart* refer to the royal *court* in contrast to a menial *cart,* thus reinforcing the poet's asserted indifference to *wealth* or status. The original text reads *loath,* but since it is used as a verb, the modern spelling of *loathe* is given here. However, in early modern English *loathe* did not have so intense a connotation of aversion as it does today (*OED* 8: 1071). Line 19 could thus be translated: *I [neither] like [nor dislike] the [royal] Court [nor menial] cart.* That is, the poet disdains *extremes* of *feeling* (especially as between *wealth* and status or their absence, as also suggested by lines 2, 18, and 20-22). See parallels to lines 16-19.

Strongest parallels:

(2) *I force not* Croesus' wealth *a straw*

> "*I force not* argument *a straw,*/ Since that my case is past the help of law" (*Lucrece* 1021-22).

> For the search "*I force not* near *a straw,*" EEBO (1473-1623) returns only two hits, to two imprints of *Lucrece.*

(16-19) *I wait not at the mighty's gate.*
I scorn no poor, nor fear no rich,
I feel no want nor have too much.
The Court ne cart I like ne loath

> Compare, again, lines already quoted in relation to E.O. 18.1, expressing an essentially identical thought in parallel grammatical structures (e.g., *I seek not, I wait not*):

>> *I seek not to wax great by others' waning,*
>> *Or gather wealth, I care not with what envy.*
>> *Sufficeth that I have maintains my state*
>> *And send the poor well pleased from my gate.*
>>   (*2 Hen. VI* 4.10.19-22)

> Cf. "The *poor* mechanic porters crowding in/ Their heavy burdens at his narrow *gate*" (*Hen. V* 1.2.203-04).

(18) *I feel no want nor have too much*

> "I live with bread like you, *feel want*" (*Rich. II* 3.2.175); "You *have too much* respect upon [i.e., concern for] the world" (*Merch.* 1.1.74); "Why, Paris *hath*

color enough . . ./ Then Troilus should *have too much*" (*Troil.* 1.2.95, 97); "yet you/ *Have too much*" (*Win.* 2.1.56-57); "I *have too much* believed mine own suspicion" (*Win.* 3.2.149).

As discussed above, the archaic *ne . . . ne* (line 19) means "neither . . . nor." There appears to be one analogous usage in canonical Shakespeare: "He, good prince [Pericles], having all lost, By waves from coast to coast is tost. All perishen of man, of pelf [i.e., all other people and goods being lost], *Ne* aught escapend but himself [i.e., *Nor* anyone escaping but Pericles himself]" (*Per.* 2.0.33-36).

Seven other appearances of *ne* in canonical Shakespeare appear to involve common usages in Latin and French where it has a somewhat different meaning, or as an abbreviation or equivalent of the English words "neigh" or "nay" (Spevack 872).

Additional parallels:

(1) *I joy not in no earthly bliss*

> "By *the hope I* have of *heavenly bliss*" (*3 Hen. VI* 3.3.182); "I know you *joy not in a love discourse*" (*Two Gent.* 2.4.124).

(3) *Care, I know not what it is*

> "Madam, *I know not,* nor I greatly *care not*" (*Rich. II* 5.2.48); "My aunt Lavinia Follows me everywhere, *I know not* why . . . ./ My Lord, *I know not, I,* nor can I guess" (*Titus* 4.1.1-2, 16); "Nay, by my troth, *I know not,* but *I know* to be up late is to be up late" (*Twelfth* 2.3.4-5); "Why I should fear *I know not,/* Since guiltiness *I know not*" (*Oth.* 5.2.38-39).

(3) I *know not what it is*

> "Your ladyship *is ignorant what it is* (*LLL* 2.1.101); "You *know not what it is*" (*A&C* 3.13.122); "Thou *knowest not what it is*" (*LLL* 3.1.157); "But *what it is,* that *is not* yet *known.*" The phrase *know not what it is* returns seventy hits in fifty-seven *EEBO* records before 1623; *I know not what it is,* eighteen hits in eighteen records; *you know not what it is,* thirty-one in twenty-seven.

(4) *I fear not* fortune

> "*I fear not* my ring" (*Cym.* 1.4.98).

(4) I fear not *fortune*

> *Fortune* is one of Shakespeare's most profoundly explored philosophical concepts; he uses the word 457 times, e.g., "Am I not an inch of *fortune* better than she?" (*A&C* 1.2.58); "'Tis paltry to be Caesar;/ Not being *Fortune,* he's but *Fortune's* knave" (*A&C* 5.2.2-3).

(5-6) *My mind is such as may not move/ For* beauty bright nor *force of love*

> "She *moves me not, or not removes*, at least,/ *Affection's edge in me*" (*Shrew* 1.2.70-71); cf. "If this letter *move him not*, his legs cannot" (*Twelfth* 3.4.159).

(6) *nor force of love*

> "And *love* you 'gainst the nature of *love—force ye*" (*Two Gent.* 5.4.58); "If this inducement *force her not to love*" (*Rich. III* 4.4.386); "This flower's *force* in stirring *love*" (*Dream* 2.2.69).

(7) *I wish* but what *I have at will*

> "Why, now *thou hast thy wish*. Wouldst *have* me weep? Why, now *thou hast thy will*" (*3 Hen. VI* 1.4.143-44); "Whoever *hath her wish, thou hast thy will*" (*Sonnets* 135.1).

(8) *I wander not* to seek for *more*

> "*I wander* from *the jewels* that I love" (*Rich. II* 1.3.270).

(8) *to seek for more*

> "*Nor seek for* danger/Where there's *no profit*" (*Cym.* 4.2.163).

(10) *In greatest storms* I sit on *shore*

> "When from thy *shore the tempest* beat us back,/ I stood upon the hatches *in the storm*" (*2 Hen. VI* 3.2.102-03).

(11) And laugh at those that *toil in vain*

> "And all the rest *forgot for which he toiled*" (*Sonnets* 25.12); "*bootless toil* must recompense itself/ With its own sweat" (*Kins.* 1.1.153-54).
>
> The locution *in vain*, which occurs three times in these de Vere poems (see also E.O. 5.32 and 9.26), appears forty times in canonical Shakespeare (Spevack 1421).

(12) To get what must be *lost again*

> "O, learn to love; the lesson is but plain,/ And once made perfect, *never lost again*" (*Venus* 407-08).

(13) *I kiss* not where I wish to *kill*

> "He thought to *kiss* him, and hath *killed* him so" (*Venus* 1110); Cf. "What follows more she *murders with a kiss*" (*Venus* 54).

(14) I feign not love where most I hate

> The line is strongly evocative of "Though I be Strange" (E5, Vol. II), especially line 25, which exactly reverses the present sentiment, "So where *I like, I list not vaunt my love*."

(15) *I break no sleep to win my will*

> "*Break not* your *sleeps* for that" (*Ham.* 4.7.30); cf. "*broke* their *sleep*" (*2 Hen. IV* 4.5.68, and *Cor.* 4.4.19); "Shall I go *win my* daughter to thy *will*?" (*Rich. III* 4.4.426).

> See also E.O. 15.6 (*break thy sleeps*).

(20-21) *extremes . . . worst of all . . . golden mean betwixt them both*

> "No midway/ 'Twixt these *extremes* at all" (*A&C* 3.4.20); "'*Twixt two extremes* of passion, joy and grief" (*Lear* 5.3.199); "'*Twixt my extremes* and me this bloody knife/ Shall *play the umpire*" (*R&J* 4.1.62); "*Alexas*. Like to the time o' the year *between the extremes*/ Of hot and cold, he was *nor sad nor merry. Cleopatra. O well-divided disposition!*" (*A&C* 1.5.51-53).

(20) *worst of all*

> "Nay, to be perjured, which is *worst of all;*
> And, among three, to love the *worst of all*" (*LLL* 3.1.195).

(22) Doth *surest* sit and *fear* no *fall*

> "They well deserve to have /That know the strong'st and *surest* way to get" (*Rich. II* 3.3.200-01); "Ours is the *fall*, I *fear*" (*Timon* 5.2.17); "Does *fall* in travail with her *fear*" (*Per.* 2.0.52); "My love and *fear* glued many friends to thee, And now I *fall*" (*3 Hen. VI* 2.6.5-6).

> *Surest* appears once (here) in these de Vere poems and twice (as quoted above) in the Shakespeare canon (Spevack 1235).

(23-24) *This is my choice*, for *why* I find/ *No wealth is like* the quiet mind

> "If I do *fail in fortune* of *my choice*" (*Merch.* 2.9.15); "*This is my* treasurer: let him speak, my lord" (*A&C* 5.2.142); "she will *find the error* of her choice: she must have change, she must: therefore put *money* in thy *purse*" (*Oth.* 1.3.351-52).

(24) *No wealth is like* the quiet mind

> "*No jewel is like* Rosalind" (*As You* 3.2.89).

Previous Commentaries: None.

E.O. 19. What Is Desire Which Doth Approve?

1	What is Desire which doth approve,
2	To set on fire each gentle heart?
3	A fancy strange, a God of Love,
4	Whose pining sweet delight doth smart;
5	In gentle minds his dwelling is.
6	What were his parents? Gods or no?
7	That living long is yet a child;
8	A goddess son? Who thinks not so?
9	A god begot, a god beguiled;
10	Venus his mother, Mars his sire.
11	Is he a god of peace or war?
12	What be his arms? What is his might?
13	His war is peace, his peace is war;
14	Each grief of his is but delight
15	His bitter ball is sugared bliss.
16	What be his gifts? How doth he pay?
17	When is he seen? or how conceived?
18	Sweet dreams in sleep, new thoughts in day,
19	Beholding eyes, in mind received;
20	A god that rules and yet obeys.
21	Why is he naked painted? Blind?
22	His sides with shafts? His back with brands?
23	Plain without guile, by hap to find
24	Pursuing with fair words that withstands,
25	And when he craves he takes no nays
26	What labours doth this god allow?
27	What fruits have lovers for their pains?
28	Sit still and muse to make a vow
29	T' their ladies, if they true remains;
30	A good reward for true desire.

Structure: Six stanzas of five lines of iambic tetrameter with alternating couplets and a final line that rhymes with other final lines, *is/bliss, sire/desire, obeys/nays,* bearing a close structural and thematic resemblance to E.O. 15, "Who Taught Thee First to Sigh?" and E.O. 11, "When wert thou Born, Desire?"

Textual sources: Although classified by May as a poem "wrongly attributed to Oxford" (83), the provenance, style, and thematic emphases of the poem all support Grosart and Looney's prior attributions of it to the Earl, as is recognized by Kurt Kreiler also. It survives in at least two MS variants, Ra and Hy, the latter of which attaches the subscription "Ewph," i.e., Euphues, the title character of John Lyly's prodigiously popular *Euphues* series (f.p. 1580-81). According to May, the subscription is intended to "perhaps indicate John Lyly," and "there is no reason to connect it with Oxford" (84). This is a surprising claim in view of Oxford's well documented connections to both Lyly and the *Euphues* novels, one of which was dedicated to Oxford. Lyly was long ago identified as the Earl's secretary and confidante by Warwick Bond in his 1905 edition of Lyly's collected works.

Explanatory notes: On the problem of Euphues and Oxford, see Ogburn (1984), 625-31, who concludes that the *Euphues* novels (owed their "origin to conversations Lyly heard in Oxford's company and its finished form" was "nursed and with great love brought up by Oxford for no lesser time than a year" (627). That Oxford is later glanced at in such titles as Nashe's *Menaphon*, subtitled "Camillas alarum to slumbering Euphues," which identifies Euphues as a person and not a fictional interlocutor in Lyly's novels, the book in which the poem first appears in print, and to which Oxford contributed dedicatory verses (misc. 2) under the sobriquet "Henry Upchear."

(24) That withstands. Possibly a mistranscription.

Strongest parallels:

(1, 6, 6, 17) What is Desire. . .? . . . What were his parents? . . . A god *begot . . . how conceived?*

Comparison of multiple lines from the Oxford poem (Figure 11), as Esther Singleton enchantingly observed ninety years ago, reveals a common factor of "unique melancholy rhythm," "musical lilt" and "choice and delicate touch" (225):

E.O. 19.	***Merch*. 3.2.63-69**
Is he a god of peace or war?	Tell me where is fancy bred,
What be his arms? What is his might?	Or in the heart, or in the head?
His war is peace, his peace is war;	How begot, how nourished?
Each grief of his is but delight	Reply, reply.
His bitter ball is sugared bliss.	It is engender'd in the eyes,
	With gazing fed; and fancy dies
What be his gifts? How doth he pay?	In the cradle where it lies.
When is he seen? or how conceived?	Let us all ring fancy's knell.
Sweet dreams in sleep, new thoughts in day.	

Figure 11: Lines from E.O. 19 compared to *Merchant* Song.

(8) Who *thinks not so?*

> The phrase *thinks not so* occurs four times in Shakespeare, e.g., "Demetrius *thinks not so*" (*Dream* 1.1.228); "She *thinks not so*; peruse this writing else" (*Per.* 2.5.41).

> Strikingly, the phrase *thinks not so* returns only eight hits in three *EEBO* records (1473-1623).

(15) *bitter . . . sugared bliss*

> Another favorite Shakespearean antithesis, e.g., "Thy *sugar'd tongue* to *bitter* wormwood taste" (*Lucrece* 893). The phrase is quite rare. The *EEBO* search "*sugared* near *bliss*" returns only seven hits in seven records (1473-1623).

Other parallels:

(1) *What is desire . . .?*

> "*What is love?* 'tis not hereafter;/ Present mirth hath present laughter" (*Twelfth* 2.3.47-48).

(1) *desire* which *doth approve*

> "So thou be good, slander *doth but approve*/ Thy worth the greater" (*Sonnets* 70.4-5); "My love *doth* so *approve* him" (*Oth.* 4.3.19).

(2) To *set on fire* each *gentle heart*

> "Ha, majesty! how high thy glory towers,/ When the *rich blood* of kings is *set on fire!*" (*John* 2.1.350-51); "Affection is a coal that must be cool'd;/ Else, suffer'd, it will *set the heart on fire*" (*Venus* 387-88).

(2) each *gentle heart*

> "You, ladies, you, whose *gentle hearts* do fear/ The smallest monstrous mouse that creeps on floor" (*Dream* 5.1.219-20); "Lose not so noble a friend on vain suppose/ Nor with sour looks afflict his *gentle heart*" (*Titus* 1.1.440-41); "*Each heart* in Rome does love and pity you" (*A&C* 3.6.92).

(3) A *fancy strange*

> "There is no appearance of *fancy* in him, unless it be *a fancy* that he hath to *strange disguise*" (*Much Ado* 3.2.31-33); "nature wants *stuff*/ To vie *strange forms with fancy*" (*A&C* 5.2.97-98).

(3) *God of love*

> "O *god of love!*" (*Much* 3.1.47); "The *god of love,*/ That sits above" (*Much* 5.2.26-27).

(4) *pining* sweet delight

> "The *pining maidens* groans" (*Hen. V* 2.4.107); "The grosser manner of these world's *delights*/. . . To love, to wealth, to pomp, *I pine and die*" (*LLL* 1.1.29-30).

(5) In *gentle minds*

> "Since men prove beasts, let beasts bear *gentle minds*" (*Lucrece* 1148).

> *EEBO* returns only thirty-three hits in thirty records (1473-1623) for the search *gentle minds*.

(6) What *were* his parents? Gods *or no*?

> "My prime request,/ Which I do last pronounce, is, O you wonder!/ If *you be* maid *or no*?" (*Tem.* 1.2.426-28); "*I'll be* your servant,/ Whether you will *or no*" (*Tem.* 3.1.85-86); "be even and direct with me, whether *you were* sent for *or no*" (*Ham.* 2.2.287-88).

(7) that living long *is yet a child*

> "*Love is too young* to know what conscience is" (*Sonnets* 151.1).

(13) *his war* is *peace*, his *peace is war*

> Another favorite Shakespearean antithesis: "*War! war! no peace! peace is* to me *a war*" (*John* 3.1.113); "Tarquin's eye may read the mot afar,/ How he *in peace* is wounded, *not in war*" (*Lucrece* 830-31).

(14) Each *grief* of his is but *delight*

> The *grief/delight* antithesis occurs in several speeches in Shakespeare, e.g., "My legs can keep no measure in *delight*,/ When my poor heart no measure keeps in *grief*" (*Rich. II* 3.4.7-8).

(18) *sweet dreams* in *sleep*

> "The *sweetest sleep*, and fairest-boding *dreams*" (*Rich. III* 5.3.227); "Thus have I had thee, *as a dream doth flatter,/ In sleep* a king, but waking no such matter" (*Sonnets* 87.13-14).

(19) each *grief* of his is *but delight*

> "My legs can keep no measure in *delight*,/ When my poor heart no measure keeps in *grief*" (*Rich. II* 3.4.7-8).

(20) a god that *rules* and yet *obeys*

> "He now *obeys*, and now no more *resisteth*,/ While she takes all she can, not all she listeth" (*Venus* 563-64).

(21) *Why is he naked painted? Blind?*

> "*Fortune is painted blind*, with a muffler afore her eyes, to signify to you that Fortune is *blind*" (*Hen. V* 3.6.30-32); "Love looks not with the eyes, but with the mind/ And *therefore is* wing'd *Cupid painted blind*" (*Dream* 1.1.234-35).

(22) His sides with *shafts*?

> "*Cupid* all arm'd . . . loosed his *love-shaft* smartly from his bow . . ./ But I might see young *Cupid's fiery shaft*/ Quench'd in the chaste beams of the watery moon" (*Dream* 2.1.161-65)

(22) His back with *brands?*

> "Two winking *Cupids/* Of silver, each on one foot standing, nicely/ Depending on *their brands*" (*Cym.* 2.4.89-91).

(24) pursuing with *fair words*

> "Dear lord, you are full of *fair words*" (*Troil.* 3.1.47); "By *guileful fair words* peace may be obtain'd" (*1 Hen. VI* 1.1.77).

(25) and when *he craves*

> "Go tell their general we attend him here,/ To know for what he comes, and whence he comes,/ And what *he craves*" (*Per.* 1.4.79-81); "*He craves* a parley at your father's house" (*Titus* 5.1.159).

(25) *doth* this god *allow*

> "She . . ./ *Doth* grace for grace and love for love *allow*" (*R&J* 2.3.85-86).

(26-27) *What labours* doth this god allow?/ *What fruits* have lovers for their *pains?*

> "The *labouring man* that tills the fertile soil/ And reaps the *harvest fruit* hath not indeed/ *The gain, but pain*" (E.O. 1.22-23).

(28) *sit still and* muse

> "She would *sit still and* weep" (*Per.* 5.1.189).

(28) to *make a vow*

> "Now, by my sceptre's awe, I *make a vow*" (*Rich. II* 1.1.118).

(30) *reward* for true *desire*

> "I *desire nothing* but the *reward* of a villain" (*Much* 5.1.243).

Previous Commentaries: Looney 1920 (146-47); Singleton (224-225).

E.O. 20: "If Women Could Be Fair and Yet Not Fond"

1	If women could be fair and yet not fond,
2	Or that their love were firm, not fickle still,
3	I would not marvel that they make men bond
4	By service long to purchase their good will.
5	But when I see how frail those creatures are,
6	I muse that men forget themselves so far.
7	To mark the choice they make and how they change,
8	How oft from Phoebus they do flee to Pan;
9	Unsettled still, like haggards wild they range,
10	These gentle birds that fly from man to man.
11	Who would not scorn and shake them from the fist,
12	And let them fly, fair fools, which way they list?
13	Yet for disport we fawn and flatter both,
14	To pass the time when nothing else can please,
15	And train them to our lure with subtle oath,
16	Till weary of their wiles ourselves we ease.
17	And then we say when we their fancy try,
18	To play with fools, oh what a fool was I.

Structure: Three six-line stanzas of iambic pentameter rhyming ABABCC.

Textual sources: Grosart (420); Looney (1921, Miller ed. 1975, 1: 595); May (1980, 40-41; 1991, 284). Printed anonymously, along with E.O. 18 and E.O. 18b, in William Byrd's 1588 *Psalmes, sonets & songs of sadnes*. May: Possibly by Oxford #III. Looney's title: "Woman's Changeableness."

Explanatory notes:

(1)   *Fond* bears here the archaic meaning of "foolish" or "foolishly affectionate" (not the bland modern sense of merely "affectionate"); the archaic meaning of *fond* could also, more intensely, connote madness or imbecility (*OED* 6: 5-6).

(8)   *Phoebus* is an epithet for *Apollo* (see E.O. 3.6), Greco-Roman god of the sun. *Pan*, in Greek mythology, is the god of wild woodlands, fields, and shepherds, strongly associated with fertility and sexuality.

(9)   *Haggard* (a term of art in falconry) refers to a wild adult *hawk* (typically female) caught for training (see also E.O. 9.14); it is thus mainly a noun in this context (not to be confused with the adjective indicating an exhausted

appearance) (*OED* 6: 1013). In early English falconry literature, *hawk*, *haggard*, and *falcon* usually refer to females (a male hawk is known to falconers as a "tiercel").

Strongest parallels:

(3) I *would not marvel* that they make men bond

> You *must not marvel*, Helen, at my course (*All's Well* 2.5.58).

(6) *Forget themselves*

> "Horatio!- or I do *forget myself*" (*Ham.* 1.2.161); "Gloucester, teach me to *forget myself!*" (*2 Hen. VI* 2.4.27); "you *forget yourself*" (*Caes.* 4.3.29); "thou dost *forget thyself*" (*John* 3.1.134); "Shall I *forget myself* to be *myself?*" (*Rich. III* 4.4.420).

(7-8) To mark the *choice they make* and how *they change, How oft from Phoebus they do flee to Pan*

> "*She must change* for youth: when *she is sated with his body,* she will find the error of *her choice. She must have change, she must*" (*Oth.* 1.3.349-52); "So excellent a king [Hamlet's late father], that was to this *Hyperion to a satyr* [referring to his uncle, the new King Claudius, hastily married to his widowed mother] . . ./ *Within a month* . . . *She married. O, most wicked speed,* to post/ With such dexterity to incestuous sheets!" (*Ham.* 1.2.139-40, 153, 156-57).

> *Apollo* (or *Phoebus*) is often associated with the Greek sun god Helios, who in turn is the son of *Hyperion* (one of the Titans). *Satyrs*, in Greek mythology, are the priapic male companions of Dionysus—like *Pan* (with whom they long ago became associated), typically depicted with goatish hindquarters, genitals, and insatiable sexual appetites.

> Hamlet's famous diatribe ("*Hyperion to a satyr*") thus essentially accuses his mother (in only slightly different terms) of *flee[ing] from Phoebus to Pan.* Oxfordians, of course, have long noted that de Vere, at the impressionable age of twelve, experienced the death of his father and, within a year or less, his mother's remarriage—perhaps unduly prompt and even unseemly as it may have appeared to a grieving pubescent son (see, e.g., Anderson 16-18, 37).

(9) *like haggards wild they range*

> "I know *her* spirits are as coy and *wild As haggards* of the rock" (*Much* 3.1.35-36); "If I do prove *her haggard,/* Though that *her* jesses were my dear heartstrings,/ I'd whistle *her* off and let *her down the wind/ To prey at fortune*" (*Oth.* 3.3.260-63).

> See also the parallels to line 15 (*train them to our lure*) and to E.O. 9.14 (*The haggard hawk with toil is made full tame*). As discussed in connection with

the latter, falconry was an aristocratic sport and status symbol during the Shakespearean era.

These passages also belong to a larger Shakespearean wild/tame antithesis, e.g., as in *Venus*: "Like a wild bird being tamed with too much handling" (560).

The parallels to line 9 (which refers generically to *women* as *wild haggards*) may not be quite as strong as those to E.O. 9.14, though line 9 and *Much* do exhibit a triple word parallel (*like/as wild haggards*). Line 9 and *Oth.* also present a specifically similar image of women *ranging*, or roaming freely like *wild* birds.

The notable passage in *Shrew* ("to man my *haggard*," etc.) echoes line 9, as it does (even more strongly) E.O. 9.14. Since that passage also connects tellingly to line 15, the quotation is provided below.

(15) *train them to our lure*

> The reference to a *lure* makes clear that line 15 continues the falconry simile. Line 15, like E.O. 9.14, parallels the *Shrew* passage—and, given the close association between *training* and *taming (as well as "manning") the haggard* (or *shrewish woman*), the very title of that play: "*My falcon* now is sharp and passing empty,/ And till *she* stoop *she* must not be full-gorged,/ *For then she never looks upon her lure./ Another way I have to man my haggard,/ To make her come and know her keeper's call*" (*Shrew* 4.1.190-94).

> Line 15 also (again) recalls the passages in *Much* and *Oth.* quoted in connection with line 9 and E.O. 9.14. See again the additional discussion of the *haggard hawk* parallels in the Introduction.

> In a gender-flipping contrast (see also E.O. 9.14), Juliet imagines herself as a falconer luring Romeo:

> "*Juliet.* Hist! Romeo, hist! O for a falc'ner's voice/ *To lure* this tassel-gentle back again!" (*R&J* 2.2.159-60).

(18) To play with *fools*, oh what a *fool was I*

> Nor did I wonder at the lily's white,
> Nor praise the deep vermilion in the rose;
> They were but sweet, but figures of delight,
> Drawn after you, you pattern of all those.
> Yet seem'd it winter still, and, you away,
> As *with your shadow* I *with these did play*. (*Sonnets* 98.9-14)

Many further parallelisms could be cited, e.g., "'And when it hath the thing it hunteth most,/ *Tis won* as towns with fire, *so won, so lost*" (*LLL* 1.1.145-46). See lines 17-18 below under "additional parallels."

Additional parallels:

(1) If women could be *fair* and yet not *fond*

"In truth, *fair Montague,* I am *too fond*" (*R&J* 2.2.98); "why art thou old *and yet not* wise?" (*Lucrece* 1599).

(2) Or that their love were *firm*, not *fickle* still

"*Fair* is my love, but not so *fair* as *fickle*" (*Pass. Pilg.* VII.1); "*firm* and sound of heart,/ And of buxom valour, hath, by cruel fate,/ And giddy Fortune's furious *fickle* wheel" (*Hen. V* 3.6.25-27).

(4) By *service* long to *purchase* their *good will*

"I entreat *true peace of you,* /Which I will *purchase* with my duteous *service*" (*Rich. III* 2.1.63-64); cf. "*purchase* us a *good opinion*" (*Caes.* 2.1.145).

(5) how *frail those creatures are*

"*Frailty,* thy name *is woman*" (*Ham.* 1.2.146).

(6) *I muse* that men forget themselves so far.

"*I muse* your majesty doth seem so cold" (*John* 3.1.317); "*I muse* you make so slight a question" (*2 Hen IV* 4.1.65).

(6) *men forget themselves* so far

"Most necessary 'tis that *we forget*/ To pay *ourselves* what to *ourselves* is debt" (*Ham.* 3.2.193); "Horatio!— or I do *forget myself?*" (*Ham.* 1.2.161). The phrase *forget myself* occurs at least another twelve times in Shakespeare.

(7) *to mark the choice they make* and how they change

"*To mark the* full-fraught man *and* best indued" (*Hen. V* 2.2.139); "Let music sound while he doth *make his choice*" (*Merch.* 3.2.43); "*Make choice* of whom your wisest friends you will" (*Ham.* 4.5.205).

(7) and *how they change*

"Look ye, *how they change!*" (*Hen. V* 2.2.73).

See also the parallels to lines 7-8 above.

(11) *Who would not* scorn and shake them from the fist

"*Who would not* wish to be from wealth exempt,/ Since riches point to misery and contempt?" (*Timon* 4.2.31-32); "I *would not spare* my brother in this case/ If he should *scorn* me so apparently" (*Errors* 4.1.77-78).

(12) And let them fly *which way they list*

> "And let them take it *as they list*" (*R&J* 1.1.41).

(13) Yet *for disport we* fawn and flatter both

> "*We* make ourselves fools, *to disport ourselves*" (*Timon* 1.2.136).

(13) *we fawn and* flatter both

> "How I would make him *fawn and beg and seek*" (*LLL* 5.2.62).

(14) to *pass the time when nothing else can please*

> "I, in this weak piping time of peace,/ Have no delight *to pass away the time*" (*Rich. III* 1.1.24-25); "you *shall have time* to/ wrangle in *when* you have *nothing else to do*" (*A&C* 2.2.105-06).

(14) when *nothing* else *can please*

> "*Nothing pleaseth* but rare accidents" (*1 Hen. IV* 1.2.207); "Nor I nor any man that but man is/ With *nothing shall be pleased*, till he be eased/ With *being nothing*" (*Rich. II* 5.5.39-41); "*No shape but his can please* your dainty eye" (*1 Hen VI* 5.3.38); "He sees his love, and *nothing else* he sees,/ For *nothing else* with his proud sight agrees" (*Venus* 287-88).

(15) with *subtle oath;*

> Compare Sonnet 138:
>
> When my love *swears* that she is made of truth,
> I do believe her, though I know she lies,
> That she might think me some untutored youth,
> Unlearned in the world's false *subtleties*. (1-4)

(16) Till weary of our whiles, *ourselves we ease*

> "Then *when ourselves we see* in ladies *eyes*,/ Do we not likewise see *our learning* there?" (*LLL* 4.3.313-14).

(17) And *then we* say *when we* their fancy try,

> "*When we* grow stronger, *then we'll* make our claim:
> Till then, 'tis wisdom to conceal our meaning" (*3 Hen. VI* 4.7.59-60).

(18) to *play with fools*

> "Let me *play the fool*" (*Merch.*1.1.79); "thus we *play the fools* with the time, and the spirits of the wise sit in the clouds and mock us" (*2 Hen. IV* 2.2.142-43).

(18) *o what a fool was I*

> "*How much a fool was I/* To be of such a weak and silly mind" (*Venus* 1015-16).

(18) to *play with fools*, o what *a fool was I*

> Concluding a speech with such a paradox and use of isocolonic structure is common in Shakespeare, e.g.:

> "*Pursued* my humour *not pursuing* his,
> And *gladly shunn'd* who *gladly fled from me*."
> (R&J 1.1.129-30)

Previous commentaries: Looney (139-40, 163-64); Singleton (88-90); Ogburn (380-81, 518); Sobran (266-67); Brazil & Flues; May (2004, 223-24, 228); Goldstein (2016, 53-54).

E.O. 21: "Cupid's Bow"

1. In peascod time when hound to horn gives ear while buck is killed,
2. And little boys with pipes of corn sit keeping beasts in field,
3. I went to gather strawberries though when woods and groves were fair,
4. And parched my face with Phoebus, lo, by walking in the air.
5. I lay me down all by a stream and banks all overhead,
6. And there I found the strangest dream, that ever young man had.
7. Methought I saw each Christmas game, both revels all and some,
8. And each thing else that man could name or might by fancy come,
9. The substance of the thing I saw, in silence pass it shall,
10. Because I lack the skill to draw, the order of them all.
11. But Venus shall not 'scape my pen, whose maidens in disdain
12. Sit feeding on the hearts of men, whom Cupid's bow hath slain.
13. And that blind Boy sat all in blood, bebathed to the ears,
14. And like a conqueror he stood, and scorned lovers' tears.
15. I have more hearts (quoth he) at call, than Caesar could commaund.
16. And like the deer I make them fall, that overcross the lawnd.
17. I do increase their wand'ring wits, till that I dim their sight.
18. 'Tis I that do bereave them of their joy and chief delight.
19. Thus did I see this bragging Boy advance himself even then,
20. Deriding at the wanton toys, of foolish loving men,
21. Which when I saw for anger then my panting breast did beat,
22. To see how he sat taunting them, upon his royal seat.
23. O then I wished I had been free, and cured were my wound;
24. Methought I could display his arms, and coward deeds expound.
25. But I perforce must stay my muse, full sore against my heart,
26. For that I am a subject wight, and lanced with his dart.
27. But if that I achieve the fort, which I have took in charge,
28. My hand and head with quivering quill, shall blaze his name at large.

Structure: Twenty-eight lines of rhyming couplets with internal rhyme at half-lines through the first sixteen lines.

Textual sources: Originally published in a longer version in *Churchyardes chance* (1580), D1ʳ-D2. May (1980, 41-42; 1991, 284-86). Looney prints as by de Vere the much longer, carefully revised and expanded version published in *England's Helicon* as "The Shepheard's Slumber," by Ignoto (see Volume II, C.11). May: Possibly by Oxford #IVa-IV (82). Looney's title: "Desire." A retainer in the household of the Earl of Surrey and his Countess, the 17th earl of Oxford's aunt Frances de Vere, Churchyard was a popular but mediocre poet and author of books on history and religion, royal entertainments, encomia, and epitaphs. May (1980, 82) is among those who recognize the potential significance of Churchyard's association with Oxford as early as 1567 (as late as 1592, when Oxford was unable to cover Churchyard's rent at Mistress Penn's flophouse, Churchyard was still dependent on Oxford's patronage [Anderson 245-46]). In 1572 Churchyard contributed verses to *Cardanus Comforte* (see E.O. 1).

Although he lists this poem as "possibly by Oxford," May bases his conclusion on the unexamined assumption of Oxford being a weaker poet than Churchyard, and thereby ducks the obvious problem of why John Flasket, Anthony Munday, Nicholas Ling, and A.B. would *all* assign to "Ignoto" in 1602 a vastly superior version of a poem published as Churchyard's twenty years earlier unless they had good reason to believe it was not written by Churchyard. Even a meager acquaintance with Churchyard's usual poetic standards induces a serious doubt that the "Ignoto" version is by Churchyard. Churchyard's biography is, however, closely intertwined with Oxford's and it is highly likely that a number of Oxford's poems first appeared in print in books ostensibly written in their entirety by Churchyard.

Explanatory notes:

(1)   A *peascod* is the pod of a *pea* plant (*OED* 11: 404-05), so *peascod time* would mean the harvest season for that crop. The symbolism also suggests association with the male *codpiece*.

(7)   *Revels*, a word used eighteen times in Shakespeare, here refers to the sequence of court performances during the winter liturgical calendar between Christmas and Shrovetide. See, especially, R. Christopher Hassell (1979) for a classic study of the imprint left by this liturgical calendar on many plays of the period.

(12)   *Cupid*, in classical mythology, is the god of love and desire.

(17)   The term *wits* as used here refers to intelligence or mental sharpness, not humor (*OED* 20: 432-34).

(25)   The nine *Muses*, in Greek mythology, are the inspirational goddesses of poets and other writers, artists, and scholars.

(26)   A *wight* is a person (male or female), with some connotation of commiseration or contempt (*OED* 20: 328).

Strongest parallels:

(1) In *peascod time*

> "these nine and twenty years, come *peascod-time*" (2 *Hen. IV* 2.4.383).

> The phrase *peascod time* is extremely rare. An *EEBO* search (1473-1623) re–turns only three hits in three records: Churchyard (1580), *Dream* (in both quarto and folio), and Ignoto in *Eng. Hel.* (for this much longer and more crafted version of the poem, see section on Ignoto poems in *Eng. Hel.*, Vol. II).

(1) when *hound to horn gives ear*

As Caroline Spurgeon notes, Shakespeare "especially loves, and describes repeatedly, the re-echoing sound of the *hounds and horn*" (328): "the musical confusion/ Of *hounds* and echo in conjunction" (*Dream* 4.1.110-11). He is especially attracted by the "doubling and mocking quality" (328) when "the babbling echo mocks *the hounds*/replying shrilly to the *well-tuned horns*, as if a double hunt were heard at once" (*Titus* 2.3.17-19). See also, "Adonis comes with *horn* and *hounds*" (*Pass. Pilg.* IX.6); "She *hearkens for his hounds and for his horn*" (*Venus* 868); "Whiles *hounds and horns* and *sweet melodious birds*/ Be unto us as is a nurse's song/ Of lullaby to bring her babe asleep" (*Titus* 2.3.27- 29); "with *horn and hound we'll give* your grace bonjour" (*Titus* 1.1.494). EEBO (1473-1623) returns only eight hits in eight records for the search "*hound* near *horn*," two of them to Shakespeare and two of them to this poem as published in Churchyard in 1580 and in *Eng. Hel.* in 1600.

(2) *boys* with *pipes of corn sit keeping beasts in field*

"And *in the shape of Corin sat* all day,/ Playing on *pipes of corn*" (*Dream* 2.1.66-67); "When *shepherds pipe on oaten straws*" (*LLL* 5.2.903). For the search *pipes of corn* EEBO (1473-1623) returns only five hits in five records. These include the "Churchyard" and *Eng. Hel.* versions of the poem, and the two hits to *Dream*. Only Peter Woodhouse in *The Flea* (1605) is added to this list via a poem "In laudem Authoris," signed "R. P. Gent": "As other Shepherds done with *pypes of Corne*" (A4r). *Corin* was a name commonly used by poets for a shepherd *boy*, i.e., an apprentice poet.

(4) *parched my face with Phoebus*

"Think on *me*,/ That am *with Phoebus*' *amorous pinches black*/ *And wrinkled deep in time*?" (*A&C* 1.5.27-29); cf. "*parch in Afric sun*" (*Troil.* 1.3.369); "*Lo!* whilst I waited on my tender lambs, And *to sun's parching heat displayed my cheeks*" (*1 Hen. VI* 1.2.77).

Phoebus (also referenced in E.O. 14.31, 17.24, and 19.8) is an epithet for *Apollo*, Greco-Roman god of the sun. There are twenty-three references to *Phoebus* (including one spelled "Phibbus") in canonical Shakespeare (Spevack 976-77). *Apollo* is referenced once in these de Vere poems (E.O. 3.6) and twenty-nine times in canonical Shakespeare (Spevack 54).

(6) And there *I found the strangest dream, that ever young man had*

"This is *the strangest tale that ever* I heard" (*1 Hen. IV* 5.4.154); "*I have had a dream, past the wit of man* to say what *dream* it was" (*Dream* 4.1.205); "the *rarest dream that e'er dulled sleep*" (*Per.* 5.1.161); "*Strange dream, that gives a dead man leave to think*" (*R&J* 5.1.7).

(12-13) Feeding on the hearts of men, whom *Cupid's bow* hath *slain*./ And *that blind*

Boy sat all in blood, bebathed to the ears

> "*Bathed in* maiden *blood*" (*Titus* 2.3.232); "let us *bathe our hands in* Caesar's *blood*" (*Caes.* 3.1.106); "*bathe my dying honour in the blood*" (*A&C*, 4.2.6); "The mailed Mars shall on his altar *sit Up to the ears in blood*" (*1 Hen. IV* 4.1.117); "Out, damned spot! Out, I say!/ . . . . Yet who would have thought the old man to have had *so much blood in him?*/ . . . . What, will these hands ne'er be clean?" (*Mac.* 5.1.32, 35-37, 40).

> While the last of the five echoes lacks the explicit double parallels to *blood* and *bathe* (or *ears*), Lady Macbeth is desperately seeking to wash off (*bathe*) her victim's *blood*; the vividly horrific impression left by all the samples is of inundation *in blood*. See also: "*slain in* Cupid's *wars*" (*Per.* 1.1.38); cf. "*Cupid's bow*" (*Venus* 581); "*Cupid's strongest bow*" (*Dream* 1.1.169); "*Cupid's bow-string*" (*Much* 3.2.10).

(27-28) But if that I *achieve the fort* [i.e., his beloved], which I have took in charge,/ My hand and head *with quivering quill,* shall *blaze* his name at large

> "He hath *achieved a maid* . . . that excels *the quirks of blazoning pens*" (*Oth.* 2.1.61, 63); cf. "*the half-achieved Harfleur* [a French port]" (*Hen. V* 3.3.8).

Additional parallels:

(3) when *woods and groves* were fair

> "The hunt is up, the morn is bright and grey,/ The fields are fragrant and *the woods are green*" (*Titus* 2.2.1-2); "Ye elves of hills, brooks, *standing lakes and groves*,/ And ye that on the sands with printless foot/ Do chase the ebbing Neptune" (*Tem.* 5.1.33-35).

(7) *Methought I saw*

> "*Methought I heard* a voice cry 'Sleep no more! Macbeth doth murder sleep'" (*Mac.* 2.2.32-33); "*Methought I saw* a thousand fearful wrecks;/ Ten thousand men that fishes gnaw'd upon" (*Rich. III* 1.4.24-25); "*methought I heard* the shepherd say, he found the child" (*Win.* 5.2.78).

(7) each *Christmas game*

> "A *Christmas gambold*" (*Shrew* ind.2.134-35).

(8) each thing else that *man could name*

> "Nay, you must *name* his *name*, and half his face must/ be seen through the lion's neck . . . I am *a/ man* as other men are; and there indeed *let him name/ his name*, and tell them plainly he is Snug the joiner" (*Dream* 3.1.36-46).

(9)*The substance* of *the thing I saw,* in silence pass it shall

> "If aught within that little *seeming substance,*/ Or all of it, with our displeasure piec'd,/ And no*thing* more, may fitly like your Grace,/ She's there, and she is yours" (*Lear* 1.1.198-201); "Each *substance of a grief* hath twenty shadows,/ Which *shows like* grief itself, but is not so" (*Rich. II* 2.2.14-15).

(10) Because *I lack the skill* to draw

> "I have not the skill" (*Ham.* 3.2.362); "If *I have any skill*" (*Kins.* 5.2.53); "*I have no skill* in sense to make distinction" (*All's Well* 3.4.39); "*I have not much skill* in grass" (*All's Well* 4.5.21); "Had *I sufficient skill* to utter them" (*3 Hen. VI* 5.5.13); "with *the little skill I have*/ Full well shalt thou perceive how much I dare" (*Titus* 2.1.43-44).

(11) But Venus *shall not 'scape my* pen

> "And who *shall scape* whipping?" (*Ham.* 2.2.530); "thou *shalt not escape* calumny" (*Ham.* 3.1.136); "in sooth you *scape not so*" (*Shrew* 2.1.240); "we *shall not scape* a brawl" (*R&J* 3.1.3); "the villain *shall not scape*" (*Lear* 2.1.80).

(14) like a *conqueror he stood*

> "Did forfeit . . . all those lands/ Which *he stood* seized of to the *conqueror*" (*Ham.* 1.1.88-89).

(14) he . . . *scorned lovers' tears*

> "My manly eyes did *scorn* an humble *tear*" (*Rich. III* 1.2.164); cf. "Hunting he *loved,* but *love he laughed to scorn*" (*Venus* 4); "So mild that patience seemed to *scorn his woes*" (*Lucrece* 1505); "Why should you think that I should *woo in scorn? Scorn* and derision never come in *tears*" (*Dream* 3.2.122-23).

(15) "I have more hearts," quoth he [the blind *Boy* Cupid], "*at call, than Caesar could command*"

> "Sextus Pompeius/ *Hath given the dare to Caesar and commands*/ The empire of the sea" (*A&C* 1.2.179-81); "His . . . ministers would prevail/ *Under the service of a child* as soon/ As i' th' *command of Caesar*" (*A&C* 3.13.22-25).

> Considering the references in lines 14-15 to *conqueror* and *Caesar,* compare, e.g.: "Shall *Caesar* send a lie?/ Have I in *conquest* stretched mine arm so far/ To be afeared to tell greybeards the truth!" (*Caes.* 2.2.65-67); "O mighty *Caesar!* Dost thou lie so low?/ Are all thy *conquests,* glories, triumphs, spoils,/ Shrunk to this little measure?" (*Caes.* 3.1.148-50); "she which by her death our *Caesar* tells/ I am *conqueror* of myself" (*A&C* 4.14.61-62); "A kind of *conquest Caesar* made here" (*Cym.* 3.1.22-23).

> One would expect, of course, to see references to *Caesar's* conquests in a play like *Caes.* But it is noteworthy that de Vere refers three times to *Caesar* in these twenty poems (in a rather unexpected context here; see also E.O.

5, lines 9 and 18), while Shakespeare devotes an entire play to the Roman leader and refers to him dozens of times in almost half the plays in the canon (Spevack 166-67).

(16) *like the deer* I make them *fall*

"Here wast thou bayed, brave *hart;* Here didst thou *fall* . . . How *like a deer* strucken by many princes/ *Doth thou here lie!"* (*Caes.* 3.1.204-10).

(17) *dim* their *sight*

"Gazing on that which seems to *dim* thy *sight"* (*2 Hen. VI* 1.2.6).

(18) *bereave them of their* joy and chief *delight*

"*Bereave him of his* wits with *wonder"* (*1 Hen. VI* 5.3.195); cf. "*joy delights in joy"* (*Sonnets* 8.2); "And I in *deep delight* am chiefly drown'd" (*Pass. Pilg.* VIII.11).

(19) *Thus did I see* this bragging Boy

"The forward violet *thus did I chide"* (*Sonnets* 99.1).

(19-20) *this bragging Boy* [Cupid] . . . Deriding at the *wanton toys*, of foolish loving men

"To *toy*, to *wanton*, dally, smile, and jest" (*Venus* 106); "*toys/* Of feathered Cupid" (*Oth.* 1.3.268-69).

Shakespeare associates *wanton* with *Cupid* and *boys* on several occasions (Spevack 1440), e.g.: "the weak *wanton Cupid"* (*Troil.* 3.3.222); "As flies to *wanton boys* are we to th' gods; They kill us for their sport" (*Lear* 4.1.36-37).

(21) Which when I saw *for anger* then *my panting breast* did *beat*

"What, shall we suffer this? let's pluck him down:/ *My heart for anger* burns; I cannot brook it" (*3 Hen. VI* 1.1.59-60); "The *colour in thy face/* That even *for anger* makes the lily pale . . . / Shall plead for me and tell my loving tale" (*Lucrece* 477-80).

(22) upon his *royal seat*

"The rightful heir of England's *royal seat"* (*2 Hen. VI* 5.1.178); "in the *seat royal* of this famous isle" (*Rich. III* 3.1.164); cf. "this the *regal seat"* (*3 Hen. VI* 1.1.26); "Have shaken Edward from the *regal seat"* (*3 Hen. VI* 4.6.2); "the *supreme seat"* (*Rich. III* 3.7.118); "the *seat of majesty"* (*Rich. III* 3.7.169).

(23) *O then I wished I had been* free

"O Cressida, how often have *I wished me thus!* (*Troil.* 3.2.61); "*I would I had been* there" (*Ham.* 1.2.234).

(23) *cured* were *my wound[s]*

"*Cureless are my wounds"* (*3 Hen. VI* 2.6.23); "with a *wound* I must be *cured"*

(*A&C* 4.14.78); cf. "A smile *recures* [i.e., *cures*] the *wounding* of a frown" (*Venus* 465); "the deer /That hath received some *unrecuring* [i.e., *incurable*] *wound*" (*Titus* 3.1.89-90).

(24) *coward* deeds *expound*

"To *expound* his *beastly* mind" (*Cym.* 1.6.152-53). *Expound/-ed* occurs six times in Shakespeare.

(25) *But I perforce must stay my muse*

"But my Muse labours" (*Oth.* 2.1.127); "*my sick Muse doth give another place*" (*Sonnets* 79.4); "*My tongue-tied Muse* in manners *holds her still* [i.e., politely *stays quiet*]" (*Sonnets* 85.1); "*Alack what poverty my Muse brings forth* . . . O blame me not if *I no more can write!*" (*Sonnets* 103.1, 5).

(25) full sore *against my heart*

"And then *against my heart* he sets his sword" (*Lucrece* 1640).

(26) *For that I am* a subject wight

"*For that I am* some twelve or fourteen moonshines/ Lag of a brother?" (*Lear* 1.2.5-6).

(27) if that I *achieve the fort* which I have took in charge

Cf. Oxford June 1585 letter: "yet am I as one that hath *long besieged a fort* and not able to compasse the end or reap the fruit of his travail" (Fowler 342).

(28) My hand and head with *quivering quill*

"Her maid is gone, and she prepares to write,/ First *hovering* o'er the paper with her *quill*" (*Lucrece* 1296-97); "By her fine foot, straight leg and *quivering thigh*/ And the demesnes that there adjacent lie" (*R&J* 2.1.19-20).

(28) shall *blaze his name* at large

"The heavens themselves *blaze forth the death of princes*" (*Caes.* 2.2.31); "Red cheeks and fiery eyes *blaze forth the wrong*" (*Venus* 219).

(28) his name *at large*

"And hear *at large* discoursed all our fortunes" (*Errors* 5.1.396); "Discover more *at large* what cause that was,/ For I am ignorant and cannot guess" (*1 Hen. VI* 2.5.59-60); "As more *at large* your grace shall understand" (*2 Hen. VI* 2.1.173).

Previous commentary: Sobran (266-70).

Essays and Appendices

Assessing the Linguistic Evidence for Oxford

Gary Goldstein

In October 2016 the German publisher Verlag Laugwitz brought out a collection of my essays on the authorship, *Reflections on the True Shakespeare*, which included two chapters on the linguistic correspondences between Oxford's twenty known poems and seventy-seven private letters and the language of the Shakespeare canon. I sent a copy to Steven May, Professor of English Emeritus at Georgetown College (Kentucky) and modern editor of Oxford's poetry, requesting the favor of a critical response, which he recently provided. In addition to his modern edition of Oxford's poetry, May wrote about Oxford's verse in his book *The Elizabethan Courtier Poets (1991)*, and reviewed Alan Nelson's biography of Oxford, *Monstrous Adversary* (2005), for *Shakespeare Quarterly*, so he is widely considered among Stratfordian academics to be a leading authority on Oxford.

Unfortunately, analyzing his detailed response to my argument that Oxford's poetry is Shakespeare's juvenilia, Oxfordians will discover a continuing refusal to seriously consider any evidence that is not *prima facie* — in other words, mathematical — proof, when advancing the Oxfordian argument.

An Overview

For decades, Oxfordian scholars have focused on two lines of evidence in making the case for Oxford's authorship—the public testimonials by Oxford's contemporaries regarding his poetry and drama, and the biographical parallels between the Shakespeare plays and particular aspects of Oxford's life. In counterpoint, Stratfordian academics claim the testimonials are too generic to be more than the flattering tributes generally paid to noblemen such as Oxford who served as patrons (Oxford had thirty books dedicated to him and was patron of two acting troupes for twenty years).

As to any biographical parallels, they make two arguments. First, that such parallels are purely coincidental, because writers in Shakespeare's time did not base their creative works on personal experience or observation, but rather on imagination and—especially in Shakespeare's case—other writers' works. Second, that if there are any true parallels, they were inserted by Shakespeare to ingratiate himself with Oxford, or possibly for commercial compensation from him so that de Vere could promote himself with fellow courtiers and officials of Elizabeth's government. Missing from modern Oxfordian arguments are the philological parallels in both his poetry and his private letters and the language of the canon. To illustrate, I will provide several examples.

Linguistic Parallels in the Poetry

Among J. T. Looney's core arguments was that the lyrical verse of Oxford was deeply interwoven with that of Shakespeare's in literary style, psychology and moral disposition. By way of example, he contrasted Oxford's Echo poem, "Sitting Alone Upon My Thought," with stanzas from *Venus and Adonis* (139).

E.O. 17	**Shakespeare**
Three times, with her soft hand, full hard on her left side she knocks, And sigh'd so sore as might have mov'd some pity in the rocks; From sighs and shedding amber tears into sweet song she brake.	And now she beats her heart whereat it groans, That all the neighbor caves as seeming troubled, Make verbal repetition of her moans She marking them begins a wailing note And sings extemporally a woeful ditty.
[This is followed by the echoing]	[This is again followed by the echoing]

In each case a female pours out her woes and is answered by echoes from caves; in each, the echoing is preceded by three identical conceptions in identical order: She beats her heart, the caves are moved to pity, and she breaks into song, after which comes the echo. In the same vein, compare the correspondences between the final three lines of Oxford's poem "Even as the wax doth melt," which was first published in *Paradise of Dainty Devices* (1576), with verse from *Romeo and Juliet*, which first appeared in print in 1597 (1.1.112).

E.O. 2

That with the careful culver climbs the worn and withered tree,/ To entertain my thoughts, and there my hap to moan, /That never am less idle, lo, than when I am alone.

Shakespeare

And stole into the covert of the wood;/ I, measuring his affections with my own,/ That most are busied when they're most alone.

Here we have three lines expressive of identical ideas in an identical order: the hiding in the woods, the internal life of thought and affection, and the third lines, which are an exact paraphrase of one another. These are not mere commonplaces of the period; they demonstrate a similar psychology of thought. Further evidence of this shared poetic sensibility was noted by the Shakespeare scholar Sidney Lee, who wrote that Oxford's ditty about desire finds its analog in Shakespeare's *The Merchant of Venice:*

E.O. 11

When wert thou born, Desire?/ In pomp and prime of May/ By whom, sweet boy, wert thou begot?/ By fond Conceit, men say.

***Merchant of Venice* (f.p. 1600)**

Tell me, where is fancy bred, Or in the heart or in the head? (3.2.63-64).

Writing ten years before Looney's *Shakespeare Identified,* Lee (1910) observed that these verses by Oxford and Shakespeare are written "in a kindred key" (227).

More famous still is Oxford's philosophical poem, "Were I a King." Comparing this short poem to Shakespeare's verse, we find explicit parallels in theme and vocabulary from two of the history plays.

E.O. 16

Were I a king, I could *command content*

Shakespeare

Was ever king that joy'd an earthly throne, And could *command no more content* than I?
                    (*2 Hen. VI* 4.9.2)

Were I obscure, hidden should be my cares . . . /A doubtful choice, of these three which to crave, *A kingdom*, or a *cottage*, or a *grave*.

The king shall be contented . . . I'll give my . . . Gorgeous palace for *a hermitage* . . ./ And my large *kingdom* for a little *grave*, A little, little *grave*, an obscure *grave*.
                    (*Rich. II* 3.3.145)

In the chapter on Oxford's poetry in *Reflections on the True Shakespeare*, I provide many more examples of Oxford's verse echoing that of Shakespeare's in terms of language and philosophical ideas.

In his 1980 edition of Oxford's poetry, Professor May argued that the verbal parallels with Shakespeare's poetry were nothing more than poetic commonplaces to be found throughout the works of Elizabethan writers: Elizabethan poets drew upon a broad, common range of motifs, rhetorical devices, allusions and adages, so that, given the relative abundance of Shakespeare's verse, it would be surprising indeed to fin d a contemporary poet whose themes and phrasing did not correspond at some point and in some way with a passage or two by the Bard (May 1980, 11-12). May did not actually try to prove the validity of this objection until 2004 in an essay. When he did, he provided only a single poetic commonplace for each of three poems that he selected: *haggard hawks, the lily* and *the rose*, and the trope called *amplification*.

However, the Oxfordian case is grounded upon more than a handful of literary correspondences; it is instead based on a pervasive similarity to Shakespeare's works in the characteristics of diction, cohesion and unity, and also in the similes employed. May's most recent critique, which is more elaborate, was laid out in his email to me in March 2017, in response to my book:

> Yes, I did go over much of your book, especially the chapter on "Shakespeare's Juvenilia." I'd like to say I found your argument about the cumulative weight of the parallel passages persuasive, but I don't, and I feel sure the profession won't either for reasons of its flawed methodology: First, the argument assumes that Shakespeare repeated himself, expressing the same ideas over and over with similar wording.
>
> Did he? I don't think he did.
>
> Second, if any of the verbal parallels with Oxford's poems are, in fact, unusual, weren't most of them in print and available for Shakespeare to plagiarize? Third, where the wording in your examples is quite similar, it is evidence of a single authorship ONLY if you can demonstrate that Oxford, Shakespeare, and no one else used these phrases. But that isn't the case.
>
> I ran a few through *EEBO* searches with the following results between 1580 and 1610:

the world afford	6 hits
affords	24 hits
ebbs and flows	258 hits
sad despair	23 hits
heaven . . . hell	45 hits

Others don't need to be tested: "patience perforce" and "fain would I," for instance, are well known commonplaces in Elizabethan English. In short, the occurrence of this phrasing in the work of any two authors, or ten authors, or in anonymous writings of the period cannot be used to establish authorship because it was ubiquitous. No matter how many examples you find, the repetitions have *no evidentiary value* [our emphasis].

First, it should be noted that May did not address the linguistic evidence contained in Oxford's letters, probably because he cannot explain how a commoner could access a nobleman's private correspondence. Second, his belief that Shakespeare would not dwell upon the same ideas in his poetry over time is actually evidence in favor of the artist's creative development as he matured. Third, the examples that May selected to find "commonplaces" were two- and three-word clusters rather than specific examples of unusual metaphors and similes. Obviously, these simple phrases were "commonplace." He completely avoided the unusual linguistic parallels since these were not commonplaces.

Perhaps May's critical position regarding Oxford's verse continues to be colored by his opinion of the man, revealed in his review of Alan Nelson's polemical *Monstrous Adversary* for *Shakespeare Quarterly*: "Oxford's career unfolds as the story of a teflon earl, a supreme egotist whose self-indulgence caused misery and even death to those who got in his way. It is a fascinating account, yet de Vere suffered no serious consequences for a lifetime of irresponsible and illegal behavior. His biography stands as a striking example of Elizabethan deference to noble birth without regard for the ignoble life that followed" (214). In the same review May was equally contemptuous in his assessment of the Oxfordian hypothesis, writing that, "The earl of Oxford's biography warrants a review in *SQ* only in part because the authorship controversy so ardently pursued by 'Oxfordians' poses a challenge to Shakespeare studies equivalent to that leveled at the biological sciences by creationism."

The Linguistic Evidence in Oxford's Letters

Based on the preceding information, I think the best way to advance the hypothesis is to focus on the literary correspondences between Oxford's writings and the Shakespeare canon, especially between his unpublished letters and the Shakespeare canon. Unlike some of Oxford's poetry, which was published during Shakespeare's time, there is no way for academics to claim that Shakespeare could plagiarize the ideas and language contained within private correspondence by the country's senior Earl written to the country's Lord Treasurer, Lord Burghley, and to its Secretary of State, Robert Cecil. The following examples were culled from the work of William Plumer Fowler and Joseph Sobran.

Compare both the ideas and vocabulary in Oxford's private letters, on a line-by-line basis, with the language and ideas in the plays and poems of Shakespeare.

As Roger Stritmatter of Coppin State University recently commented (personal communication) on the use of forensic linguistics to determine authorial identity, "As soon as you are able to compare strings of words, and see the same idea in the same grammatical structure but just with different surface features, and the surface features in each case follow their own sound pattern logic, you have a good idea that you might be working with the same author."

Oxford	**Shakespeare**
To bury my hopes in the *deep abyss* and *bottom* of despair.	In the *dark backward* and *abysm* of time. *Tem.* 1.2
	In the *deep bosom* of the ocean *buried*. *Rich. III* 1.1
In all *kindness* and *kindred* *More family than friendly*	A little *more than kin*, and *less than kind*. *Ham.* 1.2
An end according to mine *expectation*.	*Our expectation* hath this day *an end*. *Hen. V* 3.3
It is my hap according to *the English proverb* to starve like the horse, *while the grass doth grow*.	Ay, sir, but *while the grass grows—the proverb* is something musty. *Ham.* 3.2
I serve her Majesty, and *I am that I am, and* by alliance near to your Lordship, but free.	No, *I am that I am, and* they that level/At my abuses reckon up their own. *Sonnets* 121
To bring *all my hope* in her Majesty's gracious *words* to *smoke*.	This *helpless smoke of words*. *Lucrece* 1027
To *bury* and *insevill* your works in the *grave of oblivion*.	And *deeper than oblivion do we bury*/The incensing relics of it. *All's Well* 5.3
But now *time* and *truth* have *unmasked* all difficulties.	*Time's* glory is to calm contending kings To *unmask* falsehood and bring *truth* to light. *Lucrece* 939-40
Having passed *the pikes* of *so many adversaries*.	Of *bristly pikes* that ever threat *his foes*. *Venus* 620

When *the serpent* lay hid *in the herb*.

Look like *the innocent flower*
But be *the serpent* under it.
Mac. 1.5

Decked with pearls and precious stones.

Decked with diamonds and Indian *stones*.
3 Hen. VI 3.1

Finis coronat opus [The end crowns the work].

The end crowns all.
Troil. 4.5

La fin couronne les oevres.
2 Hen. VI 5.2

All's well that ends well. Still, the *fine's* the *crown*. What'er the course, *the end* is the renown.
All's Well 4.4

Will make *the end answerable to the rest of* your most *friendly proceeding*.

If *his own life answer the straightness of* his *proceeding*.
Meas. 3.2

Were but a feigned *friend* to our *proceedings*.
3 Hen. VI 4.2

Of equal *friendship* and *proceeding*.
Hen. VIII 2.4

But the world is so cunning as of *a shadow* they can *make a substance*, and of a *likelihood* a *truth*.

He takes *false shadows* for true *substances*.
Titus 3.2

What is your *substance*, whereof you are made, / That millions of strange *shadows* on you tend?
Sonnets 53

For *truth is truth* though never so old, and *time cannot make that false which was once true*.

For truth is truth to the end of reckoning.
Meas. 5.1

Is not *the truth the truth*?
1 Henry IV 2.4
A truth's a truth.
All's Well 4.5

The multiple allusions to the truth in the Shakespeare plays sound like oblique plays on the motto of the de Veres, *Vero nihil verius*, "nothing is truer than truth."

No two writers are likely to overlap this much in their choice of words and concepts, even those words which show no special distinction, let alone words like "truth" which here express, in both texts, a play on the Oxford heraldic motto.

[Reprinted with modification from *Shakespeare Oxford Newsletter* 53:2 (Spring 2017), 22-25.]

A complete database of Oxford's known correspondence may be found at www. oxford-shakespeare.com.

Verse Parallels between Oxford and Shakespeare

Robert R. Prechter

In numerous articles, including three for *The Oxfordian*, E.Y. Elliott and Robert J. Valenza—Professors of American Political Institutions, and Mathematics, respectively, at Claremont McKenna College—have argued that the poetry of Edward de Vere is nothing like that of Shakespeare. Their conclusion is based on computer analyses. In "The Shakespeare Clinic and the Oxfordians" (2010), the authors singled out for mockery one of Oxford's poems from *A Paradise of Daynty Devices* (1576). They contrasted the final stanza with a passage in *Hamlet*, referring to the two sources' "glaring stylometric mismatches" (149).

They asked and answered: "Is there a stylometric match with each other? Anything but" (138). Elliott and Valenza concluded: "The styles seem to be worlds apart" (2000, 90), and reported that Shakespeare scholars agreed with their position, as "nine out of ten of the top scorers on our Shakespeare Golden Ear test" (2010, 138) apparently finding nothing in common with this poem and the verse of Shakespeare. They also repeat May's stark assertion, "nothing in Oxford's canonical verse in any way hints at an affinity with the poetry of William Shakespeare" (2004, 242).

But the collector of the verses in *Paradise*, Richard Edwards, died in 1566, suggesting that Oxford probably wrote the poems published in the 1576 first edition before age sixteen. Among the most effective counters to Elliott and Valenza is that one hardly expects teenage poetry to read like mature verse, especially after years of theatrical experience and feedback.

Stylistic Affinities

Remarkably, however, it turns out that there are stylistic affinities between Oxford's work and Shakespeare's. Elliott and Valenza, whose algorithms of course do as they are told, simply overlook what they were not instructed to find.

The human mind is different from a computer. It is weaker in some ways and superior in others. Perhaps the computers used in Elliott and Valenza's stylometric studies are not yet programmed with the kinds of literary matches that a human mind can discern. The best poem to illustrate this is precisely the one they feature as their Exhibit A, "The Loss of My Good Name":

> Framed in the front of forlorn hope, past all recovery
> I stayless stand t'abide the shock of shame and infamy;
> My life, through lingering long, is lodged in lair of loathsome ways,
> My death delayed to keep from life the harm of hapless days;
> My sprites, my heart, my wit and force in deep distress are drowned;
> The only loss of my good name is of these griefs the ground.
>
> And since my mind, my wit, my head, my voice and tongue are weak
> To utter, move, devise, conceive, sound forth, declare and speak
> Such piercing plaints as answer might, or would, my woeful case,
> Help crave I must, and crave I will, with tears upon my face
> Of all that may in heaven or hell, in earth or air, be found
> To wail with me this loss of mine, as of these griefs the ground.
>
> Help gods, help saints, help sprites and powers that in the heaven do dwell,
> Help ye that are to wail, ay wont, ye howling hounds of hell,
> Help man, help beasts, help birds and worms that on the earth doth toil,
> Help fish, help fowl that flocks and feeds upon the salt-sea soil,
> Help echo that in air doth flee, shrill voices to resound
> To wail this loss of my good name, as of these griefs the ground.

The text above has been edited in minor ways, though none that affect my reading. Apart from the title, which I supply, the *Paradise* rendition (E.O. 30 in the collection) begins, somewhat mysteriously: "Fraud is the front of Fortune." Aside from its obscurity, the line itself is missing a beat. My conclusion is that it's probably a publishing or printing error. The alternate first line, "Framed in the front of forlorn hope," which fits the poem's fourteeners, is the one I accept as accurate. Poems were generally untitled in the 16th century, so scholars usually refer to them by their first lines. Since this one is uncertain, I have opted to call it "The Loss of My Good Name," after its repeated theme.

Parallels and Connections

Contrary to Elliott and Valenza, there turn out to be a number of connections between Oxford's youthful poem and lines from Shakespeare. Let's begin by examining one item from each stanza. In the first stanza, Oxford uses alliteration in "My *l*ife, though *l*ingering *l*ong, is *l*odged in *l*air of *l*oathsome ways." Who else alliterates the letter *l* while connecting *life* and *lingering*, as well as *loathsome* with a type of *lair*? Here is Shakespeare in *Cymbeline*: "feed on *life* and *lingering*" (5.5.19), and in *2 Hen. VI*: "lean-faced Envy in her *loathsome* cave" (3.2.174). In the second stanza, Oxford presents a list of verbs: "To utter, move, devise, conceive, sound forth, declare and speak." Who else does it? Here is Shakespeare in *All's Well That Ends Well*: "they . . . do wear . . . muster true gait, eat, speak, and move" (2.1.33). Observe that two of the verbs are the same.

In the final stanza, the one that Elliott and Valenza most disparage, Oxford writes: "Help gods, help saints, help sprites [spirits] and . . . ye . . . hounds of hell." Compare this with Shakespeare's *1 Hen. VI* : "Now help, ye charming spells and periapts[1] And ye choice spirits that admonish me" (5.3.79). Shakespeare also strings together two-syllable clauses in *Rich. III*: "Earth gapes, hell burns, fiends roar, saints pray" (4.4.182). Notice how similar Shakespeare's line is to Oxford's language in terms of parallel construction, with commas separating the iambs, each comprising two single-syllable words, two identical across the poems and a third (*sprites/fiends*) also strikingly similar.

These two brief quotes from Shakespeare utilize five of Oxford's associated words: *Help, ye, saints, spirits* and *hell*, as well as *earth*, which shows up in his poem two lines later. What may be Shakespeare's most mature play, *The Tempest*, reprises the idea of calling on various supernatural beings: "Ye elves of hills, brooks, standing lakes and groves,/ And ye that on the sands with printless foot . . ." (5.1.123). As Oxford does in line two of stanza three of his poem, Shakespeare addresses these entities once with the word *ye* standing alone and once using *ye* with a noun (*ye* and *ye* . . . *hounds* in Oxford's line, and *Ye elves* and *ye* in Shakespeare's). In each case the expressions are five poetic feet apart. Cyrus Hoy considered the word *ye* rare enough in Shakespeare that he used its appearance to claim for John Fletcher (erroneously in my view) portions of *Henry VIII*. Yet Shakespeare uses this less-utilized pronoun in both instances to echo Oxford's poem—in *1 Henry VI* and *The Tempest*—and each time it appears twice, as it does in the second line of Oxford's third stanza.

Oxford defaulted to earlier usages when mining previously rendered verbal ideas for new and improved constructions. What about Oxford's refrain, "as of these griefs the *ground*"? Many people attach *ground(s)* to actions or attitudes such as "*grounds* for divorce," "*grounds* for an argument" or "*grounds* for holding a grudge." But they

---

[1] Periapts: amulets used to ward off disease or evil.

rarely use the term in reference to emotions, such as "*grounds* for joy" or "*grounds* for sadness." Perhaps Oxford linked *ground* and *grief* because they alliterate. Regardless, the pairing is unusual. Who else uses it? In Shakespeare's 2 *Henry IV* Westmoreland says he does not see how Mowbray has "*any ground* to build *a grief* on" (4.1.27).

Observe that Shakespeare uses the singular form, as Oxford does. In five other such constructions, Shakespeare uses the plural form, as in "I did proceed on just *grounds*" (*Othello* 5.2.101). In 146 out of the 166 times that Shakespeare uses the singular *ground*, it means earth; only twice it is the past tense of grind (in *Romeo and Juliet* and *Pericles*), and the remaining eighteen times it means *basis*, as in de Vere's poem.

But even then, it mostly refers to actions, conditions or attitudes, as in "The *ground* of your ill-will" (*Richard III* 1.3.168). Only twice in the canon does Shakespeare link *ground* with an emotional state other than sadness and unrelated to a grudge, and each occurs only once, in *Cymbeline* (4.2.96): "on good *ground* we fear"; and in *Coriolanus* (2.2.89): "They hate upon no better a *ground*." Within this context, it is notable that Shakespeare links *ground(s)* to *grief* or to the synonym *woe* fully four times: "the *grounds* and motives of her *woe*" (*A Lover's Complaint*, Stanza 9); "We see the *ground* whereon these woes do lie;/ But the true *ground* of all these piteous woes" (*Romeo and Juliet* 5.3.179-80); and in the passage quoted above from 2 *Henry IV*: "any *ground* to build a *grief* on." Oxford and Shakespeare made the same mental connection in referring to a ground for misery.

A Youthful Poet

We can go even further. The entire poem holds up well as a work by a youthful poet who retained some of his compositional proclivities into maturity. He expresses the same ideas; he links the same words; and he employs the same rhythms. The following list presents each line from Oxford's poem, in order, followed by similar Shakespearean constructions:

Oxford	**Shakespeare**
Framed in the front of forlorn *hope, past all recovery*	For grief that they are *past recovery*: For, were there *hope* to conquer them again *2 Hen. VI* I.1.16-17

I stayless stand t'abide the shock of *shame and infamy*	My *shame and guilt* confounds me. *Two Gent.* 5.4.63
	Here in the streets, desperate of *shame and state* *Twelfth* 5.1.45
My *life*, through *lingering* long, is lodged in *lair of loathsome ways*	Should by the minute feed on *life and lingering* *Cym.* 5.5.86
	lean-faced Envy in *her loathsome cave* *2 Hen. VI* 3.2.13
	Within a loathsome dungeon, there to pine *1 Hen. VI* 2.5.66
	Let him keep his *loathsome cabin* still *Venus* 658
shame and infamy...*My death* delayed...	*Shame* serves thy life and doth *thy death* attend *Rich. III* 44.59
	His days may finish ere that hapless time *1 Hen. VI* 3.1.7
My sprites, *my heart, my wit and force* in deep distress are drowned	Iago doth give up/ The execution of *his wit, hands, heart* *Oth.* 3.3.72-3
	What *heart, head, sword, force, means*, but is Lord Timon's? *Timon* 1.2.97
The only loss of *my good name*	But he that filches from me *my good name*...makes me poor indeed. *Oth.* 3.3.41-2
	Let *my good name* . . . be kept unspotted *Lucrece* 820-21
is *of these griefs the ground*	it not appears to me... That you should have an inch of *any ground To build a grief on* *2 Hen. IV* 4.1.51-3

And since *my mind, my wit, my head, my voice and tongue* are weak To *utter, move, devise, conceive, sound forth, declare and speak*

They . . . do *wear . . . muster true gait, eat, speak, and move* . . . Methinks in thee some blessed spirit doth speak His powerful sound within an organ weak.

All's Well 2.1.38

So many miseries have crazed my voice, That my *woe-wearied tongue* is mute and dumb

Rich. III 4.4.12

It ascends me into *the brain*; . . . which, delivered o'er to *the voice, the tongue*, which is *the birth*, Becomes excellent *wit.*   *2 Hen. IV* 4.3.192-94

If thou hast any *sound, or use of voice, Speak* to me.

Ham. 1.1.167-68

speak all good you can *devise* of Caesar

Caes. 3.1.98

More suits you *to conceive* than I *to speak* of

As You 1.2.69

could with a ready guess *declare*, Before the Frenchman *speak*   *Hen. V* .1.71-72

Such *piercing plaints* as answer might, or would, *my woeful case*

That hearing how *our plaints* and prayers *do pierce*

Rich. II 5.3.56

the traitor Stands *in worse case of woe*

Cym. 2.4.89-90

Help crave I must, and *crave I will*, with tears upon my face

Hence will I to my ghostly father's cell, *His help to crave*   *R&J* 2.2.29-30

Poor soul, *thy face* is much abused *with tears*

R&J 4.1.14

Of all that may *in heaven or hell*, in *earth or air*, be found

Whether *in sea or fire*, in *earth or air*

Ham. 1.1.41

Bring with thee *airs from heaven* or blasts from *hell*

Ham. 1.4.53

Thou hast as chiding a nativity *As fire, air, water, earth,* and *heaven* can make

Per. 3.1.22-23

Am I *in earth, in heaven, or in hell*?

Errors 2.2.101

Help gods, help saints, help sprites and powers that in the *heaven* do dwell *Help ye* that are to wail, ay wont, ye *howling hounds of hell*

Now help, ye charming spells and periapts;/ *And ye* choice *spirits* that admonish me

1 Hen. VI 5.3.69-71

Earth gapes, hell burns, fiends roar, saints pray
Rich. III 5.4.9

O you powers That give *heaven* countless eyes
*Per.*1.1.32-3

A pair of *cursed hell-hounds* and their dam!
Titus 5.2.138

Help man, help beasts, help birds and worms that on the earth doth toil, help fish, help fowl that flocks and feeds upon the salt-sea soil

What have we here? a man or a fish? ...any strange beast there makes a man
Tempest 2.2.67-68

Courteous destroyers, affable wolves, meek bears, You fools of fortune, trencher-friends, time's flies, Cap and knee slaves, vapors, and minute-jacks! Of man and beast the infinite malady
Timon 3.6.191-94

My *flocks feed* not
Pass. Pilg. XVII.1

Of the ravin'd *salt-sea* shark
Mac. 4.1.56

Help *echo* that in air doth flee, *shrill voices* to *resound*

shrill echoes from the hollow earth.
Shrew Ind.2.46
shrill-voiced suppliant
Rich. II 5.3.118

How *sighs resound*
Pass. Pilg. XII.23

To *wail this loss* of my good name

wise men ne'er sit and *wail their loss*
3 Hen. VI 5.4.13

Conclusions

What are we to make of claims that "nothing in Oxford's canonical verse in any way hints at an affinity with the poetry of William Shakespeare"? Are there truly "glaring mismatches" between the two sources? Is there "anything but a match" between them? Are they "worlds apart"? Elliott and Valenza ask, "How could anyone suppose that the two passages were written by the same person?" (2000, 90). Apparently one discerning scholar out of the ten top-scoring "Golden Ear" testees thought so, and good for him. An ideal study would entail conducting the same type of search using the canons of all other playwrights of the era, and maybe all the poets, too. For now, however, no complete canons are searchable. Individual plays and poems are available, but the task of combing through seems prohibitively tedious. Nevertheless, as a check against the potential charge that the above parallels are commonplace or data-mined, I decided to conduct a preliminary test.

A useful foil for the searches conducted above is the canon of Christopher Marlowe, a prolific Elizabethan playwright and one whom some people actually believe was Shakespeare. I searched each one of Marlowe's seven plays and his epic poem—

Tamburlaine Part 1, Tamburlaine Part 2, Dr. Faustus, Edward the Second, Dido Queen of Carthage (co-written with Thomas Nashe), *The Massacre at Paris, The Jew of Malta* and *Hero and Leander*—for fourteen constructions common to Oxford and Shakespeare that are easy to search: *shame* and *[noun]*; *life* near *lingering*; *[my] good name*; *grief[s]* near *ground*; *voice* near *tongue*; *plaint[s]* near *pierce*; *case* near *woe[ful]*; *help* near *crave*; *earth or air*; *help* [nonproper noun] as a cry; *feed* near *flocks*; *salt-sea*; *shrill* near *voice*; and *wail* near *loss*.

As it turns out, Marlowe gets positive hits on only two of these constructions. There is one instance of *help/crave*: "crave the help of shepherds," from *Hero and Leander*; and there are three instances of *shame and*: "shame and duty," "shame and servitude" and "shame and dishonor," which are from *Tamburlaine Part 1, Tamburlaine Part 2* and *Dr. Faustus*, respectively. Another possible instance in *Tamburlaine Part 2* is "earth and all this airy region." However, I deem it too far from Oxford and Shakespeare's compact "earth or air" to fully qualify.

The paucity of Oxford's paired words in the Marlowe canon is not the only exemplary instance. *Shrill* (twelve times in Shakespeare), *wail* (twenty-four times in Shakespeare) and *salt* (fifty-one times in Shakespeare) fit Oxford's use of these words, but don't show up at all in Marlowe. In Shakespeare's two main narrative poems, *woe* shows up twenty-eight times, *wail* three times and *plaint* once. But there is not a single *plaint, woe* or *wail* in the whole of *Hero and Leander*. Nor do Marlowe's characters ever bewail the loss of their "good names." Even considering that his canon is one-fifth the size of Shakespeare's, this seems a barren result.

Having read all of the plays published during the Elizabethan era, I would predict just as few connections between Oxford's poem and Ben Jonson's or Thomas Heywood's writings. Marlowe, Jonson and Heywood, the next best playwrights of the Elizabethan and Jacobean eras, employ quite different habits of language. Between the ages sixteen and forty-five, Oxford became more proficient in literary composition, and it shows. But so do his roots.

[Reprinted with modification from *The Oxfordian* 14 (2012), 148-55].

A Methodological Afterword

Bryan Wildenthal and Roger Stritmatter

In this Volume I the twenty-one "canonical" Oxford poems have been placed in literary and historical context as the juvenilia of Shakespeare, including annotations revealing many *hundreds* of parallels — of vocabulary, idiom, diction, acoustic pattern, proverb, and literary figure — between them and the works of Shakespeare. William Plumer Fowler's 1986 *Shakespeare Identified in Oxford's Letters* had already, thirty-three years ago, demonstrated the existence of many such congruences between "Shakespeare" and the Earl of Oxford's surviving correspondence. Effectively banned in academia, the book is poorly known even by otherwise expert authorities in early modern studies even if it is becoming an underground classic among the Oxfordians.

A leading objection to the Oxfordian theory is that de Vere was a mediocre or even "bad" poet. It is widely claimed that his few surviving early lyrics fail to show the promise, originality, sophistication, or literary polish of the mature works of Shakespeare. We have tested this theory against the poems themselves, examining the frequency and detailed specificity of their echoes in the later Shakespearean works.

The case for the close similarity of word, phrase, and idea between "Shakespeare" and de Vere's surviving work has been empirically contested at least since Charles Wisner Barrell's 1946 "The Playwright Earl Publishes 'Hamlet's Book,'" which was already documenting in Oxford's preface to *Cardanus Comforte* (E.O. 1, this volume; Volume II, Appendix G) a work "crammed from beginning to end with thought-patterns, words and phrases of the most direct and striking Shakespearean quality" (39). The preface, he later wrote, "gives us . . . the creative credo of the young Shakespeare . . . a truly noble credo, worthy in all essentials of the spirit that animates the Shakespearean masterpieces" ("Proof," 61).

The argument that de Vere's early poetry was "bad" not only ignores the opinions of de Vere's own contemporaries but reflects a lack of familiarity with his critical role in the development of the early Elizabethan lyric voice through such publications as *The Paradise of Dainty Devices* (1576). According to one leading orthodox scholar, Steven May, Oxford was "the earliest titled courtier poet who can be identified in Elizabeth's reign" (1980, 5); he "deserves recognition not only as a poet but as a nobleman with extraordinary intellectual interests and commitments" (8), one recognized in his time for his "lifelong devotion to learning" (8). A generous patron of poets, artists, philosophers, and historians (8-9), as well as a promoter of Castiglione's ideals of sprezzatura in *Courtier*, he remained in close communication with fellow writers, reading their works in draft (9) and contributing detailed and erudite literary notes to such foundational works as Thomas Watson's *Hekatompathia* (1581), the first published volume of English sonnets (Arber 1870). Such unusual generosity must have accounted for much of the oft-criticized "squandering" of Oxford's inherited fortune, since, as May concedes, "with some part of this amount Oxford acquired a splendid reputation for nurture of the arts and sciences" (9).

In fact, a careful study of the two bodies of work turns on its head the superficial argument that de Vere cannot have been Shakespeare *because* he was such a bad poet. In fact, the echoes explored here prove that Shakespeare habitually reverted to imagery, ideas, figurative language, and diction pioneered in de Vere's earlier lyrics. Based on the available evidence, there seem to be only two choices: Either Shakespeare was inordinately fond of, and deeply influenced by these poems, or the same man wrote both in two different phases of his literary development.

Oxford's Early Poetry in Literary History

Since much (if not all) of de Vere's known poetry predates by some years the literary explosion led by Spenser and Shakespeare, his proper place in the history of the English lyric must be assessed by what is otherwise known of the poetry being written in England between 1560 and 1590. From this perspective, Oxford's role as a leading innovator and experimental poet also confirms and contextualizes the abundant praise voiced by his contemporaries about his literary talent.

Steven May, the leading orthodox (Stratfordian) scholar of de Vere's poetry, has set forth in a series of publications (May 1975, 1980, 1991 & 1999, and 2004), a wide range of commentary and bibliographical study of Oxford as a courtier poet. May (1991) praises the "innovation" of de Vere's poems (E.O. 2 to 9) published in *The Paradise of Dainty Devices* (1576). Those lyrics, May agrees, were written at the latest by the early 1570s, when Oxford was "still in his early twenties . . . . De Vere's eight poems in the *Paradise*," May declares, "create a dramatic break with everything known to have been written at the Elizabethan court up to that time" (53).[2] More generally, de Vere's known verse reveals "a competent, fairly experimental poet," that his poems

---

[2] See also on this topic, May 1980, 68-69.

show great variation in style—noting that the sixteen he viewed as most likely de Vere's use "eleven different metrical and stanzaic forms," including a Shakespearean sonnet (E.O. 15)—and that all the poems "are unified and brought to well-defined conclusions" (1980, 13). May notes that Oxford sometimes used "simple" methods to achieve a "sense of design" (13), and then observes:

> More complex is the weaving of a double refrain into the conventional fabric of E.O. 6, while the surprising and unconventional endings of E.O. 7 and 9 show Oxford playing upon the received tradition in imaginative ways. De Vere's poetry . . . did more than just supply his fellow courtiers with pleasingly ornamental trifles. . . . He is [Queen Elizabeth's] first truly prestigious courtier poet. (13-14)

May supplies ample evidence that de Vere's verse "compare[s] favorably with that of his 'drab' age contemporaries; it is, for example, varied in conception and execution in a manner well beyond the relentless plodding of Breton, Turberville, and Churchyard" (1980, 14).[3] By "age contemporaries," May apparently meant de Vere's poetic cohort, not necessarily his age-mates. Although May sometimes disagrees, de Vere appears to have written most of his known poems when he was only in his teens and twenties. Nicholas Breton (1545–1626), George Turberville (*c.* 1540–*ante* 1597), and Thomas Churchyard (*c.* 1520–1604) were, by contrast, all five to thirty years older than de Vere, a youthful prodigy outshining them all.

This favorable assessment of Oxford as an original and highly competent lyric poet is matched in the critical history of his reception before 1920. Alexander B. Grosart, the distinguished and prolific 19th century editor of early modern verse, in 1872 perceived in de Vere's poems the same qualities that had led Elizabethan and Jacobean literary critics William Webbe (1586),[4] George Puttenham (alleged author of *The Arte of English Poesie* (1589)), Francis Meres in *Palladis tamia* (1598),[5] and Henry Peacham (1622)[6] to rank Oxford among the foremost courtier poets. In a

---

[3] See also Goldstein 2016, 47-48.

[4] Webbe (1586): "I may not omitte the deserved commendations of many honourable and noble Lords, and Gentlemen, in her Maiesties Courte, which in the rare devises of Poetry, have been and yet are most excellent skylfull, among whom the right honourable earl of Oxford may challenge himselfe to ye title of *most excellent among the rest*" (9V; our emphasis).

[5] As Meres states (1598): "The best among us for comedy be Edward Earle of Oxford, Maister Rowely . . . Master Edwardes. . .Iohn Lilly, Lodge, Gascoyne, Green, Shakespeare, Thomas Nash, Thomas Heywood, Anthony Mundye our best plotter, Chapman, Porter, Wilson, Hathaway, and Henry Chettle" (283v).

[6] Peacham states (1622):"In the time of our late Queen Elizabeth, which was truly a Golden Age (for such a world of refined wits, and excellent spirits it produced, whose like are hardly to be hoped for, in any succeeding age) above others who honoured poesie with their pennes and practice (to omit her Majesty, who had singular gift

famously mysterious comment half a century before Looney first proposed de Vere in 1920 as the true Shakespeare, Grosart noted: "An unlifted shadow somehow lies across his memory," adding that his known poems "are not without touches of the true Singer and there is an atmosphere of graciousness and culture about them that is grateful" (359).

To Oxford University Professor William J. Courthope in the second (1897) volume of his monumental study, *A History of English Poetry* (312), de Vere "was a great patron of literature, and headed the literary party at Court which promoted the Euphuistic movement. His own verses are distinguished for their wit, and in their terse ingenuity reflect something of the coxcombry which seems to have been a leading feature of his character." Closely and rather curiously paraphrasing Shakespeare's Falstaff (2 *Hen. IV* 1.2.9-10), Courthope added that de Vere "was not only witty in himself, but the cause of wit in others" (313).

Even Sir Sidney Lee, the leading Shakespeare biographer of the late 19th and early 20th centuries (as well as adamant Stratfordian) acknowledged that de Vere was "the best of the courtier poets in the early years of Elizabeth's reign" and "wrote verse of much lyric beauty" ("Vere" 228).

Oxford's reputation as one of the foremost lyrical poets of the Elizabethan age survived into the early 20th century before being challenged by scholars anxious to preserve the reputation of the Stratfordian theory of Shakespeare authorship. In a revealing coincidence, the attack on Oxford's reputation as a poet corresponds historically to his emergence, since 1920, as the preferred alternative author (see, e.g., Shahan & Whalen 251-52; Goldstein 2016, 47; Waugh 82-83). May (1991) affirms that Oxford was "the premier Elizabethan courtier poet" (52) and "the chief innovator due to the range of his subject matter and the variety of its execution. . . . [His] experimentation provided a much broader foundation for the development of lyric poetry at court [than Edward Dyer's]" (54).

Paradise of Dainty Devices Detailed

Although disputed, it has even been suggested that some of de Vere's poetry might have appeared under George Gascoigne's name (compare, e.g., Ward's 1926 and Miller's 1975 editions of *A Hundreth Sundrie Flowres*, Ogburn 513-19, and Kreiler, with Prechter 2010). Whether this argument is correct, it is certainly true to say that controversy, scandal and subterfuge have haunted these poems since their first publication in the most popular anthology of Elizabethan times, *The Paradise of*

---

therein) were Edward Earl of Oxford, the Lord Buckhurst, Henry Lord Paget, our Phoenix the noble sir Phillip Sidney, M. Edward Dier, M. Edmund Spencer, and M. Samuel Daniel, with sundry others whom (together with those yet living, and so well known) not out of Envie but to avoid tediousness I overpasse. Thus much of poetry" (O2r). Interestingly, while prominently featuring Oxford, Peacham fails to list "Shakespeare."

Dainty Devices (1576) (Figure 12). Seven editions were published during the twenty-four year period 1576-1600. Ninety-nine poems appeared in the first edition, with twenty-six added (Delahoyde 84) to subsequent printings.

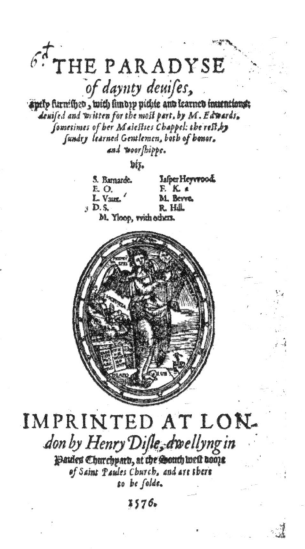

Figure 12. Title page of 1576 first edition of *Paradise of Dainty Devices* showing authors' names and initials, removed from the title page in all subsequent printings.

According to the book's own editorial apparatus, *Paradise* was originally edited by Richard Edwardes, then the master of the Children of the Chapel and of the Queens Revels (Chambers I: 23-61), who died in 1566, ten years before it appeared in print; if that editorial claim is true and complete, then the "E.O." poems it contains were all written before de Vere was sixteen, not twenty-six, an inference supported by the greater maturity and self-confidence of several anonymous poems added to subsequent editions.

Modern scholars sometimes seem mystified by the anthology's popularity, but when one compares the poetry of this volume with what came after one will realize that, aside from Spenser, there was no one else this lyrically inventive on the scene. This, of course, also explains why so many of Oxford's contemporaries lavishly praised his poetry and comedy. They were writing about the young "Shakespeare."

We should not underestimate the impact this anthology had on Elizabethan poetic consciousness or the impact of the first edition's impulse to place the names of nine contributing poets, including Oxford's initials, E.O., on the title page (Figure 12). The volume was widely read, and to a significant number of Elizabethan readers it would have seemed wholly plausible that Oxford himself continued to add more poems to the later editions, including at least some of a daringly autobiographical character (See especially Volume II.E).

Of the nine named or initialed poets, only two were members of the nobility: E.O. and L. Vaux (1509-1556), and of these two, only "E.O." was living at the time of its publication.

As Ruth Loyd Miller has suggested,

> The London literary world was not so large that the initials E.O. would not identify the author of seven poems appearing therein as Elizabeth's exuberant, irrepressible Lord Great Chamberlain of England. For him to publish, or permit his poetry to be published, under his name or identifiable initials, and his name to appear on the title-page of the publication, went against the social canon of his class. By this he was deeply compromised in name and fame. (I: 558-559)

The extent to which Oxford broke with tradition by publishing his association with the muses during his own lifetime (and at only twenty-six years of age), crossing the class divide by exhibiting his literary talent as a commercial product circulated to the general public, is confirmed not only in a body of scholarship on what is called the "stigma of print,"[7] but is already unequivocally stated in the most important of all Elizabethan works of literary criticism, the anonymous *Arte of English Poesie* (1589):

> But in these days. . . poets and poesie are despised, and the name become, of honorable infamous, subject to scorne and derision, and rather a reproach

---

[7] A standard authority on this stigma of print is J.W. Saunders's "The Stigma of Print: A Note on the Social Bases of Tudor Poetry," published in 1951 in the first issue of *Essays in Criticism*. In a more current reappraisal of Saunders's value, Daniel Traister (1990) argues that while the essay appeared many years ago, "it remains a small classic. The passage of time has failed to diminish its significance, while subsequent scholarship has made the issues it raises and its conclusions increasingly worth consideration by scholars in several fields. [Saunders's] footnotes, in fact, contain the seeds of important articles and books that, years after his work appeared, were to elaborate points that Saunders had tossed off almost casually in a few sentences" (2).

than a prayse . . . who so . . . shewes himselfe excellent in it, they call him in disdayne a phantasticall: and a light headed. . . . Now also of such among the Nobilitie or gentrie as be very well seene in many laudable sciences, and especially in making of Poesie, it is so come to passe that they have no courage to write, and if they have, yet are they loath to be knowen of their skill. So as I know very many notable Gentlemen in the Court that have written commendably, and suppressed it agayne, or els suffered it to be published without their owne names to it: as if it were a discredit for a Gentleman to seeme learned, and to shew himselfe amorous of any good Arte. (I.8, Arber 33-34, 37)

. . . And in Her Majesty's time that now is are sprong up another crew of Courtly makers Noble men and Gentlemen of her Maiesties owne servants, who have written excellently well as it would appeare if their doings could be found out and made publicke with the rest, of which number is first that noble Gentleman Edward Earle of Oxford. . . . That for Tragedie, the Lord of Buckhurst, and Maister Edward Ferrys for such doings as I have sene of theirs do deserve the hyest price: Th' Earle of Oxford and Maister Edwardes of her Maiesties Chappell for Comedy and Enterlude . . . (I.31, Arber 75-77)

Their public exposure of the inner emotional life of their powerful young author, a young man born to the life of the manor and the aristocratic sports of hawking and hunting as well as being heir to the most coveted ceremonial title in early modern England — The Lord Great Chamberlain of England — may have stimulated sales but also provoked political and cultural backlash. As W.W. Greg recounts it, he was an impecunious bad boy poet, an Elizabethan Lord Byron on steroids. De Vere was also a comic playwright, patron of the theatre, and aficionado of Italian and French style in both fashion and poetics, a man who marched to the beat of a drummer most could not hear.

These poems, subscribed with the minimalist "E.O." cryptonym, sent ripples of consternation through the London intelligentsia of the 1570s. As Ruth Loyd Miller summarizes the fallout visible in the bibliographical record:

> The 1573 publication of Thomas Bedingfield's translation of *Cardanus Comforte* with a flourish of individual endorsement advertising Oxford's patronage with the unprecedented statement that the book was published "by the commaundement of the right Honourable Earl of Oxenforde" constituted a daring departure from Elizabethan social norms. In Court circles it unquestionably caused a lifting of eyebrows and a repetition of such phrases as *Phantasticall, light headed,* and *what next*? (I: 559)

Such adjectives followed the earl of Oxford throughout his lifetime, and undoubtedly account for a large portion of the angst expressed in *Shake-speares Sonnets*, where the speaker of several (e.g., 71-76, 102), admits his shameful transgression of Elizabethan societal norms regarding aristocratic publishing and — much worse —

slumming in the public theatres, a social milieu regarded by prominent Puritan critics as the spawning ground of Satan. As Miller continues:

> After the 1576 edition of *Paradise*, which carried his initials on the title-page, and signed to seven poems, the literary nobleman never again expressed his convictions so openly regarding the creative worker's manifest duty to guide public thought into those channels that gave the Shakespearean Age its cosmopolitan dynamics. All the names and initials, except that of Edwardes, which had appeared on the title-page of the 1573 edition, were removed from the title-pages of all subsequent editions from 1578 through 1600, and discreetly inserted on the verso of the title-page. (I: 559)

Oxford's Known Poetry as Juvenilia

De Vere probably wrote most of his extant acknowledged poetry when he was still in his teens and twenties, as John Shahan & Richard Whalen (2009), among many others, have argued.[8] May (2004) professes to dispute that proposition, concluding that "the authentic canon of de Vere's poetry is a great embarrassment to the [Oxfordian] movement because it so manifestly contradicts the claims of Looney and his followers that the Earl's verse in any way resembles the poetry of William Shakespeare. The chasm between the two poets is immense" (232). Yet May (1991) had also already conceded that the "poems date primarily from [de Vere's] heyday at court during the 1570s" (270), when he was in his twenties.

Oxford actually established a presence at court while still a teenager during the 1560s. He became a ward of Queen Elizabeth's most powerful advisor, Sir William Cecil (later Lord Burghley), in 1562 at the age of twelve. See E.O. 4 (and Appendix to that poem), discussing reasons to think de Vere may have written it in 1563 at the age of thirteen. Eight de Vere poems (E.O. 2 to 9) were first published in 1576 in *The Paradise of Dainty Devices*. But since Richard Edwards, who apparently compiled manuscripts on which that volume was based, had died in 1566, all the poems in the 1576 edition may well date from de Vere's adolescence (as we shall see, there is evidence that de Vere added some later poems to subsequent editions of the popular poetry anthology).

May (1991) has conceded that "[t]here is little reason" to date any of de Vere's acknowledged verse "later than the 1580s," when he was still only in his thirties (270). Indeed, May's 1991 book, while referring glancingly to de Vere throughout, discusses him most extensively in chapter 2, "Courtier Verse Before Sidney" (41-68), covering the period only up to the late 1570s and dating de Vere's composition of his most "innovati[ve]" known verses to the early 1570s (53). May has also agreed that de Vere's known poems must be only a fragment of his corpus (1980, 12; 1991, 32).

---

[8] E.g., Looney 1920, 125.

These points are in considerable tension with his later claim (2004) that de Vere's poetry "rules out" a Shakespearean connection (221).

The Oxfordian view, generally speaking, is that de Vere probably wrote or revised the works credited to "Shakespeare" about a full generation later, during his forties and fifties. No work was published under the "Shakespeare" name until 1593 (*Venus and Adonis*), the year Oxford turned forty-three. The first canonical Shakespeare plays, or possible early versions of them, were not published, even anonymously, until the early 1590s (e.g., *The Troublesome Reign of King John* in 1591, and *Titus Andronicus*, *The Taming of a Shrew*, and *The First Part of the Contention Betwixt the Two Famous Houses of York and Lancaster*, later known as *2 Henry VI*, in 1594). No canonical play is known to have been published under Shakespeare's name until 1598, when Oxford turned forty-eight.

As discussed by Cheryl Eagan-Donovan (2017), scholars studying many great poets—Walt Whitman, Arthur Rimbaud, and Sylvia Plath, to name just a few diverse examples—have noted how dramatically they may change and develop their voices over time. Not just the extent, but the pace and timing of development, may vary greatly. Some poets blossom from immaturity to mastery while still precociously young (Rimbaud is a famous example), and some (like Whitman) much later, in middle age.

The first edition of Whitman's *Leaves of Grass* (1855), a radical break with anything he (or anyone) had written before, appeared when he was thirty-six. The expanded 1860 edition, first presenting some of his greatest work, came out when he was forty-one. The year Oxford turned forty-one, interestingly, was 1591—the very year the first version of *King John* was published (albeit anonymously) and just two years before works published under the name "Shakespeare" started appearing. A leading expert on Whitman notes that the great American poet's "[b]iographers and critics have unanimously accounted his early poetry [published into his early thirties] . . . very bland stuff, indistinguishable from the countless chunks of poetasting produced to satisfy . . . [newspaper] weeklies and dailies. . . . These [early] poems never rise above the arch or maudlin" (Schmidgall 4).

Allowing for these two key likelihoods — that de Vere's known poetry is only a fragment of his corpus and is merely part of his juvenilia — goes far to bridge the disjunction perceived by May and other orthodox critics. De Vere had more than sufficient time to grow and develop as a writer—in effect, *to become* Shakespeare—between his mid-twenties and his mid-forties (see, e.g., Ogburn 390-97).

Selection of Poems

This study builds upon and amplifies the pioneering studies of de Vere's poetry published by J. Thomas Looney in 1920 (121-71) and 1921 and Joseph Sobran in his 1997 *Alias Shakespeare* (231-70), both of which we gratefully acknowledge. We also supplement and corroborate William Plumer Fowler's remarkable 1986 book, *Shakespeare Revealed in Oxford's Letters*, which followed a similar methodology to reach similar conclusions based on de Vere's surviving epistolary prose.[9] Long before Fowler, moreover, Charles Wisner Barrell (October 1946) had already gathered impressive evidence that "Shakespeare's thought and imagery dominate Oxford's statement of creative principles" in his preface to Thomas Bedingfield's *Cardanus Comforte* (1573) — a book termed by orthodox scholar Hardin Craig "Hamlet's Book."

Previous editors of de Vere's poetry have disagreed over the size and variety of his literary corpus. For example, the editions compiled by Grosart (1872), Looney (1921), May (1975, 1980, and 1991), Sobran (1997), Chiljan (1998), Brazil & Flues (2002), and Kreiler (2013) (in German), have varied markedly in the number of poems they attribute to him. Grosart included twenty-two poems and Looney forty-seven, but both Grosart and Looney were unaware of E.O. 12, 13, 18, and 20 included here. Chiljan included twenty-six poems, Brazil & Flues twenty-five, May only sixteen (plus four "possibly" by Oxford, for a total of twenty—rejecting or failing to consider many identified by Looney but including four he omitted), and Sobran twenty (following May's selection and order).

If May has sometimes shown excessive zeal in questioning de Vere's authorship of some poems, such as the "echo" verses (E.O. 17), apparently written about Oxford's mistress, Anne Vavasour, his approach to the problem of the attribution of Oxford's poetry has generally been thoughtful and systematic. In the case of E.O. 17, he details several strong reasons (convincing in our view) to credit de Vere (1980, 79-81). May deserves particular notice for his important study (1975) detailing the evidence for de Vere's authorship of Poem E.O. 18 ("My Mind To Me a Kingdom Is"), one of the best-loved lyrics in the English language.

One reason for the larger size of Looney's edition was that he became the first to suggest that de Vere's poems include not only those appearing over the initials "E.O." or attributed to him in MS, but also a number of other poems published under various pretexts or pseudonyms. The "E.O." poems were mostly published in *The Paradise of Dainty Devices* (1576; Rollins ed. 1927) or attributed to de Vere in manuscript.

Evaluating the Poetic Parallels

May (2004) criticizes Oxfordians for detecting Shakespearean echoes in a few poems mistakenly (in his view) credited to de Vere (222, 224-25). More interestingly, poems of which Looney was unaware in the 1920s but that May now assigns to Oxford (E. O. 12, 13, 18-18b, and 20) are notably rich in parallels to Shakespeare. (May identified

---

[9] See also, e.g., Sobran 271-86, also discussing de Vere's letters, as well as Gary Goldstein's 2016 and 2017 overviews of de Vere's poetic and epistolary parallels to the Shakespeare canon, Robert Prechter's 2012 analysis of the parallels to E.O. 4, the surveys of various poetic parallels by Robert Sean Brazil & Barboura Flues in 2002, Cheryl Eagan-Donovan in 2017, and Bonner Miller Cutting's 2017 analysis of de Vere's letters petitioning for control of the tin monopoly.

E.O. 12 and 13 as "probably" written by de Vere, and E.O. 18 and 20 as "possibly" so.) Remarkably, these poems account for many of the most telling parallels identified in this study. Looney's perception of telling similarities between de Vere's known writing and that of "Shakespeare" has thus been corroborated by poems *identified by May, which Looney did not even consider*. This is only one of several intriguing cases in which evidence coming to light since Looney's pioneering work has strengthened his Oxfordian hypothesis.

Considering all these factors, no special probative weight should be attached to any particular parallel or parallels in isolation from the larger fact pattern. Some may be part of the common idiom of Elizabethan poetics while others clearly have a more idiosyncratic value (as identified in many particular cases through the control of running *EEBO* searches to determine frequency of particular words or phrases in the entire data base of early modern English books); what ultimately matters is the large quantity of different types of parallelisms, including use of particular rhetorical figures when combined with parallel syntax or vocabulary. Nor should these parallels be considered exhaustive. Further connections certainly await discovery through more careful and refined methodologies, merging linguistics and literary study.

May's only actual analysis of any specific Oxford-Shakespeare parallels appears in a short section of his 2004 article (223-29), where he effectively accuses Oxfordians of cherry-picking similarities between the two bodies of writing (222-23). Alas, *medice cura te ipsum*. Ironically, May limits his own analysis to only a handful of parallels and does not fully explore even those, missing the vastly greater number he could have addressed had he consulted Sobran's extensive 1997 study, which he either overlooked or ignored, or even taken seriously the 1986 findings of Fowler's book on the de Vere letters.

There would seem to be some tension, moreover, between May's (1991) classification of de Vere as a poet who, in *The Paradise of Dainty Devices* (1576), "create[d] a dramatic break with everything known to have been written at the Elizabethan court up to that time" (53) and his later claim (2004) that "Oxford's verse [was]. . . *without distinction* [in] the mid[16th]-century tradition of Tudor poetry" (223; our emphasis), or that "Oxford has no more claim to be the true author of Shakespeare's works than any other of the hundreds of poets" writing during that period (232). By 2004, writing for the first time more explicitly about authorship, May even cites the formerly "drab" Turberville (1980, 14) as one of many poets now allegedly *indistinguishable* from de Vere as a supplier of various motifs, words, and styles also appearing in the Shakespeare canon, which May now argues were "ubiquitous" (2004, 227) in Elizabethan verse, asserting further that "Oxford's verse, in short, lacks any unique features of style, theme or subject to connect it to Shakespeare's poetry" (225).

May's 2004 article, written for a University of Tennessee symposium on authorship, lavishes attention on Looney's identification of a pattern of Oxford-Shakespeare parallels involving the "haggard" hawk (falconry) motif (E.O. 9 and 19), as applied to willful women. To May, this pattern, first explored by Looney, has become an irrelevant "commonplace in Elizabethan verse" (224).

The empirical data fails to substantiate May's contention. An *EEBO* search (1473-1900) returns only nine hits in eight sources for the term "haggard hawk," four of them to works by George Turberville, including three in the poems attached to Turberville's *The booke of falconrie or havvking* (1575 & 1611). To support his characterization of the motif as "commonplace," May (2004, 223-249) cites six poems by others, though one (by John Grange, 244) does not refer to haggards at all, only the more generic term "Unmanned hawks." One point of Looney's argument, as May himself acknowledged, was the distinctiveness of the word "haggard," a noun which, as used here, refers to a wild adult hawk, typically female, caught for training (*OED* 6: 1013).

An *EEBO* search with an earlier time frame (1473-1600) returns only four hits in three sources for the term "haggard hawk," including Oxford in *Paradise of Dainty Devices* and two works of Turberville, with whom de Vere, as May himself acknowledged, was closely associated over a significant period of time, suggesting not only that the phrase was far from a commonplace but that Turberville, de Vere, and "Shakespeare" belonged, with respect at least to this idiomatic element, to a shared linguistic network with only a limited number of other participants.

Properly viewed in context, such data suggest that the "haggard hawk" parallels between de Vere and Shakespeare are actually much more significant than May insists; we believe he was profoundly mistaken to dismiss them as irrelevant coincidences (See details in notes to E.O. 9 and 19). How many other proposed Shakespeare "candidates" can pass even this elementary test? None. There is no evidence that any of them associated the motif of the behavior of the "haggard hawk" with human emotions or situations, as both de Vere and "Shakespeare" do. May fundamentally misses the broader relevant points, already stressed by Looney in 1920: first, the sheer *quantity* of all the interlocking parallels between Oxford's known poetry and the Shakespeare canon; second, the sometimes unusual or even idiomatic *quality* of many specific parallels; and, finally and most importantly, the overall *combination* of quantity *and* quality in the observed intertextuality.

The "haggard hawk" echoes alone reveal that de Vere, in three separate references in two of these twenty-one surviving early poems — and Shakespeare, in at least six separate references in five very different plays: *The Taming of the Shrew*, *Much Ado About Nothing*, *Othello*, *Twelfth Night*, and *Romeo and Juliet* (seven references in six plays if we count *Edward III*) — share a fascination with the aristocratic sport of falconry and its terms of art as metaphors for human behavior. The three de Vere references use the haggard mainly to illustrate the wooing and "taming" of strong-willed women (though with some gender ambiguity in E.O. 9). So do the four references in *Shrew*, *Much Ado*, and *Othello*. Perhaps reflecting some degree of personal and artistic growth as compared to the time when de Vere wrote his youthful lyrics, Shakespeare also flips the genders — in *Romeo and Juliet*, *Twelfth*

Night, and *Edward III*—to use falconry in the context of describing or luring a male, with Juliet imagined as a female falconer.

Do the "drab" George Turberville et al. offer anything remotely comparable? We invite readers to compare for themselves the five references to haggards by other poets as cited by May. While his first example (244), attributed to Turberville ("wild . . . As though you were a haggard hawk . . . Live like a haggard . . . and for no luring care"), bears a clear comparison to language of E.O. 19, the passage by itself falls short of the strong parallels between Shakespeare (especially *The Taming of the Shrew*) and E.O. 9 and 19 (especially taken together) with regard to *taming* a haggard as a paternalistic metaphor for winning over a female lover.[10]

If a comparable set of falconry parallels exists between Shakespeare and any other early modern English writer, we are not aware of it and May has not pointed it out.

A more interesting parallel to both de Vere and Shakespeare's usage (although the word "haggard" does not appear in it) is the song lyric printed as the conclusion to Clement Robinson's 1584 *Handful of Pleasant Delights*, "The Louer compareth himself to the painful Falconer. To the tune, 'I loued her ouer well'" (Rollins 71-72). This song, written in forty alternating lines of four and three iambic feet, features in swift succession several key words in Shakespeare's lexicon of hawking: *bell-falcon, range, lure, stoop, gorged*. But as the poem is anonymous, the poem's usefulness in defending May's core idea of the "commonplace" character of Shakespeare's hawking passages is quite limited.

May further attempts (2004, 224, 245-47) to discredit the Shakespearean parallels to the "damask rose" references in Poems E.O. 14 (line 26) and E.O. 17 (line 6). Those echoes, like the haggard hawk parallels, were first explored by Looney (1920, 141-45). Unquestionably the pervasive popularity of *white* (or lily) and *red* (or rosy) imagery in Elizabethan poetry (a trend reinforced by the heraldic imagery of the so-called "war of the roses," in which the white rose symbolized the house of York and the red that of Lancaster) to describe facial beauty limits the conclusions that can be drawn from such examples in isolation from other, more tellingly idiosyncratic comparisons. As May shows (and as can be confirmed on *EEBO* where, in contrast to the "haggard

---

[10] Another example cited by May (245), by George Whetstone ("The haggard then that checked of late, Will stoop to fancy's lure"), connects rather weakly to the taming theme, but more like crass bribery, as Whetstone describes his swain raiding his "novice purse" to woo his lady with "trifling chain[s,] A caul of gold and other knacks." May's three other examples are weaker still by comparison (one might even say "drab"). They do not connect to the theme or language of taming or the language of haggards ranging wild. Compare, for example, E.O. 19 (line 9) and its parallels to *Much Ado About Nothing* and *Othello*, with May (2004, 245, 249) (George Gascoigne, "haggard hawks mislike an empty hand"; John God, "her body['s] . . . haggard wonts"; and again Turberville, "a haggard kite").

hawk," a search returns thirty-seven hits in twenty-six records before 1600), the white and red damask rose was a popular Elizabethan motif.

Yet these "damask rose" echoes are still very significant considering how they fit into the broader patterns of intertextuality linking these poems to Shakespeare. As Looney noted (141-42), E.O. 14 "is the only poem in the De Vere collection in which the writer lingers tenderly and seriously on the beauty of a woman's face; and . . . his whole treatment turns upon the contrast of white and red, the lily and the damask rose." Looney observed the "striking fact . . . that the only poem of 'Shakespeare's' [*Lucrece*] in which he dwells at length in the same spirit upon the same theme is dominated by the identical contrast" (142).

No similarly strong parallels are suggested in any of the examples by other poets (such as Turberville), regarding white and red facial imagery as cited by May (246-47). Looney correctly concluded (145) that E.O. 14 and *Lucrece*, by contrast, "form an excellent example." They do indeed resonate tellingly. (See Poems E.O. 14 and E.O. 17 for full details on these and other parallels.)

For obvious reasons, May misunderstands and exaggerates Looney's reliance on the damask rose parallels. Looney did briefly discuss them, but he then immediately and very carefully "emphasize[d] a principle which is vital to the argument . . . namely, that *we are not here primarily concerned with the mere piling up of parallel passages*. What matters most of all is mental correspondence and the general unity of treatment which follows from it" (145; emphasis added).

It is possible, to be sure, that Looney may have been overly impressed with some structural or stylistic similarities he noticed between the de Vere poems and the Shakespeare canon. Though a diligent schoolteacher and rigorous scholar, he did not pretend to have deep expert knowledge of Elizabethan poetry and was, moreover, writing before modern bibliographical tools and practices were well developed. However, conceding May's reasonable premise that some structural or stylistic echoes were widespread in the poetry of the time (1980, 11-12; 2004, 223-30) cannot in itself refute Looney's conclusion; far less can it negate the stunning array of parallels summarized and explored here. Looney barely scratched the surface. May focuses briefly on a few leaves on a few trees, but fails to see the forest.

May and other orthodox critics cannot have it both ways. In one view, the echoes between de Vere and Shakespeare are allegedly *irrelevant, coincidental, and meaningless*, indicative of nothing more than a shared set of Elizabethan literary idioms common to the writers of the day. In the other, as May now suggests, the echoes are not meaningless at all, but *highly original and distinctive* enough to support a charge of Shakespeare's plagiarism of de Vere's poems. The new suggestion seems to be that Shakespeare — star of poets, soul of the age! — was influenced to a remarkable and unusual degree by the early verse of a supposedly mediocre courtier poet that was circulating up to a full generation before Shakspere of Stratford arrived in London. In fact, May now suggests, Shakespeare may have been so impressed by young de Vere's work that he might have consciously and extensively "plagiarized" it![11] Who knew?! We suggest it is more likely they were the same person at different stages of life and artistic development.

To be sure, it is common ground that the author Shakespeare (whoever he was) borrowed plots and ideas from many others. Doubtless he borrowed language too, as well as structural and stylistic ideas. He was certainly influenced by other writers, just as he influenced many. In some cases, as with Christopher Marlowe, the influence seems to be important and to have gone both ways. The lines between literary influence, borrowing, and outright theft (plagiarism) may often be blurred. Writers in cultures and times different from our own did not necessarily have the same attitudes toward all this that we have today.

In any event, May's latest suggestion seems to be that de Vere was, at the very least, a remarkably influential and important Elizabethan poet. This suggestion, that Shakespeare plagiarized de Vere, necessarily focuses even more attention on the compelling and extensive parallels between de Vere's early work and the Shakespeare canon. We look forward to May and other orthodox scholars pursuing this fascinating suggestion.

Given his record of fairness,[12] it is ironic how greatly May has overstated the extent to which the Oxfordian theory—even as originally framed by Looney, much less in its much more fully developed present form—*relies upon* the poetic parallels explored here. On the contrary, such comparisons exist within a much wider and more comprehensive assemblage of evidence, perhaps most cogently symbolized in James Warren's *Index to Oxfordian Publications* (4th ed. 2017), which documents more than 350 books and over 9,000 articles contributing to the Oxfordian synthesis, with publications of Oxfordian books and articles expanding outward into the cybersphere like sparks from an intergalactic explosion in 1920.

While one may therefore reasonably debate whether the many Shakespearean echoes of de Vere's poems conclusively *in themselves* demonstrate de Vere as Shakespeare, in combination with all the other proofs established in books by Looney, Ogburn,

---

[11] In personal communication to Goldstein (cited in Goldstein 2017), May writes: "Second, if any of the verbal parallels with Oxford's poems are, in fact, unusual, weren't most of them in print and available for Shakespeare to plagiarize?" (23).

[12] Few of May's colleagues are aware, as May himself acknowledges, that Oxfordians have "made worthwhile contributions to our understanding of the Elizabethan age" (1980, 10). In the same early study, May noted that other orthodox scholars "tend to belittle . . . the Oxfordian movement, yet its leaders are educated men and women . . . sincerely interested in Renaissance English culture. Their arguments for De Vere are entertained as at least plausible by hosts of intellectually respectable persons" (10).

and Anderson (to name only three of the most well known and influential), they are, at the very least, highly suggestive of common authorship. In combination with the imposing array of biographical, literary and linguistic evidence supporting the Oxfordian theory, the echoes form an important part—but one part only—of that larger fact pattern. As Looney observed, "first one thing and then another fits into its place with all the unity of an elaborate mosaic the moment we introduce Edward de Vere as the author of the Shakespeare writings. Is this too the merest coincidence?" (1920, 160).

Writing seven years before May's 2004 article, Sobran made the case in terms that neither May nor any orthodox writer has yet rebutted. (May missed an excellent opportunity in 2004.) Sobran fully grasped the argument briefly suggested by May in 1980 (11-12) and elaborated in 2004 (223-30): that the Oxford-Shakespeare parallels might allegedly "be assigned to coincidence and poetic convention" (Sobran 232).

But May's 2004 article failed even to cite Sobran's forty-page comparative analysis of de Vere's poems (1997, 231-70)—the central issue addressed by May's article—even though Sobran's study was by far the most extensive of its kind (until now) and was issued by a major mainstream publisher (Simon & Schuster's Free Press) at a time when Sobran was a nationally known political columnist. Ironically, he graciously credited May himself with unspecified assistance in the preparation of the book: "I have yet to ask a favor . . . that [May] has failed to grant instantly . . ."(301).

Perhaps May was unaware of Sobran's book, as suggested by May's wildly inaccurate statement that "[a]fter the publication of my edition of Oxford's verse in 1980, reference to the Earl's poetry all but disappeared from Oxfordian polemic" (2004, 232). In any event, May's 2004 article followed the all-too-common orthodox tendency in failing even to respond to important skeptical scholarship. As Sobran summed up in 1997:

> [S]ome critics rank [de Vere's poems] as brilliant and accomplished. . .
> [though] few would call them works of genius. How, then, can they be
> Shakespeare's? Perhaps because they are early poems. . . . We must bear in
> mind that whoever wrote *The Tempest* was at one time capable of writing
> *Titus Andronicus*, a play so inferior to Shakespeare's mature work that its
> authorship was formerly in doubt. (231-32)

The crucial question is whether the parallels between Oxford's twenty-one established poems and Shakespeare's work are more numerous and detailed than can reasonably be assigned to coincidence and poetic convention. The poems exhibit hundreds of intriguing resemblances to Shakespeare's phrasings, far too many to be dismissed as insignificant. The kinship is evident in their themes, turns of phrase, word associations, images, rhetorical figures, various other mannerisms, and, above all, general diction.

Not all of the parallels, obviously, are of the same order of significance as evidence. Some are trivial or conventional; others are highly distinctive and idiosyncratic. But, while we may disagree over the weight that should be attached to particular parallels, the sheer number and variety of them contradicts May's assumptions and disqualifies his more dogmatic conclusions.

"Overhearing" the Songs

Preparing this book has been a gratifying experience. Much of the contents consist of song lyrics, not poems designed to stand on their own. It might be said of these and their author, as MacCracken, Pierce and Durham have said of Shakespeare: "One of the most attractive features in his lyrics is their spontaneous ease of expression. They seem to lilt into music of their own accord, as naturally as birds sing. . . . The author, though primarily a dramatist, could be among the greatest of song writers when he tried" (71).

Harold Bloom observes that Shakespeare "grew by overhearing himself," rewriting what he had already written to make it better. The footnotes to the later poems continue the process of documenting the evolution of Shakespeare's mind through the revisions and reconfigurations he wrought on the discovered ingredients of the earlier ones. They point backward to their common idioms and ideas as seen in the "canonical" Oxford poems and forward into the mature works of the "Shakespeare" period.

The poems are the product of a literary imagination that was compulsively experimental in its expression; together they exhibit an impressive range of rhetorical constructions, yet suggest a highly dynamic and plastic unity. Bloom's "overhearing" came most readily through the author's enlarging capacity for inhabiting the situational world of the plays, writing parts for unique characters of his own invention, engaging a level of polyvocality that lyric poetry, no matter how accomplished, cannot supply. But what the lyric poem lacks Oxford, Ignoto and Shepherd Tony make up for it by their inventiveness in creating new dramaturgical opportunities for polyvocality and new modes of authorial self-reflexivity in poetry.

Motifs such as the echo (E.O. 17) or genres like pastoral dialogues ("Phillidaes Love call to her Coridon, and his replying" or "The Shepheard's Description of Love"), or even the various personae in such poems as "The Nimph's Reply to the Shepherd" or the distinctively dialogical character of the Lyly songs, which operatically disperse their lines to several singers, all testify to an underlying impulse to break through the barriers of the lyric tradition toward the operatic drama, anticipating such forms as those found in the mature *As You Like It* in such songs as Jaques' "Under the Greenwood Tree" or "Blow, blow, thou Winter Wind."

But whether thought of as poems or songs, the works are self-aware, rhythmically dynamic, erudite and musical, as well as guided by a unique brand of literary *sprezzatura*. In them we overhear the literary foreground of the great works that were still to come when these poems were being written in the 1570s and 1580s. They serve as a conduit between "Shakespeare" and the rest of the Elizabethan and ancient world. Much of what "Shakespeare" did better, E.O. , Shepherd Tony or Ignoto did first, and the raw elements of phrases, figures and idioms that form the substructure of Shakespeare's compositional method are already evident in these poems.

Golding's observation of the young de Vere's fascination with "the Histories of auncient tyme, and thinges done long ago" is deeply manifested in these poems, which carry the deep imprint of the past in them. As already noticed, the writer is on familiar terms not only with Ovid, but also Seneca. The mysticism of "My Mind to Me a Kingdom Is" (E.O. 18) draws on the Senecan principle that "it is a vast kingdom, to be able to cope without a kingdom" (*Thyestes* 470).

But de Vere was evidently alert to world-transforming ideas of his own generation; Montaigne's rediscovery of subjectivity impressed on him the concept of self-reflexivity, how the soul "can be turned upon itself; it can keep itself company" (Frame 177). The early and productive influence of Montaigne's "Of Solitude" shows in E.O. 2, with prominent echoes in *R&J* given in the commentary to that poem. Here in Montaigne Oxford encountered, perhaps for the first time, the ancient proverb of the recondite Latin satirist Persius: "Your knowledge is nothing unless another knows it." Elsewhere, however, the speaker adopts a posture of Senecan dissimulation (cf., *Thyestes* 491-511, *Phaedra* 915-22), confessing "I am not as I seem to be," a declaration with far-reaching echoes in Shakespeare (see E.O. 5).

While some poems individually may seem uninspired or formulaic at first glance, the overall production, the manifestation of "a mind reflecting on ages past," is exponentially more than the sum of its parts. The variety of the forms, strategies, and themes, and states of being of the "canonical" poems is truly impressive. In E.O. 5 the Earl even pictures himself as a defeated Hannibal, so it is perhaps not surprising that one of Queen Elizabeth's nicknames for him was her "Turk," or that he would go on to write *Othello*.

Perhaps most intriguing of all these poems, at least from a purely literary point of view, is Oxford's 1572 prefatory poem to *Cardanus Comforte* (E.O. 1), from which this book takes its title. Although written according to a strict formula of mid-line caesura that would already sound old-fashioned by 1602, it is not only a remarkably astute sociological analysis of class injustice, it is also among the earliest explicit articulations of reader-response theory in English.

As Looney always stressed, it is only through the accumulation of evidence that we approach verification of a theory. As quoted earlier, Looney advocated the principle of holistic multidisciplinary inquiry on which we also rely to guide this entire edition of de Vere's early poems and their echoes in the Shakespeare canon. The density and quality of so many parallels of thought, diction, and poetic idiom between these poems and the later works of "Shakespeare" suggest that the former constitute an essential part of Shakespeare's literary juvenilia. We invite you, dear readers, to venture onward and explore or rediscover these poems for yourselves, and to enjoy them as we have on their own merits as well for what they can tell us about the development of Shakespeare's creative genius.

Appendix A: *EEBO* hits — Canonical Oxford Poems of Vol. I

Phrase	Occurrences in *EEBO* (1473-1623)
I am not glad	2 hits/2 records
rolling restless stone	2 hits/2 records (both Sh.)
roll the restless stone (as in E.O. 6)	5/5, including E.O. 6 (includes variant spellings and forms *rowle, rowles,* and *rolleth*).
kingdom near *cottage* near *grave*	8 hits/8 records (all to E.O. 16)
stricken deer	None (only E.O. 9 and *Ham.*)
winged with desire	2 hits/2 records (Shakespeare & E.O.)
I force not near *a straw*	2 hits/2 records (both to *Lucrece*, none to E.O. 18)
did print	4 hits/4 records
sails and *love*	4 hits/4 records
pipes of corn	5 hits/5 records
come by fits	6 hits/6 records (includes variant forms *comes, commeth,* and *cometh*)

when wert thou	9 hits/8 records
hound near *horn*	8 hits/8 records
Thousand cupids	13 hits/8 records
taught near *thy tongue*	9 hits/9 records
pluck near *weed*	11 hits/9 records
quiet breast	10 hits/10 records
I muse why	12 hits/11 records
her soft hand	12 hits/12 records
each passion	13 hits/12 records
When I am alone	14 hits/14 records
who taught thee	14 hits/14 records
Thy mortal foe	16 hits/14 records
blushing near *morning*	16 hits/14 records
I am abused	15 hits/15 records
these beauties	19 hits/17 records
make me die	30 hits/19 records
speedy haste	22 hits/20 records
happy star	24 hits/20 records
carnation near *colour*	30 hits/24 records
Thy nurse	28 hits/25 records
gentle hearts	28 hits/27 records
eyes do see	30 hits/27 records
pluck near *weeds*	35 hits/30 records

Appendix B: Echoes of Oxford's "Were I a King"

These three poems appear in various MS sources as imitations of E.O. 16. Although their authorship is uncertain, and at least one has been attributed to Oxford as well as to Sir Phillip Sidney, they attest to the wide currency and influence of Oxford's six-line epigram. The poems are numbered following the presentation in Hannah (147-48), where E.O. 16 is given as I.

II. Answered thus by Sr. P. S.

Wert thou a king, yet not command content,
Sith empire none thy mind could yet suffice
Wert thou obscure, still cares would thee torment;
But wert thou dead, all care and sorrow dies.
An easy choice, of these three which to crave;
A kingdom or a cottage, or a grave.

Although attributed to Sidney in Chetham MS 8012, which prints all four epigrams that echo "Were I a King," this is first published by Horace Walpole in 1798 with distinction as also by de Vere:

> The two following POEMS by *EDWARD VERE*, Earl of OXFORD, mentioned in page 329, were communicated to me from an ancient MS. Miscellany, and I believe have never been printed.
>
> WEARE I a kinge, I mighte comande contente,
>   Weare I obscure, unknowne should be my cares,
> And weare I deade, noe thoughtes could me torment,
>   Nor woordes, nor wronges, nor love, nor hate, nor feares.
>   A doubtfull choyse for me of three things one to crave,
>   A kingdome, or a cottage, or a grave.
>
> Wearte thou a kinge, yet not comande contente,
>   Wher empire none thy mind could yet suffice,
> Wearte thou obscure, still cares would thee torment,
>   But wearte thou dead, all care and sorrow dyes.
>   An easy choyse of three things one to crave,
>   Noe kingdome, nor a cottage, but a grave.
>
>   VERE, finis.

(Walpole, Vol. 1:551)

III. Another, of Another Mind

A king? Oh, boon for my aspiring minds!
A cottage makes a country swad[13] rejoice
And as for death, I like him in his kind.
But God forbid that he should be my choice!
A kingdom or a cottage or a grave –
Nor last, nor next, but first and best I crave;
The rest I can whenas I list enjoy,
Till then salute me thus, – Vive le Roy!

F.M.

IV. Another, of Another Mind

The greatest kings do least command content
The greatest cares to still attend a crown;
A grave all happy fortunes doth prevent,
Making the noble equal with the clown:
A quiet country life to leave I crave;
A cottage, then: no kingdom, nor a grave.

---

[13] Country clown.

Appendix C: Disputed Poems from *Astrophel and Stella* (1591) and *England's Parnassus* (1593)

To Thomas Nashe's 1591 2nd edition of Sir Phillip Sidney's posthumously published *Astrophel and Stella* as printed by John Charlewood for Thomas Newman have been added at the end a group of poems that do not appear in the text as printed in the 1590 first edition printed by John Windet for the competing publisher William Ponsonbie. Gwinne Matthew (1558?-1627) and Fulke Greville, Lord Brook (1554-1627) are listed by *EEBO* as parties of interest in the first edition, just as Nashe and Samuel Daniel are for the Newman edition.

 While it was subsequently attributed to Fulke Greville in his *Works* (1633), "Faction that ever dwells in Court" (179-80), had already been published in 1591 with the seemingly definitive subscription "*Finis* E.O." The fact that it is the edition associated with Nashe, and not that associated with Greville, immediately raises a doubt as to Greville's own credibility. Interestingly, Greville was a staunch adherent to the Sidney faction at court, which Oxford's "Euphuists" opposed.

The additional poems are noticed in the title page, which declares that in addition to Sidney's work have been added "Sundry other rare sonnets of divers Noble men and gentlemen." This statement is reproduced in the 1597 edition printed by Matthew Lownes, which retains the added poems. Twenty-six of these supplementary poems, all labeled "Sonnets" and printed in three stanzas of 4-4-6 alternating rhymes, are by Samuel Daniel. The book very carefully identifies the entire group as by Daniel, introducing the group with the legend, "The Author of this Poeme, S.D.," and then concluding the sequence with "finis, Daniel" (DP 1).

Next come a series of designated cantoes primo-quinto (1b-d), followed by "Faction that ever dwells in Court," which is signed E.O. (1e). For some time scholars have ignored the volume's specificity about its attributions and fallen to disputing the authorship of the ambiguously identified members of this sequence. "Faction that ever dwells in court" was later published as being the work of Fulke Greville, and has been accepted as his by Stephen May among others, even though both Grosart and Looney assigned it to Oxford. If Greville actually wrote it, it would be the best poem he ever wrote.

A more plausible theory, in light of the patterns of attribution in the book, as well as the individuals associated with the first two editions of the play, assigns all seven of the concluding poems to Oxford. It is obvious from the appearance of two editions of Sidney's work in less than two years' time that the text was a lucrative and marketable one. Nashe's edition, appearing shortly after that sponsored by Greville, was also political. The two editions reflect the continuing battle over Sidney's legacy, going back to Oxford and Sidney's 1580-81 tennis court quarrel, in which Greville let it be known that he was of Sidney's faction. Nashe in 1591 was closely associated with the Earl of Oxford, and would shortly dedicate *Strange News* to him under the sobriquet "Master Apis Lapis" (Barrell 1940) and personify Oxford's growing reputation as the quintessential bankrupt nobleman in *Pierce Penniless* (1592) and *Summer's Last Will and Testament* (1592).

It is evident that the strategy of the Newman edition in part depended on the title page notification of additional poems, of which Samuel Daniel evidently provided the largest number. That Fulke Greville would have supplied a poem for this edition and allowed the Earl of Oxford to attach his own initials to it seems most unlikely in view of the book's publication under the auspices of a competing court faction that Greville strenuously opposed.

That Oxford was the author of at least some of the concluding lyrics in Nashe's edition was certainly the belief of the editors of *England's Parnassus* (1593), for there "What Plague is Greater than the Grief of Mind" and "Doth Sorrow Fret Thy Soul" (Canto Quinto), along with "Love is a Discord and a Strange Divorce" (not in *Astrophel and Stella*) are reprinted as by E.O. (2a-b). For ease of future reference, these disputed poems are labelled DP1-11.

Finis, Daniel. **DP 1**

Canto primo.

HArke all you Ladies that doo sleepe,
The Fairie Queene *Proserpina*
Bids you awake, and pitie them that weepe:
      You may doo in the darke
      What the day doth forbid;
      Feare not the doggs that barke,
      Night will haue all hid.

But if you let your Louers mone,
The Fairie Queene *Proserpina*
Will send abroad hir Fairies euerie one:
      That shall pinch blacke and blew
      Your white hands and faire armes,
      That did not kindly rewe
      Your Paramours harmes.

In myrtle arbours on the downes,
The Fairie Queene *Proserpina*
This night by Moone shine leading merrie rounds,

Holds

Aſtrophel and Stella. 77

Holds a wat h with ſweete Loue,
Downe the dale, vp the hill,
No plaints nor grieues may moue,
Their holy vigill.

All you that will hold watch with Loue,
The Fairie Queene *Proſerpina*
Will make you fairer than *Dianas* Doue,
    Roſes red, Lillies white,
    And the cleere damaske hue
    Shall on your cheekes alight :
    Loue will adorne you.

All you that loue, or lou'd before,
The Fairie Queene *Proſerpina*
Bids you increaſe that louing humour more :
    They that haue not yet fed
    On delight amorous,
    She vowes that they ſhall lead
    Apes in *Auernus.*

DP 2

     Canto Secundo.

WHat faire pompe haue I ſpide of glittering Ladies,
    With locks ſparckled abroad, and roſie Coronet
On their yuorie browes, trackt to the daintie thies
VVith roabs like *Amazons*, blew as Violet :
VVith gold Aglets adernd, ſome in a changeable
Pale, with ſpangs wauering taught to be moueable.

  2 Then thoſe Knights that a farre off with dolorous viewing,
Caſt their eyes hetherward : loe in an agonie
All vnbrac'd, crie aloud, their heauie ſtate ruing ;
Moyſt cheekes with blubbering painted as *Ebonie*
Blacke, their feltred haire torne with wrathfull hand,
And whiles aſtonied, ſtarke in a maze they ſtand.

        L 3

                                    But

78 **Syr P. S. his**

3 But hearke what merry found; wha' fodaine harmonie
Looke, looke neere the groue where the Ladies doe tread
VVith their knights the meafures waide by the melodie,
VVantons whofe traue fing make men enamoured,
Now they faine an honor, now by the flender waft
He muft lift hir aloft, and feale a kiffe in haft.

4 Streight downe vnder a fhadow for wearines they lie,
VVith pleafant daliance, hand knit with arme in arme,
Now clofe, now fet aloof they gaze with an equall eie,
Changing kiffes alike, ftreight with a falfe alarme,
Mocking kiffes alike, powt with a louely lip,
Thus drownd with iollities, their merry daies doe flip.

5 But ftay now I difcerne they goe on a Pilgrimage:
Toward Loues holy land fare *Paphos* or *Cyprus*,
Such deuotion is meete for a blithefome age,
With fweet youth it agrees well to be amorous,
Let olde angrie fathers lurke in an Hermitage,
Come weele affociate this iollie Pilgrimage.

Canto Tertio.　　**DP 3**

MY Loue bound me with a kiffe
That I fhould no longer ftaie;
VVhen I felt fo fweete a bliffe,
I had leffe power to paffe away:
Alas that women do no not knowe
Kiffes make men loath to goe.

Canto Quarto.　　**DP 4**

Loue whets the dulleft wittes, his plagues be fuch,
But makes the wife by pleafing doat as much.
So wit is purchaft by this dire difeafe,
Oh let me doat, fo Loue be bent to pleafe.

Canto

Aſtrophel and Stella.   79

Canto Quinto.   **DP 5**

A Daie, a night, an houre of ſweete content,
Is worth a world conſum'd in fretfull care,
Vnequall Gods in your Arbitrement
To ſort vs daies whoſe ſorrowes endles are,
     And yét what were it? as a fading flower;
     To ſwim in bliſſe, a daie, a night an hower.

2 VVhat plague is greater than the griefe of minde,
The griefe of minde that eates in euerie vaine,
In euerie vaine that leaues ſuch clods behind
Such clods behind as breed ſuch bitter paine,
     So bitter paine that none ſhall euer finde,
     What plague is greater than the griefe of minde.

3 Doth ſorrowe fret thy ſoule? ô direfull ſpirit,
Doth pleaſure feede thy heart ? ô bleſſed man :
Haſt thou bin happie once ? ô heauie plight :
Are thy miſhaps forepaſt ? ô happie than :
     Or haſt thou bliſſe in eld ? ô bliſſe too late :
     But haſt thou bliſſe in youth ? ô ſweete eſtate.
                          Finis. CONTENT.

DP 6

                     Meglioa ſpero.

I Aſtion that euer dwelles, in Court where wit excelles,
               hath ſet defiance.
Fortune and Loue haue ſworne, that they were neuer borne,
     of one alliance.

Cupid which doth aſpire, to be God of Deſire,
          Sweares he giues lawes ;
That where his arrowes hit, ſome ioy, ſome ſorrow it,
          Fortune no cauſe.   *Fortune.*

8o   **Syr P. S. his**

Fortune sweares weakest hearts (the bookes of *Cupids* Arts)
    turnd with hir wheele,
Senses themselues shall proue : venter hath place in *Loue,*
    aske them that feele.

This discord it begot *Atheists,* that honor not :
    Nature thought good,
Fortune shou'd euer dwell in Court where wits excell,
    Loue keepe the wood.

So to the wood went I, with *Loue* to liue and die,
    Fortune's forlorne :
Experience of my youth, made me thinke humble Truth
    In desarts borne.

My Saint I keepe to mee, and *Ioane* her selfe is shee,
    Ioane faire and true :
Shee that doth onely moue passions of loue with *Loue :*
    Fortune adieu.

DP 7   *Finis* E. O.

If flouds of teares could clense my follies past,
And smokes of sighs might sacrifice for sin,
If groning cries might salue my fault at last,
Or endles mone for error pardon win;
    Then would I crie, weepe, sigh, and euer mone
    Mine error, fault, sins, follies past and gone.

I see my hopes must wither in their bud,
I see my fauours are no lasting flowers,
I see that words will breath no better good
Than losse of time, and lightning but at howers :
    Then when I see, then this I say therefore,
    That fauours, hopes, and words, can blinde no more.

FINIS.

DP 8

Loue is a difcord and a ftrange diuorce,
Betwixt our fence and reft,by whofe power,
As mad with reafon,we admit that force,
Which wit or labour neuer may diuorce.
  It is a will that brooketh no confent,
  It would refufe,yet neuer may repent.
     --- Loue's a defire,which for to waight a time,
Doth loofe an age of yeares,and fo doth paffe,
As doth the fhadow feuerd from his prime,
Seeming as though it were,yet neuer was.
  Leauing behind,nought but repentant thoughts,
  Of dayes ill fpent,of that which profits noughts.
It's now a peace,and then a fudden warre,
A hope confumde before it is conceiu'd,
At hand it feares,and menaceth a farre,
And he that gaines,is moft of all deceiu'd.
  Loue whets the dulleft wits his plagues be fuch,
  But makes the wife by pleafing, dote as much.
          E.O.

Eng. Parn. (1593): "Love is a Discord and a Strange Divorce,"
subscribed "E.O." (DP 10, M6v). The more complete version in
Menaphon (1589) also prints a fir st stanza commencing "What
thing is Love?"

DP 9

Doth forrow fret thy foule ? ô direfull fpirit,
Doth pleafure feed thy heart ? ô bleffed man.
Haft thou bene happie once ? ô heauy plight.   Are

Are thy mifhaps forepaft ? ô happie than:
Or haft thou bliffe in eld ? ô bliffe too late :
But haft thou bliffe in youth ? ô fweet eftate.
E. of O.

DP 10

What plague is greater then the griefe of minde ?
The griefe of mind that eates in euery vaine :
In euery vaine that leaues fuch clods behinde,
Such clods behind as breed fuch bitter paine.
So bitter paine that none fhall euer finde
What plague is greater then the griefe of minde.
E. of Ox.

Eng. Parn. (1593): "Doth Sorrow Fret Thy soul?" (DP 9 C3r-v)
and "What Plague is Greater than the Griefe of Mind?" (DP 10
P1r).

DP 11

552   NOBLE AUTHORS.

WHEN I was faire and younge then favoure graced me,
Of many was I foughte their miftreffe for to be,
But I did fcorne them all and anfwered them therefore,
Goe, goe, goe, feeke fome other-wher, importune me no more.

Howe many weeping eyes I made to pyne in woe,
Howe many fighinge hartes I have not fkill to fhowe,
But I the prouder grewe and ftill thus fpake therefore,
Goe, goe, goe, feeke fome other-wher, importune me no more.

Then fpake brave Venus fonne that brave victorious boy,
Sayinge, You dayntye dame, for y' you be fo coye,
I will foe pull your plumes, as you fhall fay no more
Goe, goe, goe, feeke fome other-wher, importune me no more.

As foone as he had faide, fuch care grewe in my breaft
That nether nighte nor daye I could take any refte,
Wherfore I did repente that I had faide before
Goe, goe, goe, feeke fome other-wher, importune me no more.

E. of OXFORDE.

As reproduced from Walpole's *Royal and Noble Authors* (Vol. 1: 552), this poem is improbably attributed elsewhere to Queen Elizabeth, no doubt at least in part on account of the female perspective, which is the equivalent to claiming that the author must have been a woman because he wrote parts for Juliet or Cleopatra. For other poems making use of a feminine persona, see E.O. 17, Ig. 4, Ig. extra 5, and E.O. extra 2).

Primary Works Cited

Anonymous. *England's Helicon*. London: John Flasket [1600]. Reprinted
(Arthur H. Bullen ed.), London: Lawrence & Bullen (1887, rev. 1899),
and Harvard UP, Hugh Macdonald ed. (1949), 2d printing (1962),
edited from 1600 edition with additional poems from 1614 edition.

Arber, Edward [ed.]. *The Arte of English Poesie* London: Richard Field, 1589. Reprinted
London: Bloomsbury (1869). Anonymous but widely attributed to George
Puttenham, the work is also reprinted as *The Art of English Poesy by George
Puttenham: A Critical Edition* (Frank Whigham & Wayne A. Rebhorn eds.),
Cornell UP (2007).

_____ [ed.]. *The hekatompathia or Passionate centurie of loue, diuided into two parts:
whereof, the first expresseth the authors sufferance in loue: the latter, his long
farewell to loue and all his tyrannie. Composed by Thomas Watson Gentleman;
and published at the request of certaine gentlemen his very frendes*. London :
imprinted by Iohn Wolfe for Gabriell Cawood, dwellinge in Paules Churchyard
at the signe of the Holy Ghost, [1582], carefully edited by Edward Arber. 5
Queen's Square, Bloomsbury (1870).

Barnfield, Richard. *The encomion of Lady Pecunia: or The praise of money. By Richard
Barnfeild* [sic], *graduate in Oxford*. London: Printed by G. S[haw] for Iohn
Iaggard, and are to be solde at his shoppe neere Temple-barre, at the signe of
the Hand and starre [1598].

_____. *Poems: in divers humors* [being a separately titled conclusion to *The Encomium
of Lady Pecunia*]. London: Printed by G. S[haw] for Iohn Iaggard, and are to be
solde at his shoppe neere Temple-barre, at the signe of the Hand and starre
[1598].

Bevington, David [ed.]. *Endymion. The Revels Plays*. Manchester: University Press
(1996).

Bullein, William. *Bullwark of Defence against all Sicknes, Sornes, and Woundes*. London:
Thomas Marshe (1562).

Bullen, E.H. [ed.]. *England's Helicon: A Collection of Lyrical and Pastoral Poems: Published in 1600*. London: John C. Nimmo (1887).

Bullen, E.H. [ed.]. *England's Helicon: A Collection of Lyrical and Pastoral Poems: Published in 1600*. Lawrence & Bullen: London (1899).

Byrd, William. *Psalmes, sonets, & songs of sadnes and pietie, made into musicke of fiue parts: whereof, some of them going abroad among diuers, in vntrue coppies, are heere truely corrected, and th' other being songs very rare and newly composed, are heere published, for the recreation of all such as delight in musicke: / by William Byrd, one of the Gent. of the Queenes Maiesties honorable chappell*. [London]: Printed by Thomas East, the assigne of W [sic] Byrd, and are to be sold at the dwelling house of the said T. East, by Paules wharfe [1588].

Churchyard, Thomas. *A pleasaunte laborinth called Churchyardes chance framed on fancies, vttered with verses, and writte[n] to giue solace to euery well disposed mynde: wherein notwithstanding are many heauie epitaphes, sad and sorowfull discourses and sutche a multitude of other honest pastymes for the season (and passages of witte) that the reader therein maie thinke his tyme well bestowed. All whiche workes for the pleasure of the worlde, and recreation of the worthie, are dedicated to the right honourable sir Thomas Bromley knight, lorde Chancelour of Englande*. Imprinted at London: By Ihon Kyngston [1580].

Collier, John Payne [ed.]. *Twenty-five Old Ballads and Songs: From Manuscripts in the Possession of John Payne Collier. A Birthday Gift. Printed for Presents only*. London (11th Jan. 1869).

Crawford, Charles. *England's Parnassus. Compiled by Robert Allot, 1600. Edited from the Original Text in the Bodleian Library and Compared to the Two Copies in the British Museum. With Introduction, Notes, Tables and Indexes*. Oxford: The University Press (1913).

Davison, Francis. *A poetical rapsody containing, diuerse sonnets, odes, elegies, madrigalls, and other poesies, both in rime, and measured verse. Neuer yet published. The bee and spider by a diuerse power, sucke hony' & poyson from the selfe same flower*. Printed at London : By V. S[immes] for Iohn Baily, and are to be solde at his shoppe in Chancerie lane, neere to the office of the six clarkes [1602].

Daye, Angell. *The English secretorie. VVherein is contayned, a perfect method, for the inditing of all manner of epistles and familiar letters, together with their diuersities, enlarged by examples vnder their seuerall tytles. In which is layd forth a path-waye, so apt, plaine and easie, to any learners capacity, as the like wherof hath not at any time heretofore beene deliuered. Nowe first deuized, and newly published, by Angell Daye*. At London: printed by Robert Walde-graue, and are to be solde by Richard Iones, dwelling at the signe of the Rose and the Crowne, neere vnto Holburn Bridge [1586].

Edwards, Richard. *Damon & Pythias*. (Originally Published, London: Richard Johnes, 1571; Oxford. Malone Society Reprints, 1957).

_____. *The paradyse of daynty deuises, aptly furnished, with sundry pithie and learned inuentions: deuised and written for the most part, by M. Edwards, sometimes of her Maiesties chappel: the rest, by sundry learned gentlemen, both of honour, and woorshippe. viz. S. Barnarde. E.O. L. Vaux. D.S. Iasper Heyvvood. F.K. M. Bevve. R. Hill. M. Yloop, vvith others.* Imprinted at London: By [R. Jones for?] Henry Disle, dwellyng in Paules Churchyard, at the south west doore of Saint Paules Church, and are there to be solde [1576].

Frame, Donald M. [ed.]. *The Complete Works of Montaigne: Essays, Travel Journal, Letters.* Stanford: The University Press (1957).

Gent, T.B. *A ritch storehouse or treasurie for nobilitye and gentlemen, which in Latine is called Nobilitas literata, written by a famous and excellent man, Iohn Sturmius, and translated into English by T.B. Gent. Seene and allowed according to the order appointed.* Imprinted at London: By Henrie Denham, dwelling in pater noster row at the signe of the Starre., Anno Domini [1570].

Golding, Arthur. *Thabridgment of the histories of Trogus Pompeius, collected and wrytten in the Laten tonge, by the famous historiographer Iustine, and translated into English by Arthur Goldyng: a worke conteynyng brieflie great plentie of moste delectable hystories, and notable examples, worthie not onelie to be read but also to be embraced and followed of all menne* [London]: Anno Domini. M.D.LXIIII. mense. Maii Imprinted at London in Fletestrete, nere vnto Sainct Dunstons churche, by Thomas Marshe (1564).

_____. *The .xv. bookes of P. Ouidius Naso, entytuled Metamorphosis, translated oute of Latin into English meeter, by Arthur Golding Gentleman, a worke very pleasaunt and delectable.* Imprinted at London: by Willyam Seres, [1575].

_____. *The Psalmes of Dauid and others. With M. Iohn Caluins commentaries.* Imprinted at London: By Thomas East and Henry Middleton: for Lucas Harison, and George Byshop, Anno. Do. M.D.LXXI. [1571].

Greg, W.W. [ed.]. *Fedele and Fortunio. The deceites in loue: excellently discoursed in a very pleasaunt and fine conceited comoedie, of two Italian gentlemen. Translated out of Italian, and set downe according as it hath beene presented before the Queenes moste excellent Maiestie.* At London: Printed [by John Charlewood?] for Thomas Hacket, and are to be solde at his shop in Lumberd streete, vnder the Popes head, Anno. 1585. Malone Society Reprints (1909).

Greville, Fulke. *Certaine learned and elegant vvorkes of the Right Honorable Fulke Lord Brooke, written in his youth, and familiar exercise with Sir Philip Sidney. The seuerall names of which workes the following page doth declare.* London : Printed *by E[lizabeth]. P[urslowe]. for Henry Seyle, and are to be sold at his shop at the signe of the Tygers head in St. Paules Church-yard* [1633].

Harvey, Gabriel. *Gabrielis Harueij Gratulationum Valdinensium libri quatuor. Ad illustriss. augustissimámque principem, Elizabetam, Angliæ, Franciæ, Hibernicæq[ue] Reginam longè serenissimam, atq[ue] optatissimam.* Londini : ex officina typographica Henrici Binnemani, Anno. M.D.LXXVIII. [1578] Mense Septembri.

Lee, Sidney. *The passionate pilgrim : being a reproduction in facsimile of the first edition, 1599, from the copy in the Christie Miller Library of Britwell.* Oxford: The Clarendon Press (1905).

Lyly, John. *Collected Works.* London: Edward Blount, 1632. Reprinted in *The Complete Works of John Lyly* (R. Warwick Bond ed.), Oxford University Press, three vols. (1902).

McDonald, Hugh [ed.]. *England's Helicon: Reprinted from the Edition of 1600 with Additions from the Edition of 1614.* Cambridge, MA: Harvard University Press (1962).

Meres, Francis. *Francis Meres's Treatise "Poetrie"* (from *Palladis Tamia*, London: Cuthbert Burby, 1598). Reprinted (Don Cameron Allen ed.), Illinois UP, (University of Illinois Studies in Language and Literature, vol. 16) (1933).

Miller, Ruth Loyd [ed.]. *A Hundreth Sundrie Flowres.* London: Richard Smith, 1573 [anonymous]. Reprinted as *The Posies of George Gascoigne, Esquire, Corrected, Perfected, and Augmented by the Author*, London: Richard Smith, 1575. Reprinted as *A Hundreth Sundrie Flowres* (Bernard M. Ward ed.), London: Etchells & Macdonald, 1926. 2d ed. (Miller ed.), Port Washington, N.Y.: Kennikat Press & Jennings, La.: Minos Publishing (1975).

Munday, Anthony. *Zelauto. The fountaine of fame Erected in an orcharde of amorous aduentures. Containing a delicate disputation, gallantly discoursed betweene to noble gentlemen of Italye. Giuen for a freendly entertainment to Euphues, at his late ariuall into England. By A.M. seruaunt to the Right Honourable the Earle of Oxenford.* Honos alit artes. Imprinted at London: By Iohn Charlevvood [1580].

_____. *The first [seconde] part, of the no lesse rare, then excellent and stately historie, of the famous and fortunate prince, Palmerin of England Declaring the birth of him, and Prince Florian du Desart his brother, in the forrest of great Brittaine: the course of their liues afterward, in pursuing knightly aduentures, and performing incomparable deeds of chiualrie. Wherein gentlemen may finde choyse of sweete inuentions, and gentlewomen be satisfied in courtly expectations. Translated out of French, by A.M. one of the messengers of her Maiesties chamber.* London: Printed by Thomas Creede [1609].

_____. *The famous and renovvned historie of Primaleon of Greece, sonne to the great and mighty Prince Palmerin d'Oliua, Emperour of Constantinople Describing his knightly deedes of armes, as also the memorable aduentures of Prince Edvvard of England: and continuing the former history of Palmendos, brother to the fortunate Prince Primaleon, &c. The first booke. Translated out of French and Italian, into English, by A.M.* London: Printed by Thomas Snodham [1619].

Pilkington, Francis. *The first booke of songs or ayres of 4. parts vvith tableture for the lute or orpherian, vvith the violl de gamba. Newly composed by Francis Pilkington, Batcheler of Musick, and lutenist: and one of the Cathedrall Church of Christ, in the citie of Chester.* London: Printed by T. Este, dwelling in Aldersgate-streete, and are ther to be sould [1605].

Puttenham. George [presumed author]. *The Arte of English Poesie*, see Arber, Edward.

Rollins, Hyder Edward [ed.]. *A Handful of Pleasant Delights (1584) by Clement Robinson and diverse Others.* Cambridge: Harvard University Press (1924).

_____ [ed.]. *The Paradise of Dainty Devices*. London, 1576. Reprinted (Rollins Cambridge, MA: Harvard University Press (1927).

_____ [ed.]. *The Pepys Ballads*. Harvard UP (1929). In two volumes.

_____ [ed.]. *The Poems: A New Variorum Edition of Shakespeare*. Lippincott (1938).

_____ [ed.]. *England's Helicon 1600, 1614*. 2 vols. Cambridge, Mass.: Harvard University Press (1935).

R.S. *The phoenix nest Built vp with the most rare and refined workes of noble men, woorthy knights, gallant gentlemen, masters of arts, and braue schollers. Full of varietie, excellent inuention, and singular delight. Neuer before this time published. Set foorth by R.S. of the Inner Temple Gentleman.* Imprinted at London: By Iohn Iackson [1593].

T.C. *An Hospitall for the Diseased*, London: R. Tottell [1578].

Tofte, Robert. *Alba. The months minde of a melancholy louer, diuided into three parts: by R.T. Gentleman. Hereunto is added a most excellent pathetical and passionate letter, sent by Duke D'Epernoun, vnto the late French King, Henry the 3. of that name, when he was commanded from the court, and from his royall companie.* Translated into English by the foresaid author. At London: Printed by Felix Kingston, for Matthew Lownes [1598].

Whigham, Frank and Wayne A. Rebhorn. *The Art of English Poesy by George Puttentham: A Critical Edition*. Ithaca, N.Y.: Cornell University Press (2007).

Walpole, Horace. *A catalogue of the royal and noble authors of England, with lists of their works.* Printed at Strawberry-Hill, 1758

Ward, B.M. [ed.]. *A Hundredth Sundrie Flowres From the Original Edition of 1573*. London: F. Etchells and H. Macdonald (1926).

Webbe, William. *A Discourse of English Poetrie*. London: John Charlewood for Robert Walley, 1586. Reprinted (Edward Arber ed.), London: Constable (1895).

Secondary Works Cited

Adams, John Quincy. *The Passionate Pilgrim by William Shakespeare. The Third Edition, 1612, Reproduced in Facsimile from the Copy in Folger Shakespeare Library, with an Introduction by Hyder Edward Rollins*. New York: Charles Scribner's Sons (1940).

Alter, Robert. *The Five Books of Moses*. New York: Norton (2004).

Anderson, Mark. *"Shakespeare" By Another Name: The Life of Edward de Vere, Earl of Oxford, the Man Who Was Shakespeare*. Gotham (2005).

Argamon, Shlomo, Kevin Burns & Shlomo Dubnov [eds]. *The Structure of Style: Algorithmic Approaches to Understanding Manner and Meaning*. Springer (2010).

Armstrong, Edward A. *Shakespeare's Imagination: A Study of the Psychology of Association and Inspiration*. London: Lindsay Drummond, 1946.

Aspinall, Dana E. "Menaphon: Camilla's Alarm to Slumbering Euphues in His Melancholy Cell at Silexedra. Robert Greene Brenda Cantar." *The Sixteenth Century Journal*, 1 (1998), 141-43.

Barkan, Leonard. *The Gods Made Flesh: Metamorphosis and the Pursuit of Paganism*. New Haven: Yale University Press (1990).

Barker, Jill. "Wooed by a snail: Testaceous Androgyny in English Renaissance Drama." *Imprimatur* 1: 20-30 (1995).

Barrell, Charles Wisner. "New Milestone in Shakespearean Research: Contemporary Proof that the Earl of Oxford's Literary Nickname was 'Gentle Master William.'" *Shakespeare Fellowship Quarterly*, V:4 (Oct. 1940), 49-66.

_____. "Earliest Authenticated 'Shakespeare' Transcript found with Oxford's Personal Poems." *Shakespeare Fellowship Quarterly* VI: 2 (April 1945), 22-26.

_____. "The Playwright Earl Publishes 'Hamlet's Book'." *Shakespeare Fellowship Quarterly* 7:3 (July 1946), 35-42.

_____. "Proof That Shakespeare's Thought and Imagery Dominate Oxford's Own Statement of Creative Principles: A Discussion of the Poet Earl's 1573 Letter to the Translator of 'Hamlet's Book'." *Shakespeare Fellowship Quarterly* VII:4

(Oct. 1946), 61-69.

Bednarz, James P. "Canonizing Shakespeare: The Passionate Pilgrim, England's Helicon and the Question of Authenticity." *Shakespeare Survey* 60 (2007), 252–67.

Bennett, Josephine Waters. "Oxford and *Endimion*," *PMLA* 57 (1942), 354-69.

Bennett, Nicola & Richard Proudfoot. See Proudfoot & Bennett.

Best, M.R. "A Note on the Songs in Lyly's Plays," *Notes and Queries* 12:3 (March 1965), 93-94.

Bevington, David, Martin Butler and Ian Donaldson [eds.] *The Cambridge Edition of the Works of Ben Jonson*. Cambridge: The University Press (2012), in seven volumes.

Bond, Warwick. *The Complete Works of John Lyly*. Oxford: at the Clarendon Press, in three vols (1902).

_____. "Lyly's Songs" *Review of English Studies* 6: 23 (July 1930), 295-99.

Brazil, Robert Sean & Barboura Flues, eds. "Poems and Lyrics of Edward de Vere." *Elizabethan Authors* (2002).

Burns, Kevin, Shlomo Argamon & Shlomo Dubnov. See Argamon, Burns & Dubnov.

Burrow, Colin. *Shakespeare and Classical Antiquity*. Oxford: The University Press (2013).

Byrne, M. St. Clare. "'The Shepherd Tony': A Recapitulation." *The Modern Language Review*, 15: 4 (1920) 364–73.

Cannan, Paul D. "Edmond Malone, The Passionate Pilgrim, and the Fiction of Shakespearean Authorship," *Shakespeare Quarterly* 68:2 (Summer 2017), 139-71.

Cardano [Cardanus], Girolamo. *De Consolatione* [*Cardanus Comforte*]. Venice, 1542. Reprinted (Thomas Bedingfield trans.), London: Thomas Marsh, 1573. Reprinted (rev. ed.), London: Thomas Marsh, 1576.

Carter, Albert Howard. "On the Use of Details of Spelling, Punctuation, and Typography to Determine the Dependence of Editions." *Studies in Philology*, 44:3 (1947), 497–503.

Case, Arthur E. *A Bibliography of English Poetical Miscellanies 1521-1750*. Oxford: Printed for the Bibliographical Society (1935).

Chambers, Edmund K., ed. *The Tragedy of Hamlet, Prince of Denmark*. Boston: Heath (1895).

_____. *The Elizabethan Stage*. Oxford: at the Clarendon Press. In Four vols. (1923).

Chaski, Carole. "Who's at the Keyboard? Authorship Attribution in Digital Evidence Investigations." *International Journal of Digital Evidence*, 4:1 (Spring 2005), 1-11.

Chiljan, Katherine [ed.]. *Book Dedications to the Earl of Oxford*. n.p., 1994.

_____. *Letters and Poems of Edward, Earl of Oxford*. n.p., 1998.

Clark, Eva Turner. *The Satirical Comedy Love's Labour's Lost*. New York: William Farquhar Payson (1933).

Coldiron, Ann. "The Widow's Mite and the Value of Praise: Commendatory Verses and an Unrecorded Marginal Poem in LSU's Copy of The Faerie Qveene 1590." *Spenser Studies: A Renaissance Poetry Annual*, 31-32 2017-2018.

Coleman, Robert. "Tityrus and Meliboeus." *Greece & Rome* 13:1 (1966), 79–97.

Connor, Francis X. "Shakespeare, Poetic Collaboration and The Passionate Pilgrim." *Shakespeare Survey* 67 (2014), 119–30.

Coursen, Herbert R. *Christian Ritual and the World of Shakespeare's Tragedies*. Lewisburg: Bucknell University Press (1976).

Courthope, William J. *A History of English Poetry* (in six volumes, 1895-1910). Vol. 2, New York: Macmillan (1897).

Craig, Hardin. "Hamlet's Book." *Huntington Library Quarterly Bulletin* 6 (Nov. 1934), 15-37.

Crystal, David & Ben Crystal. *Shakespeare's Words: A Glossary and Language Companion*. London: Penguin Books (2002).

Cunliffe, John W. *The Complete works of George Gascoigne in Two Volumes*. Originally published 1907, reprinted by Greenwood Press, 1969.

Cutting, Bonner Miller. "Edward de Vere's Tin Letters." *Shakespeare Oxford Fellowship*, Oct. 14, 2017 (conference presentation) (posted on YouTube Jan. 22, 2018).

_____. "Sufficient Warrant: Censorship, Punishment, and Shakespeare in Early Modern England," *The Oxfordian* 19 (2017), 69-100.

Cyr, Helen W. "Lord Oxford Said It First." *The Shakespeare Newsletter* 36.1 (1986), 11.

Danner, Bruce. "The Anonymous Shakespeare: Heresy, Authorship, and the Anxiety of Orthodoxy," in Starner and Traister (2011), 143-58.

Delahoyde, Michael. "Lyric Poetry from Chaucer to Shakespeare," *Brief Chronicles* V (2014), 69-100.

_____ [ed.]. *Anthony and Cleopatra*. Oxfordian Shakespeare Series (2015).

Doughtie, Edward. *Lyrics from English Airs 1596-1622*. Cambridge, MA: Harvard University Press (1970).

Dubnov, Shlomo, Shlomo Argamon & Kevin Burns. See Argamon, Burns & Dubnov.

Duffin, Ross W. *Some Other Note: The Lost Songs of English Renaissance Comedy*. Oxford: The University Press (2018).

Dutton, Richard. *Mastering the Revels: The Regulation and Censorship of English Renaissance Drama*. London: Palgrave Macmillan (1991).

Dyer, Rev. T.F. Thistleton. *Folk-Lore of Shakespeare*. New York: Dover (1866).

Eagan-Donovan, Cheryl. "Looney, the Lively Lark, and Ganymede: A Closer Look at the Poetry of Edward de Vere." *Shakespeare Oxford Fellowship*, Oct. 14, 2017 (conference presentation) (posted on YouTube March 23, 2018).

Elliott, Ward E.Y. and Robert J. Valenza. "Can the Oxford Candidacy Be Saved?" *The Oxfordian*, Volume III (2000), 71-95.

_____. "Oxford by the Numbers: What Are the Odds That the Earl of Oxford Could Have Written Shakespeare's Poems and Plays?" *Tennessee Law Review* 72:1 (2004), 323-96.

_____. "The Shakespeare Clinic and the Oxfordians," *The Oxfordian*, XII (2010), 138-67.

Feuillerat, Albert. *The Composition of Shakespeare's Plays* (New Haven: Yale University Press, 1953).

Fitzgerald, James. "Shakespeare, Oxford, and Du Bartas: The little known story of Edward de Vere's revelatory last poem," *Shakespeare Oxford Newsletter*, 33:1 (Winter 1997), 1, 10-14.

_____. "E.L. Oxen," *Shakespeare Oxford Newsletter*, 34:1 (Spring 1998), 10-11, 24.

Flues, Barboura & Robert Sean Brazil. See Brazil & Flues.

Fowler, Alastair. *Triumphal Forms: Structural Patterns in Elizabethan Poetry*. Cambridge: The University Press (1970).

Fowler, William Plumer. *Shakespeare Revealed in Oxford's Letters*. Randall (1986).

Frame, Donald M. *The Complete Works of Montaigne: Essays, Travel Journal, Letters. Newly Translated by Donald M. Frame*. Stanford: The University Press, 1948.

Frazer, Winifred. "Censorship in the Strange Case of William Shakespeare: A

Body for the Canon," *Brief Chronicles I* (2009), 9-28.

Garber, Marjorie. *Shakespeare's Ghostwriter's: Literature as Uncanny Causality.* New York and London: Methuen (1987).

Gascoigne, George. *A Hundreth Sundrie Flowres.* See Miller ed. (1975).

Gidley, Fran. "Shakespeare in Composition: Evidence for Oxford's Authorshp of Sir Thomas More," *The Oxfordian* VI (2003), 29-54.

Gilbert, Sky. "Was Shakespeare a Euphuist? Some Ruminations on Oxford, Lyly and Shakespeare" *Brief Chronicles* 5 (2014), 171-88.

Goldstein, Gary. "Is This Shakespeare's Juvenilia?" Goldstein, *Reflections on the True Shakespeare*, Laugwitz Verlag, 2016, in *Neues Shake-speare Journal*, special issue no. 6, 45-69.

_____. "Assessing the Linguistic Evidence for Oxford." *Shakespeare Oxford Newsletter* 53:2 (Spring 2017), 22-25.

Golding, Louis Thorn. *An Elizabethan Puritan: Arthur Golding the Translator of Ovid's Metamorphoses and also of John Calvin's Sermons.* New York: Richard R. Smith (1937).

Goodlet, John "Shakespeare's Debt to John Lyly" *Englische Studien herausgegeben von F. Kölbing,' Heilbronn,* (1881), 356-63.

Green, Nina. "Were the Letters and Youthful Poems of Edward de Vere Written in the Lexical Vocabulary of Shakespeare?" Parts 1-3, *Edward de Vere Newsletter* 57-59 (Nov., Dec., 1993 & Jan. 1994).

_____. "Does the Lexical Vocabulary of Edward de Vere's Letters and Youthful Poems Support his Authorship of *The Reign of King Edward III*?" Parts 1-3, *Edward de Vere Newsletter* 60-62 (Feb., March & April 1994).

Greg, W. W. "The Authorship of the Songs in Lyly's Plays," *Modern Language Review* I (Oct., 1905), 43-52.

Gregory, Horace. *Ovid: The Metamorphoses.* New York: The Viking Press (1958).

Grosart, Alexander B. [ed.]. *Miscellanies of the Fuller Worthies Library. In four volumes.* Printed for Private Circulation, 1872-1876 AMS Press Reprint (1970).

_____. "The Poems of Edward de Vere, Earl of Oxford," *Miscellanies of the Fuller Worthies' Library.* VI: 349-51, 359, 394-429.

_____. *The Works of Gabriel Harvey, D.C.L. In Three Volumes.* Printed for private circulation. 1884. AMS reprint 1966.

Halpom, James W. *Songs Written by or Attributed to William Shakespeare.* New York: William Morrow & Co. (1929).

Hannah, J. *The Courtly Poets from Raleigh to Montrose*. London: Bell and Daldy (1870).

Hannas, Andrew. "Gabriel Harvey and the Genesis of 'William Shakespeare,'" *Shakespeare Oxford Society Newsletter* 29: IB (Winter 1993), 1-8.

_____. "To the Editor" (re "E.L. Oxon" problem), *Shakespeare Oxford Society Newsletter* 34:1 (Spring 1998), 11.

Hassel, R. Christopher. *Renaissance Drama and the English Church Year*. Lincoln, Neb. (1979).

Haste, Ian. "The Name within the Ring: Edward de Vere's 'Musical' Signature in *Merchant of Venice*," *Shakespeare Matters* 8:2 (Spring 2009), 1, 23-26 +.

Head, Franklin H. *Shakespeare's Insomnia and the Causes Thereof*. Boston: Houghton Mifflin (1887).

Hebel, William J. "Nicholas Ling and *England's Helicon*," *Library* 4:2 (1924), 153-60.

Hess, Ron. "'Another Rare Dream': Is this an 'Authentic' Oxford poem?" *The Oxfordian* VIII (2005), 60-75.

Hobday, C.H. "Shakespeare's Venus and Adonis Sonnets," *Shakespeare Survey* 26 (1973), 103-09.

Hosley, Richard. "Anthony Munday, John Heardson, and the Authorship of 'Fedele and Fortunio.'" *The Modern Language Review* 55: 4 (1960), 564–565.

_____."The Authorship of 'Fedele and Fortunio.'" *Huntington Library Quarterly* 30:4 (1967), 315–30.

Hoy, Cyrus. "The Shares of Fletcher and his Collaborators in the Beaumont and Fletcher Canon," *Studies in Bibliography* 15 (1962), 71-90.

Johnson, Gerald D. "Nicholas Ling, Publisher 1580-1607." *Studies in Bibliography* 38 (1985), 203–14.

Jones, Emrys. *New Oxford Book of Sixteenth Century Verse*. Oxford: the University Press (1993).

Kerrigan, John [ed.]. *The Sonnets and A Lover's Complaint*. Penguin (1986).

Kreiler, Kurt, ed. & trans. *Edward de Vere, Earl of Oxford: Der zarte Faden, den die Schönheit spinn ("The thriftless thread which pamper'd beauty spins")*. Germany: Suhrkamp (2013).

Kuhl, Ernest P. "Shakspere and *The Passionate Pilgrim*," *Modern Language Notes* 34:5 (May 1919), 313-314.

Law, Robert Adger. "Two Notes On Shakespearian Parallels," *Studies in English* 9 (1929), 82–85.

Lawrence, W. J. "Music in the Elizabethan Theatre." *The Musical Quarterly* 6: 2 (1920), 192–205.

_____. "The Problem of Lyly's Songs," *TLS* (20 Dec. 1923).

Lee, Sidney. *The French Renaissance in England: An Account of the Literary Relations of England and France in the Sixteenth Century*. New York: Scribner (1910).

_____. "Vere, Edward, de, Seventeenth Earl of Oxford (1550-1604)," *Dictionary of National Biography*. London: Smith, Elder & Co. (1899). Vol. LVIII: 225-229.

Lees-Jeffries, Hester. *England's Helicon: Fountains in Early Modern Literature and Culture*. Oxford: The University Press (2007).

Leishman, J. B. "Review of *Englands Helicon* by Hugh Macdonald." *The Review of English Studies* 2:8 (1951), 381–382.

Lempriere, J. *Bibliotheca classica; or, A dictionary of all the principal names and terms relating to the geography, topography, history, literature, and mythology of antiquity and of the ancients; with a chronological table*. New York: W.E. Dean (1833).

Looney, J. Thomas. *"Shakespeare" Identified in Edward de Vere the Seventeenth Earl of Oxford*. London: Cecil Palmer (1920). Reprinted, New York: Stokes (1920). 2d ed., New York: Duell, Sloan & Pearce, 3d ed. (1948) (Ruth Loyd Miller ed.), Port Washington, N.Y.: Kennikat Press & Jennings, La.: Minos Publishing, (1975) (in two volumes), vol. 1, pp. 1-536 (citations to first American [1920 Stokes] edition unless otherwise noted).

_____ [ed.]. *The Poems of Edward de Vere*. London: Cecil Palmer (1921). Reprinted in Looney 1920 (Miller ed. 1975).

MacCraken, Henry N., F. E. Pierce, and W. H. Durham. *An Introduction to Shakespeare*. New York: Macmillan (1927).

Macmichael, Edgar M. and George Glenn. *Shakespeare and his rivals: a casebook on the authorship controversy*. Odyssey Press (1962).

Marotti, Arthur. "Patronage, Poetry, and Print," *Yearbook of English Studies: Politics, Patronage, and Literature in England 1558-1658* 24 (1991), 1-26.

May, Steven W. "The Authorship of 'My Mind to Me a Kingdom Is'." *Review of English Studies*, 26:104 N.S. (1975), 385-94.

_____, "The Poems of Edward de Vere, Seventeenth Earl of Oxford and of Robert Devereux, Second Earl of Essex." *Studies in Philology*, 87:5 (1980), 5-132.

_____. *The Elizabethan Courtier Poets: The Poems and Their Contexts*. Missouri UP (1991). Reprinted, Pegasus Press (University of North Carolina at

Asheville), 1999 (citations to 1991 edition, as 1999 reprint appears identical).

_____. "The Seventeenth Earl of Oxford as Poet and Playwright." *Tennessee Law Review* 72:1 (2004), 221-54.

_____. "*Monstrous Adversary: The Life of Edward de Vere, 17th Earl of Oxford*" (review), *SQ* 56:2 (2005), 214-16.

Maynard, Winifred. "*The Paradyse of Daynty Deuises* Revisited." *The Review of English Studies* 24:95 (1973), 295–300.

Miller, Ruth Loyd. "The Cornwallis-Lysons Manuscript." Looney 1920 (Miller ed. 1975), vol. 2 ("Oxfordian Vistas"), 369-94.

_____. "The Earl of Oxford Publishes Hamlet's Book, *Cardanus Comforte*." Looney 1920 (Miller ed. 1975), vol. 2 ("Oxfordian Vistas"), 496-507.

Moore, John Robert. "The Songs in Lyly's Plays," *PMLA* 42:3 (Sept. 1927), 623-40.

Muller, Lucian. *Development of Ancient Versification* (translated by Samuel Ball Platner). Boston: Allyn & Bacon (1892).

Nelson, Alan, *Monstrous Adversary: The Life of Edward de Vere, 17th Earl of Oxford*. Liverpool: Liverpool University Press (2003).

Nelson, Paul. "Four Anonymous Elizabethan Poems Now Attributed to Edward de Vere, 17th Earl of Oxford." Unpublished MS (1991).

Newcomber, Alphonso Gerald [ed.]. *Much Ado About Nothing.* Stanford Ca.: Stanford University Press (1929).

Nichols, John. *Progresses and Public Processions of Queen Elizabeth*. 3 vols. London: J. Nichols & son (1823).

North, Marcy. "Ignoto in the Age of Print: The Manipulation of Anonymity in Early Modern England." *Studies in Philology* (91:4) 1994, 390–416.

_____. *The Anonymous Renaissance: Cultures of Discretion in Tudor-Stuart England.* Chicago: University Press (2003).

Ogburn, Charlton (Jr.). *The Mysterious William Shakespeare: The Myth and the Reality*. Dodd, Mead, 1984. Reprinted (2d ed.), McLean, Va.: EPM Publications, 1992 (citations to 1992 edition).

Ostwald, Martin and Thomas G. Rosenmeyer. *The Meters of Greek and Latin Poetry* New York: Bobbs-Merrill (1963).

Oxford English Dictionary (OED). Oxford UP, 2d ed. 1989 (in twenty volumes).

Pallott, Donatella. "'By curious Art compild': *The Passionate Pilgrime* and the Authorial Brand," *Journal of Early Modern Studies* 5 (2016), 383-407.

Parrott, T. M. "The Authorship of 'Two Italian Gentlemen,'" *Modern Philology*

13: 5 (1915), 241–51.

Peacham, Henry. *The Compleat Gentleman*. London: Francis Constable, 1622. Reprinted (G.S. Gordon ed.), Oxford UP (1906).

Pigman, G.W. *George Gascoigne: A Hundredth Sundrie Flowres 1573*. Oxford (2000).

Prechter, Robert R. "A Deeper Look at the Arthur Golding Canon," *Shakespeare Matters* 7:1 (Fall 2007), 7-14.

_____. "*Hundreth Sundrie Flowres* Revisited: Was Oxford Really Involved?" *Brief Chronicles* 2 (2010), 43-76.

_____. "Verse Parallels Between Oxford and Shakespeare." *Oxfordian* XIV (2012), 148-55.

Proudfoot, Richard & Nicola Bennett, eds. *King Edward III*. Bloomsbury Arden Shakespeare (2017).

Prouty, C.T. *George Gascoigne's A Hundredth Sundrie Flowres*. Columbia: University of Missouri (1942).

Raby, F. J. E. *A History of Secular Latin Poetry in the Middle Ages*. Oxford: At the Clarendon Press (1934).

Ray, W. J. "Proving Oxfordian Authorship of 'Sweet Cytherea,'" *Shakespeare Matters* 10:1 (Winter 2011), 1, 13-27.

Reid, Lindsay Ann. "'Certaine Amorous Sonnets, Betweene Venus and Adonis': fictive acts of writing in *The Passionate Pilgrime* of 1612." *Etudes Epistémè : Revue de littérature et de civilisation (XV1-XVIII siècles)* 21 (2012).

Ringler, William A. and Steven M. May, *Elizabethan Poetry: A Bibliography and First-line Index of English Verse, 1559-1603*. New York: Thames Continuum (2004).

Ringler, William A., Michael Rudick and Susan J. Ringler. *Bibliography and Index of English Verse 1501-1558*. Mansell (1993).

Robertson, J.M. *The Baconian Heresy*. London: Herbert Jenkins (1913).

Roe, John. "'Willobie His Avisa' and 'The Passionate Pilgrim': Precedence, Parody, and Development." *The Yearbook of English Studies* 23 (1993), 111–25.

Rollins, Hyder Edward

"A. W. and 'A Poetical Rhapsody.'" *Studies in Philology*, 29:2 (1932) 239–51.

Saintsbury, George. *A History of English Prosody*. In two vols. London: Macmillan (1923).

Salmon, Vivian and Edwina Burness [eds.]. *A Reader in the Language of Shakespearean Drama*. Amsterdam/Philadelphia: John Benjamins Publishing (1987).

Sams, Eric [ed.]. *Shakespeare's Edward III: An Early Play Restored to the Canon.* New Haven: Yale University Press (1969).

_____ [ed.]. *Shakespeare's "Edmund Ironside": The Lost Play.* Fourth Estate (1985). Reprinted, Wildwood House (1986).

Saunders, J.W. *The Profession of English Letters.* London: Routledge & Kegan Paul (1964).

Schmidgall, Gary. *Walt Whitman: A Gay Life.* New York: Dutton (1997).

Schmidt, Alexander. *Shakespeare Lexicon and Quotation Dictionary. Third edition Revised and Enlarged by Gregor Sarrazin.* In two Vols. New York: Dover (1971).

Schoenbaum, Samuel. *Shakespeare's Lives.* Oxford University Press (1970), reprinted (rev. ed.) (1991).

Seng, Peter J. *The Vocal Songs in the Plays of Shakespeare: A Critical History.* Cambridge: Harvard University Press (1967).

Shahan, John M. & Richard F. Whalen. "Apples to Oranges in Bard Stylometrics: Elliott & Valenza fail to eliminate Oxford," The Oxfordian 9 (2006), 113-125.

_____. "Auditing the Stylometricians: Elliott, Valenza and the Claremont Shakespeare Authorship Clinic." *Oxfordian* XI (2009), 235-67.

_____. "Elliott and Valenza's Stylometrics Fail to Eliminate Oxford as Shakespeare," *Discovering Shakespeare: A Festschrift in Honor of Isabel Holden.* Concordia University (2009).

_____. Reply to Elliott and Valenza, *The Oxfordian* 12 (2010), 137-42.

Simpson, D.P. *Cassell's New Latin Dictionary.* New York: Funk & Wagnalls Co. (1959).

Simpson, John and Jennifer Speake. *The Oxford Dictionary of Proverbs.* Oxford: The University Press (2008).

Singleton, Esther. *Shakespearian Fantasias: Adventures in the Fourth Dimension.* Privately Printed, 1929.

Smith, Sarah. "The Reattribution of Munday's *Pain of Pleasure,*" *The Oxfordian* V (2002), 70-99.

Smith, Sir William. *A Smaller Latin English Dictionary. Revised edition by J.F. Lockwood.* London: John Murray. Ninth impression (1962).

Sobran, Joseph. *Alias Shakespeare: Solving the Greatest Literary Mystery of All Time.* New York: Free Press, Simon & Schuster (1997).

Sonnino, Lee A. *A Handbook to Sixteenth-Century Rhetoric*. London: Routledge & Kegan Paul (1968).

Spevack, Marvin. *The Harvard Concordance to Shakespeare*. Cambridge, MA: Harvard University Press (1973).

Spurgeon, Charlotte. *Shakespeare's Imagery and What It Tells Us*. Cambridge: The University Press (1935).

Starner, Janet Wright and Barbara Howard Traister. *Anonymity in Early Modern England: "What's in a Name?"* Burlington, Vt.: Ashgate (2011).

Sternfeld, Frederick W. and Mary Joiner Chan. "'Come Live with Me and Be My Love.'" *Comparative Literature* 22:2 (1970) 173–87.

Stevens, The Honorable John Paul. "The Shakespeare Canon of Statutory Construction." *The University of Pennsylvania Law Review*, 140 (1992), 1375-87.

Stritmatter, Roger A. "The Biblical Origin of Edward De Vere's Dedicatory Poem in Cardan's *Comforte*." *Oxfordian* I (1998), 53-63.

_____. *The Marginalia of Edward de Vere's Geneva Bible: Providential Discovery, Literary Reasoning, and Historical Consequence*. Oxenford Press, 2001 (Ph.D. dissertation, University of Massachusetts, Amherst). Reprinted, 4th ed. (2015).

_____. "A Matter of Style," in *Marginalia* (2001), 571-79.

_____. "A Law Case in Verse: *Venus and Adonis* and the Authorship Question," *Univ. of Tennessee Law Review* 72:1 (2004), 171-219.

_____. "Spenser's 'Perfect Pattern of a Poet' and the 17th Earl of Oxford." *Cahiers Élisabéthains* 77 (Spring 2010), 9-22.

Swinburne, Algernon Charles. *A Study of Shakespeare*. London: Chatto & Windus (1880).

Tomlin, Rebecca. "A New Poem by Arthur Golding," *N&Q* 59 (December 2012), 501-05.

Tufte, Virginia. *Artful Sentences: Syntax as Style*. Graphics Press LLC: Cheshire, Ct. (2006).

Traister, Daniel. "Reluctant Virgins: The Stigma of Print Revisited," *Colby Quarterly* 26:3 (June 1990), 75-86.

Vickers, Brian. *The Artistry of Shakespeare's Prose*. London: Methuen (2008).

Valenza, Robert J. See Elliott, Ward E.Y. & Robert J. Valenza.

Vanhoutte, Jacqueline. "Age in Lust: Lyly's Endymion and the Court of Elizabeth I," *Explorations in Renaissance Culture* 37.1 (Summer 2011), 51-70.

Waddell, Helen. *Medieval Latin Lyrics*. New York: Henry Holt & Co. (1929).

Wainewright, Ruth. "On the Poems of Edward de Vere," *Shakespearean Authorship Review* 16 (1966), 1-18.

Walther, H. *Das Streitgedicht in der lateinischen Literatur des Mitteltalters*. London: John Abemarle (1920).

Ward, B.M. *The Seventeenth Earl of Oxford 1550-1604 from Contemporary Documents*. London: John Murray (1928).

Ward, Bernard M. [ed.]. *A Hundreth Sundrie Flowres*. See Miller ed. (1975).

Waugaman, Richard M. "A Wanderlust Poem, Newly Attributed to Edward de Vere." *Shakespeare Matters*, 7:1 (Fall 2001), 21-23.

_____. "The 1574 *Mirour for Magistrates* is a Possible Source of 'Feath'red King' in Shakespeare's 'The Phoenix and the Turtle,'" *Cahiers Élisabéthains* 85 (Spring 2014), 67-72.

_____. *Newly Discovered Works by "William Shake-Speare," a.k.a. Edward de Vere, Earl of Oxford*. Kindle Book. 2nd edition (2017).

_____. "Did Edward de Vere Translate Ovid's *Metamorphoses*?" *The Oxfordian* XX (2018), 7-26.

Waugh, Alexander. "My Shakespeare Rise!" William Leahy, ed., *My Shakespeare: The Authorship Controversy*, Edward Everett Root (2018), 47-83.

Whalen, Richard F. See Shahan, John M. & Richard F. Whalen.

Whitman, Walt. "What Lurks Behind Shakspere's Historical Plays?" *November Boughs*, Philadelphia: McKay (1888), 52-54.

Williams, Gordon. *A Glossary of Shakespeare's Sexual Language*. London: Athlone Press (1997).

Williams, Travis D. "The Bourn Identity: *Hamlet* and the French of Montaigne's *Essais*." Notes and Queries 58:2 (2011), 254-58.

Wood, Antony. *Athenae Oxonienses (1691-92)*. Germany: George Olms (1969).

Woods, Susanne. "'The Passionate Sheepheard' and 'The Nimphs Reply': A Study of Transmission." *Huntington Library Quarterly* 34: 1 (1970), 25–33.

Wright, George T. "Hendiadys and *Hamlet*." *PMLA* 96:2 (1981), 168–93.

Zukerman, Cordelia. "Shakespeare's Comedies, *The Passionate Pilgrim*, and the Idea of a Reading Public." *Studies in English Literature 1500-1900*, 57:2 (2017), 253-74.

Index of First Lines

Index

M

U

V

W

The Snail's Head
Baltimore, Maryland.
Where the Design Meets the Mind
2019

Courtly Poets, 1870 - Anthology
(Poems By Edward
Earl of Oxford

• Fancy and Desire - P. 142
"Come hither, shepherd's Swain?"
(Also in Art of Poesy, 1589 By Puttenham)
Shorter version

• If women could be Fair, P. 143 (P. 141)
etc
(and not yet fond)
Alternate title - "A Renunciation"

• Fain Would I Sing, Etc P. 144/ (P. 79)
(but fury makes me fret) P. 145

• The Earl of Oxford to the Reader ... (1576)
" The labouring man That Tills the fertile
Soil."
(P. 27)
(from Cardanus's Comfort 1576)

At
• Epigram P. 147
" Were I a King, I could command
Content..." (P. 109)

TOTAL- 5 poems - P. 142-147

" My mind to me A Kingdom Is" - P. 121
in ~~Art~~ Anthology - By Sir Edward Dyer

Made in United States
Orlando, FL
20 October 2022

P. 132 - " Of a Contented Mind" By Thomas ~~Lord~~
Lord Vaux